SUZAN-LORI PARKS IN PERSON

D1471716

This collection of interviews offers unprecedented insight into the plays and creative works of Suzan-Lori Parks as well as being an important commentary on contemporary theater and playwriting, from jazz and opera to politics and cultural memory.

Suzan-Lori Parks in Person contains 18 interviews, some previously untranscribed or specially undertaken for this book, as well as commentaries on her work by major directors and critics, including Liz Diamond, Richard Foreman, Bonnie Metzgar and Beth Schachter. These contributions combine to honor the first African American woman to receive the Pulitzer Prize in drama, and explore her ideas about theater, history, race and gender.

Material from a wide range of sources chronologically charts Parks's career from the early 1990s to the present. This is a major collection with immediate relevance to students of American/African American theater, literature and culture. Parks's engaging voice is brought to the fore, making the book essential for undergraduates as well as scholars.

Philip C. Kolin is the University Distinguished Professor in the College of Arts and Letters at The University of Southern Mississippi, USA. He has published more than 40 books and 200 articles and is the editor of *The Southern Quarterly*.

Harvey Young is an Associate Professor of Theatre at Northwestern University, USA. His books include *Theatre & Race* (2013) and *Embodying Black Experience* (2010).

SUZAN-LORI PARKS IN PERSON

Interviews and Commentaries

*Edited by Philip C. Kolin and
Harvey Young*

Routledge
Taylor & Francis Group

LONDON AND NEW YORK

First published 2014
by Routledge
2 Park Square, Milton Park, Abingdon, Oxon OX14 4RN

and by Routledge
711 Third Avenue, New York, NY 10017

Routledge is an imprint of the Taylor & Francis Group, an informa business

British Library Cataloguing in Publication Data
A catalogue record for this book is available from the British Library

Library of Congress Cataloguing in Publication Data
Parks, Suzan-Lori
[Interviews. Selections]
Suzan-Lori Parks in person : interviews, addresses, commentaries /
[edited by] Philip C. Kolin, Harvey Young.
      p. cm.
   Includes bibliographical references and index.
   Parks, Suzan-Lori – Interviews. 2. Parks, Suzan-Lori – Criticism
   and interpretation. I. Kolin, Philip C. editor of compilation. II. Young,
   Harvey, 1975– editor of compilation.
   PS3566.A736A6 2013
   812'.54-dc23
2013022132

ISBN: 978-0-415-62491-6 (hbk)
ISBN: 978-0-415-62493-0 (pbk)
ISBN: 978-0-203-10384-5 (ebk)

Typeset in Bembo
by HWA Text and Data Management, London

Printed and bound by CPI Group (UK) Ltd, Croydon, CR0 4YY

CONTENTS

FIGURES

ACKNOWLEDGMENTS

We greatly appreciate the assistance of numerous individuals whose advice and support helped us to prepare this collection of interviews and commentaries. Liz Diamond, Bonnie Metzgar, and Beth Schachter, accomplished artists with long personal and professional relationships with Suzan-Lori Parks, were extraordinarily generous with their time and provided us with new, previously unpublished material (interviews and an essay). Una Chaudhuri offered us her wise counsel and encouragement throughout the many months we spent tracking down and securing permission for interviews with Parks. Our gratitude as well goes to the librarians and archivists who alerted us to unpublished and/or untranscribed or uncatalogued interviews, including Kathy Carbone at California Institute of the Arts and Patricia Albright, Emily Wells, and Emily Weir at Mt. Holyoke College, Parks's *alma mater*.

We are grateful to Joseph Roach and Emily Coates for allowing us to include a previously untranscribed 2005 interview with Parks and Bonnie Metzgar that was sponsored by the World Performance Project at Yale. Jonathan Kalb not only arranged, moderated, and edited a series of cutting-edge interviews with several of Parks's leading collaborators and critics but also assisted us in obtaining permission to reprint the 2004 Hunter College Forum here. The Hunter College Forum was transcribed by Leigh Ronnow and previously published online at HotReview.org.

We are thankful to numerous newspapers, academic journals, and their representatives for granting us permission to reprint the following pieces. Patti Hartigan, "Theater's Vibrant New Voice: Suzan-Lori Parks Puts Dreams into Words—and Invents a New Language for the Stage," from *The Boston Globe*, 14 February 1992: 37, ©1992. All rights reserved. Used by permission and protected by the Copyright Laws of the United States. The printing, copying, redistribution, or retransmission of this content without express written permission is prohibited. Erika Munk "The Next Stage: Is Playwright Suzan-Lori Parks the Voice of the Future?," *Washington Post*, 28 February 1993: G3. "Suzan Lori-Parks" by Han Ong was commissioned by and first published in BOMB Magazine, from BOMB 47/Spring 1994. © Bomb Magazine, New Art Publications, and its Contributors. All rights reserved. The BOMB Digital Archive can be viewed at www.bombsite.com. Michele Pearce, "Alien Nation: An Interview with the Playwright," *American Theatre Magazine*, March 1994 (Volume 11, Issue 3), 26. Published by Theatre Communications Group. Used by Permission of Theatre Communications Group. Tom Sellar, "Making History: Suzan-Lori Parks," *TheatreForum* (Summer/Fall 1996), 35–36. Una Chaudhuri, "For Posterior's Sake," *Public Access* (May 1996), 34–36. "Adrienne Kennedy by Suzan Lori-Parks" was commissioned by and first published in BOMB Magazine, from BOMB 54/Winter 1996. © Bomb Magazine, New Art Publications, and its Contributors. All rights reserved. Shelby Jiggetts, "Interview with Suzan-Lori Parks," *Callaloo* 19.2 (1996), 309–317. © 1996 by Charles H. Rowell. Reprinted with permission. Ronni Gordon, "Love and War Seen in Black and White," *Union-News* (Springfield, MA), 10 April 1997. "Suzan-Lori Parks" from *The Playwright's Voice: American Dramatists on Memory, Writing and the Politics of Culture* by David Savran. Copyright © 1999 by David Savran. Published by Theatre Communications Group. Used by permission of Theatre Communications Group. Kathy Sova "A Better Mirror: An Interview with the Playwright," *American Theatre*, March 2000 (Volume 17, Issue 3), 72. Published by Theatre Communications Group. Used by Permission of Theatre Communications Group. Rick DesRochers, "The Mythology of History, Family and Performance," *Public Access* (August 2001): 8–10. John Marshall, "A Moment with Suzan-Lori Parks, Playwright," *Seattle Post-Intelligencer*, 26 May 2003. Kevin J. Wetmore, Jr., "It's an Oberammergau Thing: An Interview with Suzan-Lori Parks," in *Suzan-Lori Parks: A Casebook*, edited by Kevin J. Wetmore, Jr. and Alycia Smith-Howard (New York: Routledge, 2007): 124–140. Shawn-Marie Garrett, "An Interview with Suzan-Lori Parks," in *Suzan-Lori Parks: Essays on the Plays and Other Works*, © 2000, edited by Philip C. Kolin by permission of McFarland & Company, Inc., Box 611, Jefferson, NC 28640): 181–190. Dave Steakley, "A Conversation with *The Book of Grace* Playwright/Director Suzan-Lori Parks and Zach Producing Artistic Director Dave Steakley, <http://www.zachtheatre.org>. Jonathan Kalb, "Remarks on Parks: A Symposium on the Works of Suzan-Lori Parks (2 Parts)," of The Johns Hopkins University Press.<http://www.hotreview.org>. We especially thank James Gleason at *The Republican*, Monique Parish at PARS International Corp., and Jim Carmody at *TheatreForum*. In addition, the artistic and managing staff of several theatre companies have answered our questions, supplied copies of interviews, and pointed us in the right direction, most notably Jocelyn Prince, formerly of the Public Theater (and now at Woolly Mammoth Theatre); David Steakley and Renelle Bedell at ZACH Theatre; and Jeff Berlin at Marin Theatre Company.

In assembling this collection, we had the privilege of working directly with many of the interviewers featured in this book. In addition to those already named, we appreciate the assistance of Erika Munk, Shawn-Marie Garrett, David Savran, Tom Sellar, and Kevin J. Wetmore, Jr..

We would like to thank our respective schools—The University of Southern Mississippi and Northwestern University—for their continuing support of our work. In particular, we thank Steven R. Moser, Dean of the College of Arts and Letters at The University of Southern Mississippi; Barbara O'Keefe, Dean of the School of Communication at Northwestern; Eric Tribunella, Chair of the English Department at USM; and our research assistants: Michael Anderson, Dawn Tracey Brandes, Nikita Core, Jeremy DeFatta, Anna Beth Williams, and Louise Edwards Neiman. Special thanks to Larissa Kennedy at the Charles Warren Center at Harvard University, where Harvey Young was a Fellow during the completion of this book.

To our editors at Routledge, we express our gratitude for their help and faith in this project—Talia Rodgers and Ben Piggott. We also appreciate the assistance of Harriet Affleck, Sarah Taylor, John Hodgson, and Louise Armstrong.

Finally, our thanks go to our families for their love and patience. Philip C. Kolin expresses his thanks to and his immense respect for his children—Kristin, Eric, and Theresa—and his grandchildren—Evan Philip, Megan Elise, and Erica Marie. Harvey Young is grateful for the support and encouragement provided by his wife, Heather Schoenfeld, and their son, Mark Ezekiel (Zeke).

"WATCH ME WORK"

Reflections on Suzan-Lori Parks and her Canon

Philip C. Kolin and Harvey Young

Suzan-Lori Parks is widely recognized as one of the most provocative and prolific dramatists of the current millennium. The winner of numerous awards, including the Pulitzer Prize for Drama and the Tony Award, Parks has given the American theater an entirely new, challenging stage language that resonates with insightful puns and historical allusions. Only three years after her college graduation and the production (as a staged reading) of her first play, her senior thesis, *The Sinner's Place* (1985), Suzan-Lori Parks's immense talent and potential to radically transform American theater were widely touted by leading theater critics. In 1989, Mel Gussow, senior critic for the *New York Times*, lauded the playwright for her "theatrical versatility" and originality. Four years later, the *New York Times* hailed her as one of "30 artists under 30 most likely to change the culture for the next 30 years," and in 1999, *Time Magazine* numbered Parks among the "100 Innovators for the Next Wave." Two years later, Parks, who by then had already won two OBIE Awards, was given a $500,000 "Genius" grant from the MacArthur Foundation. The following year, she won the Tony Award and the Pulitzer Prize for Drama. Since then, she has re-envisioned the idea of the "world premiere" and "opening night" by having her collection of more than 365 plays, *365 Days/365 Plays*, staged at over 700 theaters in the United States and approximately 100 theaters across Canada and Europe from 2006–2007, thrown back the curtain on her writing process by literally inviting audiences to "Watch Me Work," and adapted American operatic and literary classics, such as *Porgy and Bess* and *Their Eyes Were Watching God*, for the theatrical stage and the television screen. Although primarily a playwright, Parks has demonstrated exceptional talent in art forms other than theater. She is a best-selling novelist (*Getting Mother's Body*) and a screenwriter (Spike Lee's *Girl 6*). A musician, she wrote the score for *Father Comes Home from the War* and the libretto for *Ray Charles*

FIGURE 1 Suzan-Lori Parks directs a rehearsal of *The Book of Grace*, ZACH Theatre, 2011. Photo by Kirk A. Tuck. Courtesy of ZACH Theatre.

Live!—A New Musical! Parks even composed several original songs, including "The Looking Song" for her *Red Letter Plays*, *In the Blood* (1999) and *Fucking A* (2000). As a vocalist and guitarist as well, she has reincarnated herself as Sula Parks and has performed at the Public Theater and elsewhere.

Suzan-Lori Parks in Person is divided into two parts: interviews with the playwright and commentaries by the people who worked most closely with her. Interviews with Suzan-Lori Parks contextualize and even extend her dramaturgy. They provide valuable first-hand information about her influences from her childhood experiences living on a military base in Germany, to her college studies with novelist James Baldwin, to her passion and love for music. They offer insight into her thinking, sharing her ideas on everything from the collective unconscious, to jazz, to American politics, to popular film, to black cultural memory. In addition, the interviews themselves are highly engaging texts. They feel more like plays in which the playwright, alongside her interlocutors, doubles as both the author and a character. The commentaries in this book also grant readers a privileged perspective into Parks's distinctive approach to making theater. Her longtime collaborators, including directors who helmed world premiere productions, recall their first impressions of the artist, reflect on the challenges and successes of their productions, and offer insight into Suzan-Lori Parks, the person and not the playwright. In addition, prominent theater historians and critics discuss Parks's evolving legacy and her contributions to American theater. These commentaries provide historical and critical context that speak to Parks's enduring influence and the power of her theatrical voice.

Consisting of more than three decades of interviews and commentaries, this book reveals Parks to be a keen social critic, a vibrant commentator on contemporary theater, and a fascinating conversationalist through her observations on race, gender, history, and American culture. In privileging the playwright's own voice, this collection allows Parks to reflect on her iconoclastic approach to theater and her career as an artistic innovator. Through the interviews presented in this collection, we can hear the artist directly and indirectly (through the commentaries of her collaborators) talk about the inspirations for her most critically acclaimed plays and comment on the changing face of American theater. Indeed, one of the most striking things about Suzan-Lori Parks, as she appears in this collection, is the consistency of her enthusiasm and advocacy for the performing arts as a medium to tell stories that need to be told and to write histories frequently left unrecorded.

Finding my Me

Susan L. Parks, or "Susie Parks" as she was known to her college instructors, became Suzan-Lori Parks as a result of her name being spelled incorrectly on a promotional flyer: "When I was doing one of my first plays in the East Village, we had fliers printed and they spelled my name wrong. I was devastated."[1] Mortified by the error which could not be corrected in time for the performance, the young playwright adopted her director's advice, "Just keep it, honey, it will be fine." On that day and through that error, Suzan-Lori Parks was born. Although unintended, the emergence of "Suzan-Lori" was already in the works. As a high school student in Germany, Suzan-Lori Parks quickly discovered that the logic of black and white that defines interpersonal relationships in the United States was not applicable. As a college student at Mount Holyoke, she found inspiration in novelist James Baldwin's suggestion that she seemed better suited to be a playwright than a novelist, explaining that her words leap from the page and demand embodiment. From that moment on, Parks became a playwright. She enrolled in acting classes. She began to direct plays, including a student production of Ntozake Shange's *for colored girls who have considered suicide when the rainbow is enuf*. Because the language and content of her first play were considered too raw, *The Sinner's Place* was not produced at Mount Holyoke but presented as a reading at a local theater festival. After college, she went to London to study acting at The Drama Studio, and when she returned she took various jobs, including working as a paralegal. Each career was short-lived as her second play (and the first to be professionally produced), *Imperceptible Mutabilities in the Third Kingdom*, brought her immediate celebrity status within the world of experimental theater. Commercial success, including Broadway fame, eventually would follow.

A crucible of the themes and techniques that distinguish Parks's plays appears in *Imperceptible Mutabilities*. The play, which was produced as part of the 1989 BACA Fringe Festival, exemplifies Parks's distinctive stage language, her repetition and revision (or "rep and rev") dramatics, her "allegorical absurdism,"[2] use of choral voices and figures, and, perhaps, most importantly, her investigation into why and how black figures have been erased from history. In *Mutabilities*, Parks explores the wide and stinging impact of slavery in America and its effects on black identity. Victims in both slave-owning and postcolonial America, her characters ask a crucial Parks's question: "How we gonna find my Me?"[3] The title of Parks's play brilliantly uses "myth and metaphor" to raise and answer that key question. The "Third Kingdom" metaphorically refers to "the space of sea between the worlds" of freedom and bondage.[4] It is in this in-between space that African American identity can be found or, as choral figures Kin-Seer and Shark-Seer chant, "My new Self was uh 3rd Self made by thuh space inbetween."[5]

Parks's dramaturgy rewrites, reimagines, and restores a black historical presence. As Irene Backalenick stressed, too, Parks's "subject matter moves through boundless areas of time and space but in identifying with her own background is often grounded in black history."[6] Indeed, the central theme of this early play centers on the dramatization of the terrifying ways black bodies (and identity) have been fragmented, dismembered, and expunged as transgressive elements in American history. On the Middle Passage, Africans were separated from home, the place of history, memory, and the sense of self. Kin-Seer recalls: "And I was wavin. Wavin. Wavin at my uther me who I could barely see. Over thuh water on thuh uther cliff I could see my uther me but my uther me could not see me."[7] The painful voyage claimed countless lives. Bodies of the sick, the already dead, and those seeking escape went overboard and disappeared. That sense of separation and loss extends across *Mutabilities*. "Tonight I dream of where I be-camin from. And where I be camin from duhduhnt look like nowhere like I been," announces Kin-Seer, commenting on the collective loss of racial memory.[8]

In the four parts of *Mutabilities*, Parks attempts to set the record straight, or at least to bewail the fact that black history, consciousness, and identity have been lost, forgotten, and/or destroyed. The first part of the play, "Snails," dramatizes the experience of three contemporary young black girls who are ridiculed and punished by the white establishment (academic, commercial, etc.) because of their language, culture, and looks. Even more disruptive, they are seen as specimens by a white naturalist, Dr. Lutzky, who spies on the girls and then tries to eradicate them. In this moment, Parks introduces a theme, the surveillance of black bodies, that repeats across her other plays, most notably *Venus, In the Blood*, and *Topdog*. The second part of the *Mutabilities* is an extended dialogue among the five choral characters (Kin-Seer, Us-Seer, Shark-Seer, Soul-Seer, and Over-Seer) about the fate of black people in America. They have lost their names, their clothes, their selves. All that's left is their "bleechin bones." Over-Seer asks, "Who're you again?" and Soul-Seer laments, "Duh duhnt-he-know-my-name."[9]

"Open House," the third part, concentrates on the life of an old slave, Aretha, propped up on a hospital bed. She has been cruelly treated by Charles, her white master, his children, whom she reared, and Miss Faith, a sanctimonious bigot. The title of this section vibrates with Parksian irony. The "Open House" refers to a slave ship (a slaver) and the number of bodies it can force into its hold. Transported back in time, Aretha conjoins a family reunion with the arrival of slavers with their cargoes: "Gotta know thuh exact size. Thup. Got people comin. Hole house full. They gonna be kin?... How many kin I hold. Whole hold full."[10] The "whole" is polyvalent—Aretha's womb, the slave ship's belly, the abyss into which she will descend, foreshadowing Parks's fascination with homonyms: *hold, hole, whole*. The fourth part, "Greeks (or the Slugs)," continues Parks's excoriation of white society for dismembering and disremembering black history. Legless and eyeless, Sgt. Smith becomes a victim of the military establishment. The disabled sergeant, who inspired the later *Father Comes Home from the War* plays, cannot even recognize his own children ("You one of uh mines?") and is reduced to cleaning a rock. His identity—his *mine, mind*—is dismembered by the *minefield* he steps on, a symbol of how memory and historical awareness (and presence) can be taken away.

Parks makes the imperceptible stunningly perceptible, and uncomfortable. As director Liz Diamond asserts in a 2009 interview with Faedra Chatard Carpenter:

> What *Imperceptible Mutabilities in the Third Kingdom* explores is a deeply disturbing idea—that history is not the ramp envisioned by the Enlightenment... in opposition to the way Darwin's theories are traditionally understood. Their evolution doesn't necessarily signify progress... The characters are snails, or worse, slugs... shapeless little organisms with no protective shell. *IMP* gets under your skin—it's intensely funny and dramatic, and does what great theatre is supposed to do: Rock you. Invade your heart and mind.[11]

The success of Parks's first professionally produced and fully realized production anchors itself in the playwright's ability to employ language to create a physical presence with the power to intervene in the writing and remembrance of history. She creates a third space, a "Third Kingdom," on stage "where meanings converge and mutate"[12] and the past becomes present.

Language is a Physical Act

In a 1985 scholarship application to study at The Drama School in London, Parks, then a college senior, expressed her desire to study acting to become a better playwright. She wrote:

> I have chosen writing and directing and must prepare accordingly for my career. But why a school for actors?... To study drama through the medium of acting is to move from mere understanding to a physicalization of that character.[13]

An attention to the embodiment of words, which is especially evident in her frequent use of the "uh" sound, is a key feature of her playwriting. Indeed, she would affirm in "Elements of Style," "Language is a physical act, something that involves your whole blood."[14] *The Death of the Last Black Man* (1990) exemplifies Parks's highly experimental, language-driven, surrealistic theater. It was produced in 1990 at BACA Downtown in Brooklyn and directed by Beth Schachter. Parks's description of the play underscores its haunting effect on audiences—*Last Black Man* consists of "12 figures with strange names all telling this jazz poetic story about a man who died and doesn't know where he's going to go now that he's dead." Commenting on her jazz poetry, the playwright told David Savran that her characters

> talk funny because they're in a really funny place. They're walking a line between the living and the dead, or he is anyway. Most of the people in the play are dead. They really don't make sense a lot of the time because they're dead.[15]

As Parks stressed in a short article early in her career, "I do not write as people I know speak; nor have I ever heard anyone speak as I write."[16]

Like *Mutabilities*, and so many of her other plays that follow, Parks's signature style includes ingenious puns, parodies, and an outrageous sense of humor to attack and disable stereotypes of black identity. There are also elements of the minstrel show, melodrama, and even cartoons in some of her plays, particularly in *Last Black Man*. For example, Ham's long genealogy two-thirds of the way into the play parodies Biblical passages and is filled with the contemptuous names that overseers used to refer to black slaves. Moreover, by naming characters Black Man with Watermelon, Black Woman with Fried Drumstick, or Lots of Grease and Lots of Pork, Parks satirizes conventional racial portraits of African Americans. Her characters are far more complex, more nuanced than the names they carry. As Jennifer Larson reminds us, "Black Man's inability to see himself in the watermelon that names him… shows his initial disconnection with stereotypes that define him in history."[17]

The influence of Adrienne Kennedy, a playwright whom Parks would later formally interview for a magazine profile, is especially strong in *Last Black Man*. As Parks told Savran, "I am a fan of hers, particularly her *Funnyhouse of a Negro*" (1964).[18] Parks claimed, "I read it and reread it. It also had a hand in shaping what I do." Like Kennedy's *Funnyhouse*, as well as *The Owl Answers* and *A Rat's Mass*, *Last Black Man* takes audiences into a mad, surrealistic world where we find allegorical characters who war with their multiple selves. In this nightmare world, linear time and consequential logic are replaced with horrific sights and sounds of black dismemberment and fragmentation expressed in haunting poetry and framed through Roman Catholic religious rituals. Both Kennedy and Parks stage the subconscious, probing the interiority of complex characters who are persecuted in (and by) a dominating society. In some ways, Kennedy's spectacles—Sarah's noose around her neck in *Funnyhouse*—look forward to Parks's stage pageants. Like Kennedy before her, too, Parks dismantles a safe, predictable, and binary world of being alive or being dead; living then as opposed to now; and inhabiting self or others. Kennedy's Sarah has four selves including Patrice Lumumba, the Duchess of Hapsburg, Jesus, and Queen Victoria. Similarly, Black Man is reincarnated as himself in many contexts throughout the play, attesting to the veracity of Parks's epigraph from Beat poet Bob Kaufman— "When I die/I won't stay/ Dead." Time releases Black Man from chronological boundaries only to execute him more frequently, more heinously. The various tortures Black Man endures—beatings, lynching, drowning, etc.—prefigure the numerous times that the Foundling Father in *The America Play* is assassinated when he is dressed as Abraham Lincoln.

Many times, Parks's scathing humor tells a harrowing chronicle. Recounting his experience being electrocuted, Black Man cries, "They juiced me some" and then, more fully, reveals that

> They had theirselves uh extender chord. Fry uh man in thuh town square needs uh extender tuh reach em thuh electric. Hook up thuh chaiar tuh thuh power. Extender: 49 foot in length. Closer to tuh thuh power I never been. Flip on up thuh go switch. Huh! Juice begins its course.

But as he was being "juiced," Black Man got away. "First 49 foot I was runnin they was still juicing."[19] His death seems even more horrific in light of Parks's black comedy over "juicin" him as he tries to escape. Parks thus turns a gruesome sight into an absurdly funny one, undercutting the authority of a sadistic punishment. When Black Man is lynched, he remembers white spectators watching as if they were at a picnic. Parks also uses savage satire by comparing the disparity of a hanging and a picnic,[20] true to the actual history of lynching.

Parks is clearly attuned to Kennedy's surrealistic plays where time dissolves or reloops. In *Last Black Man*, for instance, Queen-then-Pharaoh Hatshepsut holds forth on the collapsibility of time:

> Yesterday, tuhday next summer tuhmorrow just uh moment uhgoh in 1317 dieded thuh last black man in thuh whole entire world. Uh! Oh Don't be uhlarmed. Do not be afeared. It was painless. Uh painless passin. He falls 23 floors to his death.[21]

Commenting on how the past looks no different from the present, Black Woman tells Black Man,

> They comed from you and tooked you. That was yesterday. Today you sit in your chair where yo sat yesterday and thuh day afore yesterday afore they comed and tooked you. Things today is just as they are yesterday cept nothin is familiar cause it was such uh long time uhgoh.[22]

Kennedy's characters, like Parks's, are imprisoned in time warps.

Like Kennedy's characters, too, Parks's are victims of a society that denies them selfhood and erases their history. Conscious of efforts to render them invisible, her characters frequently assert a desire to be heard, recognized, and remembered. Early in the play, Yes and Greens Black-Eyed Peas Cornbread instructs Last Black Man: "You should write it down because if you don't write it down then they will come along and tell the future that we did not exist. You should write it down and you should hide it under a rock."[23] When these words are repeated near the end of the play, Parks replaces "Hide it under a rock" with "You will write it down and you will carve it out of a rock."[24] This verbal shift, or revision of the words, charts the powerful ways in which black characters move from "hiding" their history to "carving it," or preserving it, thus making history and not losing it. Significantly at the end of the play, Black Man can tell Black Woman—"Remember me."[25]

As in *Mutabilites*, ancestral memory must be recorded so that it preserves the times before slavers stole Africans away from their homeland and then moves to documenting the horrors of the Middle Passage that followed. Reflecting these events in African history, Parks fittingly includes characters named Before Columbus, or a time before slavers came to Africa, and Queen-Then-Pharaoh Hatshepsut, one of the few female rulers of Egypt and a symbol of African power and empire. When Before Columbus recounts that "All those boats passed by me. My coast fell into the sea. All thuh boats. They stopped for me," referring to slavers, Queen-Then-Pharaoh Hatshepsut ironically replies, "I have not seen you since,"[26] exemplifying Parks's subversive sense of humor. Lots of Grease and Lots of Pork draws a similar conclusion, reiterated throughout *Last Black Man*—"This is the death of the last black man in the whole entire world." As Alice Rayner and Harry J. Elam, Jr. aptly stress, "The death of every black man in the past inhabits the death of each black man in the present in the sense that history is lived as present."[27] In resurrecting Black Man so many times, Parks becomes a witness to the gruesome events constituting black history, told and retold through rep and rev techniques.

As in Kennedy, too, Parks incorporates religious rituals as an instrumental part of her stage spectacles. In a 1994 interview with Han Ong, Parks declares, "Every play I write is like a religious pageant." She adds, "My plays are like passion plays where the community comes together to reenact the passion of whomever."[28] Certainly the community of black characters in *Last Black Man* is gathered to remember the deaths and resurrections of Black Man. Black Woman in particular testifies to his numerous reincarnations. Similarly, in her 1999 interview with David Savran, Parks claims, "For me plays are more like religious experiences than secular ones."[29] In this context, *Last Black Man* might be seen as an elegy, or even a black ghost play. As Liz Diamond, describing the production, underscored, "We created a whispering chorus of 'ghosts' that played as the audience entered the theatre and took their seats. These were the voices of all those 'figures' from the past, arriving and naming themselves, as they gather to teach the history of the Black Man, to get us to face it, own it, and 'write it down.'"[30]

Describing herself and Parks as "recovering Catholics," Diamond recalls that Parks and she went to "masses together" to see how church rituals could inform *Last Black Man*. As Diamond points out, in *Last Black Man*, Parks:

> wanted… the call and response of the Catholic Church which is very slow and cadenced. I don't know how to describe it musically, but it is kind of a formal, strict, metric rhythm, as opposed to the more propulsive bending rhythms you might hear in a Baptist church. And that's what we went for.[31]

The sound of bells that divides one section of *Last Black Man* from another evokes the bells rung before Mass begins and during the most sacred part of the liturgy, the Consecration. Another Catholic ritual that helped Parks shape *The Last Black Man* is the Stations of the Cross, commemorating Christ's journey to Golgotha, including the agony of carrying the cross, his three falls, meeting his mother, etc. Echoing the Stations and detailing the violence of the lynching act, Black Man remembers when he was hung on a tree and the limb broke:

> It had begun tuh rain. … ZAP. Tree bowed over till thuh brank said BROKE. Uhround my necklace my neck uhround, my neck my tree branch. In full bloom. Ithad begun tuh rain. Feet hit thuh ground in I started runnin. I was wet right through intuh through. I was uh wet that dont get dry. Draggin on my tree branch on back tuh home."[32]

Parks thus transforms a sacred religious ritual into a template for Black Man's tragic life.

Hear the Bones Sing. Write It Down.

Suzan-Lori Parks frequently mines history. As she observes, "Since history is a recorded or remembered event, theater, for me, is the perfect place to 'make' history." She adds:

> because so much of African American history has been unrecorded, dismembered, washed out, one of my tasks as a playwright is to—through literature and the special strange relationship between theater and real life—locate the ancestral burial ground, dig for bones, find bones, hear the bones sing, write it down.[33]

The playwright's fascination with the past is evident not only through her representation of historical figures onstage—such as Abraham Lincoln, John Wilkes Booth, and Saartjie Baartman among others—but also through her centering the dramatic narrative around a "black digger" or a "Negro Resurrectionist" who serves as the conduit between the audience and the world of the play. The digger, as the agent who literally unearths the past, invites the spectator into Parks's dramaturgy and, by extension, into the past as reimagined by the playwright.

The America Play, which premiered at Yale Repertory Theatre in 1993 and was later staged in 1994 at the Public Theater, is one of Parks's most challenging, political works. As the title suggests, the play focuses on her attempt to encapsulate our national character, or reputation, and to "encourage people to think about the idea of America in addition to the actual day-to-day reality of America…"[34] That idea has committed Parks to question and reconfigure one of the most central myths that underlies the American image and heritage— the persona of Abraham Lincoln. Parks has long been fascinated by the idea of America that Lincoln symbolized: "I didn't choose Lincoln; Lincoln chose me."[35] In the *America Play*, a black grave digger named Lesser Man looks so much like Lincoln, the "Great Man," that someone suggested that "he… ought to be shot." And so instead of just "speechifying" Lincoln, as he had done with little success, Lesser Man impersonates him in a show where the "public was invited to pay a penny, choose from a selection of provided pistols, enter the darkened box and 'Shoot Mr. Lincoln.'"[36]

The implications of having a black man play Lincoln are crucial to understanding Parks's interrogation of and quarrel with history. As in *Mutabilities* and *Last Black Man*, she finds that African Americans have been erased from the historical record, "dismembered" in the narratives that privilege and render present a dominant white culture.[37] Parks is a keen witness to "History—the destruction and creation of it through theatre pieces and how black people fit into all of this." Inserting a black man in the Lincoln mythic narrative changes how white America has projected and privileged itself. Defending her fiction as an antidote to historical prejudice, or the deliberate absenting of black achievement, Parks has asked, "Where is history? Because I don't see it. I don't see any history out there, and so I've made some up."[38] Making this point more emphatically, she told Michelle Pearce that the world was once "a blank slate, and since that beginning, people have been filling it with tshatshkes, which we who come next must receive and do something with."[39] Mr. Lincoln's "tshatshkes," or memorabilia, trappings, provide Parks with the theatrical images, props, and representations she needs to make history while at the same time reinstating a black presence in it.

The first act of *The America Play* is largely taken up with Lesser Man's role playing Lincoln. He and his wife Lucy had visited the "Great Hole of History" theme park on their honeymoon and he had become obsessed with playing major historical figures who paraded through the Great Hole, but none called to him more than Lincoln. Determined to celebrate their "virtual twinship,"[40] Lesser Man obsessively strove to imitate Lincoln down to the last follicle. He saved hairs from his barber's floor to make a wide assortment of beards, including a blonde one; he also wore a black frock coat, appropriate shoes, and even put a wart on his face to resemble Lincoln's. He feigned deafness in one ear to match Lincoln's malady. He searched for "faux historical knickknacks," all those "*tshatshkes*" that Parks said filled American history and that "we had to do something with."[41] But Lesser Man did not wear a stovepipe hat, since people do not like their Lincolns to wear hats inside. "Somehow [he had] to equal the Great Man in stature."[42] Because of his uncanny resemblance—a *coup de théâtre* in Parks's excoriating satire of white image-making—it was not inconceivable that he play Lincoln at Ford's Theatre—"the darkened box" of his show; he was, in another example of Parks's irony, a "dead ringer" for the Great Man.

But, tragically, Lesser Man makes his living more by dying as Lincoln than living as the sixteenth president. As Deborah Geis asserts, Parks emphasizes the "trauma" of the assassination more than its "political" consequences.[43] His black identity is simultaneously erased and bleeds through the Lincoln costume and mannerisms he adopts. His impersonations do not conceal his black heritage and, arguably, his assassination as Lincoln allows him to be murdered simply for being a black man. Throughout Act One, Parks references the events that occurred on the night Lincoln was murdered at Ford's Theatre—the distance of the president's box from the stage, John Wilkes Booth's words when he killed the President, the words others used when Lincoln lay on his deathbed. Parks even brings black actors in white face (reminiscent of Adrienne Kennedy's *Funnyhouse of a Negro*) on stage to speak the very lines from *Our American Cousin*, the play Lincoln was watching at the moment of the assassination. But while African Americans are incorporated into this particular historical episode, they also bring their own terrifying legacy to Parks's various stages—the one from which Booth jumps (the President's box), the one on which Lesser Man performs, and the one Parks's audiences watch as these various plays-within-plays unfold. As Janet Larsen usefully reminds us, Lesser Man's being "incarnated in Lincoln does not protect him from the thrills white patrons experience from shooting a black man in his own 'dark box,'"[44] thus violating his body and symbolically committing the racial crime of lynching, all perfectly legal.

The Lesser Man's obsession with and quest for being a part of history emerge from a racial joke—yet another example of the playwright's linguistic mastery—that Parks references in her interview with Han Ong. Commenting on her working relationship with director Liz Diamond, Parks recalls:

> We both love the dumb gag, the knee slapper. There's a lot of power in that, and there's a lot of really serious stuff going on in *The America Play*, but I swear I can only think of the jokes. The jokes led me to write *America*. The relationship between "nigger" and "digger" was the whole play for me. When I could allow myself to have a little chuckle about "nigger" and "digger," I knew who these people were in the play.[45]

But even though Lesser Man had witnessed history and wanted to be inscribed in its annals, he, as a black man, is deemed to be insignificant. As his wife Lucy prepares her son for the experience of being black, she tells him

> You could look intuh that Hole and see your entire life pass before you.
> Not your life but someones life from history, you know, [someone who'd
> done somethin of note, got theirselves known somehow, uh President
> or] somebody who killed somebody important, uh face on uh postal
> stamp, you know, someone from History. *Like* you, but *not you*. You know:
> *Known.*[46]

Because of the digger's blackness, he is excluded from the parade of history—he
is "not like" the historical personages he admires. The digger remains a "nigger"
in the context of Parks's joke, an onomastic inheritance he passes on to his son
Brazil, the name of a nut often contemptuously racialized. Nonetheless, Parks's
grave digger was so fascinated with these spectacles that

> the Reconstructed Historicities he had witnessed continue to march
> before him in his mind's eye as they had at the Hole … On the way home
> again the histories paraded again on past him although it wasnt on past
> him at all it wasnt something he could expect but again like Lincoln's life
> not "on past" but *past. Behind him*. Like an echo in his head.[47]

Holes—the Great Hole or its replica—become the major topic in Act Two
of *The America Play* as Brazil digs in the Foundling Father's "Hall of Wonders"
to find his father's remains and to retrieve both familial and national history.
According to Rayner and Elam, "Just as the Foundling Father in the first act
seeks recovery of an identity through repetition of the Lincoln scene, Lucy and
Brazil, in the second act, seek recovery of the body of the Foundling Father."[48]
Digging, as his father did before him, Brazil discovers insignificant souvenirs,
including a medal for faking. History is thus trivialized, "reduced to a void."[49]
The father's cruel fate is passed on to his son. All that Brazil inherits, therefore,
is an empty hole, a spade, and a couple of sound bites from his Foundling Father
on a TV, replaying his Lincoln act. Like his father, Brazil tries to recover history
in order to be a part of it. Parks insists in her interview with Shelby Jiggetts that
"History is not 'was,' history is 'is.' It is present, so if you believe that history
is in the present, you can also believe that the present is in the past. It's mostly
directional."[50] Yet Lucy deceives herself, and Brazil, by declaring, "I swannee
you look more and more and more and more like him every day."[51] Though
Brazil retrieves his father's bones and his Lincoln artifacts, he admits that the
Foundling Father was his "foe father," another Parksian pun that invites multiple
interpretations: parent (fore), antagonist (foe), and Lincoln impersonator (faux).
Like his father, Brazil inherits a faux view of history.

Parks's play *Venus*, a 1996 co-production by Yale Repertory Theatre and the
Public Theater, also investigates the historical mistreatment of black bodies. It
is the story of Saartjie (or Sarah) Baartman, a black South African woman who
was paraded throughout England and France as the "Hottentot Venus" toward
the beginning of the 19th century. It was chiefly Baartman's backside, the fatty

deposits on her rear-end that attracted a crowd and rendered her an object of curiosity for European audiences. The tour of the original, living Hottentot Venus was brief, lasting only two years before her untimely death. A plaster mold was made of her corpse, painted, and put on display for over a century. Her body was dismembered with parts, specifically her genitals, preserved, bottled, and similarly put on show. When Parks began writing *Venus*, a campaign was ongoing to convince the French government to return the remains and cast of Saartjie Baartman to South Africa.[52]

In *Venus*, the character of the Negro Resurrectionist, patterned after the gravedigger in *The America Play*, serves as the master of ceremonies. Not unlike early vaudeville performances, he introduces each of the play's thirty-one scenes before they begin. Across these scenes, the character based on Baartman agrees to travel to London with the hope of earning a fortune or, as Parks memorably writes, to "make a mint."[53] She quickly becomes the star attraction at a freak show. Her travels and exhibition as an oddity prompt an investigation into whether she is being shown against her will—considering that the transatlantic slave trade had only recently, in 1807, been banned in England. Eventually, though, she attracts the attention of the Baron Docteur to whom she proves irresistible as both a romantic partner and an object of scientific curiosity. The play ends, as it begins, with the announcement of her death and an allusion to the ongoing exhibition of the real life Saartjie Baartman: "Love stands on show in museum. Please visit."[54]

Venus marks a transition in Parks's playwriting—from explicitly experimental fare to a more conventional, linear, dramatic narrative. Nevertheless, the transformation is not complete. Elements of Parks's avant-garde aesthetic remain, specifically in the *For the Love of the Venus* sections, a play-within-the-play that satirizes sentimental dramas popular during the exhibit of the real life Baartman, her use of a chorus with shifting identities to represent the multiple communities which displayed the Hottentot Venus, and, least consequentially, her presentation of the scenes in a counting down format (from thirty-one to one).

Not only has *Venus* attracted the most scholarly attention within Parks's extensive canon, but also the most controversial. The world premiere production, directed by Richard Foreman, was overwhelmed by, as producer Bonnie Metzger observes, the competing "huge legacies and visions" of the artistic team which compromised the expression of Parks's dramaturgical voice. In particular, reviewers and audience members critiqued the presence of Foreman's signature design choices—strings criss-crossing the stage and the presence of a blinking red light—as distracting elements. In a 1996 *Variety* review of the production, Greg Evans claimed that "The story, overcome by the hyper-stylization, musters little poignancy."[55] Yet Ben Brantley, in his *New York Times* review, praised Parks and Foreman as artistic innovators who "have talent and originality to spare" before observing, "But that doesn't necessarily mean that they should be married."[56] Parks was steadfast in her public support for Foreman's choices: "Of course, Richard has his own thing going, too. But it wasn't at the expense of my play."[57] Nevertheless, the production won two 1996 OBIE awards, including one for Parks for Best Playwriting.

Venus has garnered critical attention for its nuanced engagement with history and its exploration of intersecting racial, gender, and class identities. Jean Young challenges the play for its suggestion that the real Baartman was "an accomplice in her own exploitation."[58] Indeed, Parks characterizes Venus Hottentot as not always powerless and, in select instances, as a person who has chosen to become an exhibit, an object of otherness for hire, similar to Foundling Father, Lesser Man and *Topdog's* Lincoln. As she told Tom Sellar in a 1996 interview, "It's not the story of a black woman who's victimized."[59] Although the play reveals that Baartman has agency and, therefore, is complicit in her mistreatment, it also portrays her as a person with severely limited options, not unlike Hester LaNegrita in Parks's *In the Blood* (1999). Even though Venus Hottentot consents to travel to England to escape from an impoverished lifestyle as a domestic in South Africa, she elects to continue to be staged as a freak because she lacks the financial resources to strike out on her own.

Others have celebrated the play for its ability not only to remember the harsh experiences of Saartjie Baartman, but also to embody them before new and more contemporary audiences.[60] Parks gives Baartman a second life and, perhaps more importantly, the chance to be appreciated as a young woman subjected to tremendous abuse. Despite the fact that the play similarly invokes audiences to look upon the displayed body of Venus Hottentot, this second look—distanced by time, geography, and the frame of theater—helps the audience to witness, as a replay, the historical abuse of the black body.

In *Topdog/Underdog* (2001), Parks's most commercially successfully and arguably her most critically acclaimed play, the playwright, again, stages a black man playing Lincoln. This time, she introduces her audience to him alongside his brother, a man named Booth. As the title suggests, Parks's Pulitzer Prize-winning play, which also proved a sensation on Broadway, is about the tensions that exist between two orphaned brothers with competing ambitions. In a 2001 interview with Rick DesRochers, director George C. Wolfe observed:

> *Topdog* concerns the mythology of the family. I find that in a lot of families the older brother tends to be attracted to the mythology and illusions of family and is invested in creating a scenario of the white picket fence and family picnics together…Whereas the younger brother tends to be totally invested in the phenomenon of overthrowing the older brother so as to claim enough space for himself. In addition to this dynamic, because the brothers, are abandoned in the play, the symbiotic nature of their relationship is intensified.[61]

Indeed, this dynamic intensifies between the brothers and culminates in fratricide, when Booth, fulfilling the legacy of his name, kills Lincoln. His death, another dead Lincoln, and another hole (in the head, in the family unit) exists as a traumatic replay continually reenacted across Parks's theatrical canon, going back to *Mutabilities*. It further signals a loss that speaks to the experience of African Americans: being the targets of racist violence; being ignored in the drafting of American history (and, thus, existing as a hole in history); and being viewed as a political problem or challenge (from the 3/5s Compromise—which identified African Americans as being less than whole—to the Fourteenth and Fifteenth Amendments to the US Constitution).

In *Topdog*, Lincoln and Booth live together in a small apartment. Booth is a hustler who makes money on the streets playing three-card monte. Lincoln, as we saw, works in a carnival setting impersonating a president. People pay for the right to "assassinate" the president and a black man, who coexist within the same body. Orphans, the brothers depend on one another. They are co-dependent but also fiercely in competition with one another, not unlike the brothers, Austin and Lee, in Sam Shepard's *True West* (1981). For Parks, a comparison with classical Greek theater is apt:

> [*Topdog*] is very much… in the Greek tragedy mode. Like *Oedipus*. When you go into the theater, you know what's going to happen, and yet you delight in the journey of Oedipus. So I loved *Oedipus* and *Medea* and those kinds of plays, bloody, tragic, you know, heart wrenching.[62]

Parks's decision to stage "two brothers named Lincoln and Booth and see how their story would play out"[63] invites an imagination of a likely and historically consonant conclusion. Nevertheless, the tragedy and dramatic intrigue anchor themselves not in the presence of a surprise ending but rather in watching the brothers' back-and-forth dialogue create a tension that amplifies into a homicidal impulse.

Riffing Hawthorne

In applying her unique linguistic style to read, write, and engage history, Suzan-Lori Parks often succeeds in giving voice to the least empowered. In *Last Black Man*, she fleshes out stereotypes and gives them a complex multidimensionality. In *The America Play* and *Topdog*, she allies the "Lesser Man" with the "Great Man." In *Venus*, she grants agency to a carnival "wonder." This theme also applies in her theatrical adaptations of Nathaniel Hawthorne's *The Scarlet Letter* (1850) in *In the Blood* and *Fucking A*. Superseding and escaping from the classic text, Parks uses theater to create a black female protagonist who has her own voice, family, space, and grievances. Parks's Hester thus displaces Hawthorne's Hester Prynne as the central figure in a new play that stands at "the intersection of the historical and the now."[64]

In Hawthorne, the scarlet letter, of course, alludes to the act of adultery— the sin—that Hester Pryne is accused of and for which she is ostracized by a hypocritical, repressive culture. As Philip C. Kolin points out, the title *In the Blood* is harrowingly ambiguous standing for the sexual crimes, a tainted blood heritage, social stigma, and punishment associated with the flesh.[65] Parks's Hester is also persecuted for her sexuality; but Parks exchanges Salem for a more contemporary, urban locale; her Hester LaNegrita is a homeless, illiterate welfare mother of five fatherless children, all of whom live in squalor under a bridge. This Hester does not wear the scarlet letter—A—but it is no less prominent in her life. Trying to learn the alphabet from her oldest child Jabber, whom she murders for calling her a "slut," she traces the shape of the first letter of the alphabet with her body and at the end of the play and writes it in Jabber's blood on the ground. In *Fucking A*, that Hester, whom Parks insists is a separate character entirely,[66] is an abortionist, and so the red letter A symbolically and historically links her to what she does. Red and the letter A are inseparable in Parks. The striking Theatre Communications Group (TCG) cover of *The Red Letter Plays* is, not surprisingly, scarlet with a picture of Hester with a small red "A" branded onto her right eye as she faces the reader.

The Hester of *In the Blood* is at the mercy of the system that takes advantage of her and uses her for her sexuality. Through five characters, including Hester's white friend Amiga Gringa who sells her babies for money ("Do you have any idea how much cash I'll get for the fruit of my womb?"), Parks symbolically attacks the traditional areas from which Hester should expect help but does not—the church, the medical profession, public assistance. One of her children was fathered by a despicable clergyman—the Rev. D., onomastically recalling Hawthorne's Arthur Dimmesdale—who insists she have an abortion, and despises Hester who is too poor, shabby-looking, to even enter his church. Another one of the fathers is a potential husband, Chilli (clearly inspired by Hawthorne's Roger Chillingsworth), who runs away when he discovers that Hester has five children, yet another one of Hester's treacherous lovers. Welfare, another one of society's hypocrites, denounces Hester but compelled her to be part of a *ménage à trois* with her husband. Despite this intimate encounter, Welfare insists that "we have absolutely nothing in common."[67] Nor can Hester expect aid or sympathy from the street doctor who bristles, "Five kids are a strike against you."

As in other works—most notably, *Mutabilities*, *Venus*, *Girl 6*, *Getting Mother's Body*—Parks decries the commodification of the black female body. Like the girls who are spied upon by the white naturalist in *Mutabilities,* or Venus Hottentot who was displayed, Hester's sexuality is at the center of many demeaning gazes, all of them turning her into victim, exoticized other, and "slut," a name written on the wall of her home; she also faces the threat being neutered because of having so many children. Carol Schafer refers to Hester's body, like Venus's, as being a "bloody biological battlefield."[68] Dehumanizing her, a street doctor slides under her dress, as if she were a car due for an oil change, to inspect her female parts. As if to underscore the societal forces against Hester, Parks names one of her children Trouble. Though she is selfless and would starve herself to feed her children, they do not always bring her happiness. Ironically, the actors playing Hester's offspring double with the roles of her Job-like accusers, exemplifying still another way Parks incorporates rep and rev, a double take, if you will, on how Hester is seen and treated by family and friends alike.

Far different from the surrealistic and intensely experimental style that characterized *Mutabilities*, *The America Play*, and *Last Black Man*, *In the Blood* is disruptively gritty, naturalistic. As David Krasner insists, the play "utilizes realistic settings and psychological characterizations." [69] James C. Taylor likens *In the Blood* to the "1930s social dramas of Odets."[70] Unquestionably, *In the Blood* rages against crimes in the street and the oppression of the poor and black. In productions, directors have filled the stage with urban litter, trash, symbolizing the "urban wasteland"[71] where Hester attempts to survive and protect her children. Sadly, she and they are assimilated into this trashed, fragmented world. Besides using a naturalistic setting and characters, *In the Blood* also retains traces of Parks's "Brechtian–feminist aesthetic."[72] The play's fast-paced action and "The Looking Song" cogently link *In the Blood* to Brecht's social protest dramas. It might be regarded as Parks's version of *Mother Courage*, except that Hester's courage is stretched to the breaking point.

Parks identifies Greek tragedy as a major influence on *In the Blood*. Her love of Greek theater explains why so much action occurs offstage and gets reported rather than enacted onstage as is best evidenced in *Devotees in the Garden of Love* (1992), a play in which three women watch a raging and offstage battle from a hilltop. As Parks told Kathy Sova, "The Greeks understood distance and journey; their plays often include events that happen offstage and retold to us later. In *Blood*, I use the confessions, the characters' interior monologues, to describe events that happened offstage."[73] Parks's characters, structure, and themes in *In the Blood* also resemble a Greek tragedy. Harvey Young has explored how choral segments/songs divide Parks's play, thus linking it with classical drama.[74] Schafer points out that *In the Blood* observes the so-called Aristotelian unities found in the classical Greek theater—the play is set in one place, on one day, and dramatizes one key action. Moreover, Schafer asserts, "Hester's choices allow us to perceive her as a tragic hero with a tragic flaw who brings about her own downfall."[75]

On the other hand, some reviewers maintain that Hester is more sinned against than sinning, is more a victim of social forces than a flawed tragic hero. We might ask in murdering her son Jabber does Hester rival Medea? When Hester tells Rev. D. she saw an ominous "black thing" like a hand in the sky, is she confronting an unalterable fate? Does Parks's play arouse our pity and fear, the two main emotions tragedy, according to Aristotle, was to elicit? Parks seems to answer these questions: "I just write tragedy and devastation. It's like bleeding; like they used to bleed folks. The play creates a wound that is actually the first stage in the healing process."[76] That first stage undeniably involves indicting the audience for allowing the crimes committed against Hester and her children and the second stage is deciding to do something about it.

Just as Suzan-Lori Parks imprinted her signature on Hawthorne's *The Scarlet Letter*, she seemingly did so with one of Eugene O'Neill's most powerful plays. According to Hilton Als, *The Book of Grace*, which premiered at the Public Theater in March 2010, is a "modern day riff of Eugene O'Neill's *Desire Under the Elms*." [77] Like *Desire Under the Elms*, and Parks's earlier works, *The Book of Grace* is a three-character play showing a family in crisis. Vet, the bigoted white father who works as a Texas border guard, has not seen his son, Buddy, whom he fathered with a black woman, in 15 years. When Buddy returns home from the military, carrying grenades and years of bitterness with him, he and his father clash while Vet's new wife, Grace, attempting to ameliorate every situation, welcomes Buddy. All three characters work on "books," accounts of how they see themselves and each other. In *Desire under the Elms*, as in Parks's other plays, the sins of parents haunt their children.

Many critics interpreted *The Book of Grace* as a parable on who and what constitutes America. Ben Brantley claimed that with her three characters, Parks was "dividing the American soul into three components," an idea, of course, that runs throughout Parks's earlier canon especially in *America Play* and *Last Black Man*.[78] Though not as boldly experimental or critically appreciated as these early plays, *The Book of Grace* nonetheless includes some of Parks's signature symbols, particularly fences and holes. For example, Vet digs a hole in his backyard. There also are "holes" all along the Texas border with Mexico, a point that Suzan-Lori Parks makes in an interview with Dave Steakley, later in this collection. Significantly, Vet's job as a border guard is to keep people out of America while the hole he digs seems to represent the moral and familial emptiness within his own home, as Ephraim Cabot discovers in *Desire*.

Excavating Porgy and Bess

In addition to adapting literary works such as *The Scarlet Letter*, Parks has ventured into musicals (*Ray Charles Live!*) and opera with her transformation of the Gershwins' classic *Porgy and Bess*, which premiered in 2011 at the American Repertory Theatre before transferring to Broadway. Director Diane Paulus asked Parks to join her in "excavating and shaping and modernizing the story and particularly Bess."[79] Paulus was given the go-ahead from the Gershwin estate to make the opera more accessible to larger audiences. Her aim, as well as Parks's, therefore, was to transform an American classic opera into a commercially profitable musical that would draw African American audiences into the theater. Acutely aware that the 1935 *Porgy and Bess* presented a stereotypical portrait of African American characters, along with the frequent use of the N-word, Parks "scrubbed the libretto of its retro dialect."[80] She knew what had to be changed and why to make the work politically correct:

> While the original opera triumphs on many levels, I feel the writing sometimes suffers from what I call "a shortcoming of understanding"…

In DuBose and Dorothy Heyward [who collaborated on the lyrics with Ira Gershwin] and the Gershwins' original, there is a lot of love and a lot of effort made to understand the people of Catfish Row. In turn, I've got love and respect for their work, but in some ways I feel it falls short in the creation of fully realized characters. Now, one could see their depiction of African-American culture as racist, or one could see it as I see it: as a problem of dramaturgy.[81]

Tampering with an American classic was highly controversial, an arena not new to Parks whose plays repeatedly have pushed the boundaries of theater. Parks emphasized that she and Paulus had "to make sure we had a story that lived up to its title," focusing on both Porgy and Bess. Elaborating, Parks claimed:

I feel this work more than anything is a romance, and so I wanted to flesh out the two main characters so they are not cardboard cut-out characters… I think that's what George Gershwin wanted, and if he had lived longer… he would have gone back to the story of "Porgy and Bess" and made changes, including to the ending.[82]

To underscore the romance and make Porgy and Bess more accessible to 21st-century audiences, Parks and Paulus streamlined the opera, reducing its running time from four hours to two-and-a-half; substituted spoken dialogue where recitatives were called for in the original; changed dialogue to make it more realistic; turned Porgy into a more desirable man for Bess; and made the ending more hopeful and less perplexing for audiences. As theater critic Melanie N. Lee wrote in her review, "This production makes up for the shortened and cut tongues, cut characters, loss of recitative by pumping up the drama, the dance, the laughter, and the motivations."[83] "Now there's an actual dramatic arc to 'Porgy and Bess,'" claimed Phillip Boykin who played Crown, Bess's rejected lover, reeling from whiskey and happy dust.[84] In the Parks's adaptation, "The story's primal themes—love, death, desire, home, survival… are deeply etched," argued David Rooney for his review in *The Hollywood Reporter*.[85] Not surprisingly, these are the themes that have dominated Parks's dramatic canon.

Essentially, then, Parks also added psychological depth to Bess and Porgy. "In the opera you don't really get to know many of the characters as people, especially and most problematically Bess, who goes back and forth from Crown's woman to Porgy's woman while also addicted to drugs," declared Paulus.[86] Bess's addiction is made more contemporary and, possibly, more destructive. Yet she is able to overcome her addiction and, in Parks's script, she is seen as a much more heroic and well-developed character. But of all the characters to undergo a transformation from the Gershwins' 1935 opera it is probably Porgy who changes the most. He does not ride across the stage in a goat cart but instead walks with a cane and braces. Norm Lewis, who played Porgy, remarked that "Porgy was less of an enigma in the new production. His malformed legs are explained in new dialogue, and his desire to walk and become a 'natural man for Bess.'"[87] Also commenting on Lewis's Porgy, Mark Kennedy observes, "His Porgy knows Bess is out of his league, which makes his attempt to better himself—to be a 'natural man' with a brace—even more breathtaking."[88]

In general, the critics applauded Parks's adaptation. Richard Zoglin, writing for *Time Magazine,* notes, "It's accessible—a *Porgy* for purists and for the rest of us, too…This *Porgy* is faithful to what counts most—[George] Gershwin's lush, bluesy irreplaceable score. That makes it a revival not to hound but to hail."[89] In his review, Ed Siegel went even further in praising Parks: "… not only is the new version thoroughly respectful toward the original, its changes are mostly subtle and, as far as I'm concerned, improvements on the original."[90] And Scott Brown concluded that Parks's adaptation was a "gorgeous and transportive theatrical rapture."[91]

Most vocal among the naysayers was Stephen Sondheim who blasted the production in advance of its opening, attacking Paulus and Parks for their editing and revising this classic opera. He blamed them for providing "back stories for the characters," arguing that "Porgy, Bess, Sportin' Life and the rest are archetypes and intended to be larger than life and that filling in 'realistic' details is likely to reduce them to line drawings." In sentences dripping with sarcasm, he excoriated Parks: "It is reassuring that Ms. Parks has a direct pipeline to Gershwin and is just carrying out his work for him, and that she thinks he would have taken one of the most moving moments in musical theater history— Porgy's demand, 'Bring my goat!'—and thrown it out."[92] He concluded by reminding Paulus and Parks that "there is a difference between reinterpretation and wholesale rewriting." Gesturing toward Sondheim in his review of the play, Kennedy concluded politely, "You won't miss the goat cart."[93]

Radical Inclusion

Although Parks's plays were first embraced by the experimental theater community, the theatrical ambitions of the playwright have always sought newer, wider, and increasingly popular audiences across a range of presentational formats. Her plays have premiered in bars and have been staged on Broadway. She has won both the Obie Award and the Tony Award. She has written for radio, television, and film. Indeed, Suzan-Lori Parks maintains an active and compelling presence in essentially every mass medium of communication. Perhaps no Parks creation better represents her seeming omnipresence than *365 Days/365 Plays*, a theatrical experiment that sought to redefine the idea of a world premiere by inviting professional and amateur companies across the globe to share in the premiere experience by simultaneously mounting separate productions of sections of a new play. The play, *365 Days/365 Plays*, not unlike the fictional cartoon character Voltron, exists as a series of parts that combine to create a new whole. In this case, it is approximately 365 plays, each of which is complete in itself, but together, also exist essentially as scenes in a much larger theatrical creation.

In interviews, Parks often speaks of "hearing the voices" and the spiritual influences that guide her hand in playwriting. Similarly, she found motivation to write "a play a day" for an entire year. This exercise was done privately with the playwright informing only her inner circle of friends what she was doing. As Parks has noted, "It was kind of like endurance art but it was really, really trippy because it was endurance art done in private, without an audience. Very few people knew that I was doing it."[94] Every day, she would carve out space to write her "daily devotion." On some days, her plays would exist as fully realized theatrical pieces bearing a resemblance to episodes in previous works. On other days, the play would be only a line or two, essentially a theatrical haiku. Nevertheless, she persisted in writing and in so doing developed a piece that offers uncanny insight not only into her writing process but also serves as a historical record of the events of the year.

The first play *Start Here* and, by extension, opening *365 Days/Plays*, explicitly draws attention to the craft of writing. For the reader, it is easy to imagine the playwright facing a blank page in her typewriter (or notebook) or staring at a blank computer screen—Parks regularly employs both forms of writing—and formally beginning her 365-day effort with the words "Start Here." It is perhaps even more compelling to recall the speed with which Parks wrote *Topdog* and wonder what ambitions the playwright had for this new work, which motivated her to write at least one play per day for a year. In much the way that *Topdog* riffs on a previous theme in Parks's dramaturgy, specifically the Lesser Man's replaying of Lincoln's assassination, the scores of plays in *365* frequently connect with topics Parks previously addressed. At times, some plays feel like bonus reels, material left unsaid and never produced in Parks's other plays. Despite the fact that Parks has been clear that she crafted each play from scratch, the unique markers of her dramaturgy—her physicalized language and investment in making history—appear throughout the play collection.

In staging the plays, Suzan-Lori Parks, with producer Bonnie Metzgar, elected to allow theater companies, both amateur and professional, to present one week's worth of plays at a fee of $1.00 per play. Multiple theaters would share the same week and, in so doing, would jointly (but in separate productions) stage their world premieres. With nearly 1,000 theatrical companies and groups committed to the project, Parks's play, as the *New York Times* has noted, may be the largest and most elaborate theatrical premiere ever, involving some of the "most prominent institutional theaters in the country as well as summer-stock theaters in Montana, community ensembles on the South Side of Chicago, a nursing home in Atlanta, and an abandoned movie house in the valley of the Rio Grande." As she pointed out in an interview with Joseph Roach transcribed here for the first time, Parks realized that she could have spent a handful of days, written another two-person play, and created a text that could be staged on Broadway. However, her commitment to the craft of playwriting and her respect for the muses who inspire her prevented her from pursuing the more profitable but less fulfilling avenue.

In recent years, the phrase "radical inclusion" best describes Parks's approach to theater creation. In a 2007 interview with Kevin Wetmore, she noted:

> To write a play a day for a whole year, you have to dismiss the bouncer who works the door of your creative mind. All ideas are welcome. All ideas are worthy for play-making. Somehow I wanted the production of the play cycle to dovetail with this 'radical inclusion'. But I didn't know how. So one day I'm hanging out with Bonnie Metzgar, who I've known since 1989, and we're sitting around thinking about how a production of *365* can be different and fun. And we're like, 'Maybe lots of theatres could do it – like 365 theatres!' And that was crazy. It was like saying, 'And then we're going to go to the moon!' It was just that nutty – 365 theatres doing the plays.[95]

The philosophy of not blocking the doors of inspiration ultimately led not only to the writing of *365* but to nearly 1,0000 professional, university, and community theaters jointly participating in its premiere. Furthermore, radical inclusion might be best evidence by Parks's 2012 and 2013 "Watch Me Work" performances at the ZACH Theatre in Houston and at the Public Theater in New York City. Sitting on an elevated platform in the lobby of the theater with a typewriter or notepad, Parks literally turns her "daily devotion" into a performance. Anyone can stop by and watch her work, or see her write. It is an act of generosity—allowing casual observers an opportunity to see first-hand the benefits of radical inclusion on the writing process. This staging certainly aligns with Parks's interest in the scopic—the watching of black bodies at work within her plays—from the women in *Devotees*, who themselves are spectators; to the Lesser Man and Lincoln in *The America Play* and *Topdog;* to Hester LaNegrita in *In the Blood* to the Venus Hottentot in *Venus*. The playwright becomes a character even as she scripts them. For a few hours each day, she stands (or sits) on show in the theater lobby and urges everyone to "Please visit."

Notes

1 John Marshall, "A Moment with… Suzan-Lori Parks, playwright," *Seattle Post-Intelligencer*, May 26, 2003.
2 Alisa Solomon quoted in Deborah Geis, *Suzan-Lori Parks* (Ann Arbor: University of Michigan Press, 2008), 45.
3 Suzan-Lori Parks, *The America Play and Other Works* (New York: Theatre Communications Group, 1995), 40.
4 Geis, 50.
5 Parks, *Other Works*, 55.
6 Irene Backalenick, "Suzan-Lori Parks: The Joy of Playwrighting," *Theater Week*, April 8–14, 1996: 27.
7 Parks, *Other Works*, 38.

8 Ibid., 54.
9 Ibid., 40.
10 Ibid., 42–43.
11 Faedra Chatard Carpenter, "A Parks Remix: An Interview with Liz Diamond" in Philip C. Kolin, ed. *Suzan-Lori Parks: Essays on the Plays and Other Works* (Jefferson, NC: McFarland, 2010), 195.
12 Shawn-Marie Garrett, "Figures, Speech and Form in *Imperceptible Mutabilities in the Third Kingdom*," in Kevin J. Wetmore and Alycia Smith-Howard, eds., *Suzan-Lori Parks: A Casebook* (London: Routledge, 2007), 16.
13 Suzan-Lori Parks, "Statement of Purpose," February 12, 1985. Unpublished.
14 Parks, *Other* Works, 18.
15 David Savran, *The Playwrights Voice: American Dramatists on Memory, Writing and the Politics of Culture* (New York: Theatre Communications Group, 1999), 149
16 Suzan-Lori Parks, "Thoughts on Para-literate Speech," *NWP: Journal of the New Works Project*, 1, May 1, 1989: 2.
17 Jennifer Larsen, *Understanding Suzan-Lori Parks* (Columbia, SC: University of South Carolina Press, 2012), 22.
18 Savran, 144.
19 Parks, *Other Works*, 108.
20 Ibid., 119.
21 Ibid., 111.
22 Ibid., 107.
23 Ibid., 104
24 Ibid., 131.
25 Ibid., 126.
26 Ibid., 130
27 Alice Rayner and Harry J. Elam, Jr. "Unfinished Business: Reconfiguring History in Suzan-Lori Parks's *The Death of the Last Black Man in the Whole Entire World*," *Theatre Journal* 46, no. 4 (December 1994): 451.
28 Han Ong, "An Interview with Suzan-Lori Parks," *BOMB* 47 (Spring 1994): 47–50.
29 Savran, *The Playwright's Voice*, 148.
30 Diamond quoted in Carpenter, 194.
31 Jonathan Kalb, Richard Foreman, Liz Diamond, Leah C. Gardiner, and Bill Waters, "Remarks on Parks 2," www.hotreview.org/articles/remarksparks2.htm
32 Parks, *Other Works*, 119.
33 Quoted by Robert Brustein in Jonathan Kalb, Robert Brustein, Shawn-Marie Garrett, Mark Robinson and Alisa Solomon, "Remarks on Parks 1," www.hotreview.org/articles/remarksparks1.htm
34 Michele Pearce, "Alien Nation: An Interview with the Playwright," *American Theatre*, 11.3 (March 1994): 26.
35 Academy of Achievement, "Suzan-Lori Parks Interview," June 22, 2007, http://www.achievement.org/autodoc/page/par1int-1. In other interviews, Parks has noted the odd coincidence that she and John Wilkes Booth, Lincoln's assassin, share a birthday.
36 Parks, *Other Works*, 164.
37 Alpert Awards, "Suzan-Lori Parks Playwright and Screenwriter" (1996), http://previous.alpertawards.org/archive/winner96/parks.html.
38 Pearce, 26.
39 Ibid.
40 Parks, *Other Works*, 164.
41 Ibid., 169.
42 Ibid., 171.
43 Geis, 160.
44 Larsen, 69.
45 Ong, "Suzan-Lori Parks," 47–50.

46 Parks, *Other Works*, 196.
47 Ibid., 163.
48 Rayner and Elam, 181.
49 Geis, 100.
50 Shelby Jiggetts, "Interview with Suzan-Lori Parks," *Callaloo*, 19.2 (Spring 1996): 317.
51 Parks, *Other Plays*, 190.
52 For more on *Venus*, see Harvey Young, "Touching History: Staging Black Experience," in *Embodying Black Experience* (Ann Arbor: University of Michigan Press), 119–166.
53 Suzan-Lori Parks, *Venus* (New York: Dramatists Play Service, 1995): 26.
54 Ibid., 162.
55 Greg Evans, "Venus, Joseph Papp's Public Theater Martinson Hall, May 3, 1996.
56 Ben Brantley, "Of an Erotic Freak Show and the Lesson Therein," *New York Times,* May 3, 1996.
57 Quoted in Rick DesRochers, "Mythology, History, Family, Performance," Public Access (Stagebill), August 2001, 1: 8–10.
58 Jean Young, "The Re-Objectification and Re-Commodification of Saartjie Baartman in Suzan-Lori Parks's Venus," *African American Review*, 31.4 (Winter 1997): 699.
59 Tom Sellar, "Making History: Suzan-Lori Parks," *Theatre Forum*, Summer/Fall 1996: 35–36
60 See Sara Warner, *Suzan-Lori Parks on Stage and Screen* (London: Methuen, forthcoming, 2015) and Harvey Young, "Touching History."
61 Quoted in DesRochers, 9.
62 Elizabeth Farnsworth, "Pulitzer Prize for Drama," *Online News Hour*, April 11, 2002, http://www.pbs.org/newshour/conversation/jan-june02/parks_4-11.html.
63 Ibid.
64 Kevin J. Wetmore, "It's an Oberammergau Thing: An Interview with Suzan-Lori Parks," in Kevin J. Wetmore and Alycia Smith-Howard, eds., *Suzan-Lori Parks: A Casebook* (London: Routledge, 2007): 124–140.
65 See Philip C. Kolin, "In the Blood," *The Explicator* (Summer 2006), 245–248.
66 Kathy Sova, "A Better Mirror," *American Theatre*, Vol. 17.3 (March 2000): 32.
67 Suzan-Lori Parks, *In the Blood* (New York: New Dramatists Play Service, Inc., 2000): 37.
68 Carol Schafer, "Staging New Literary History: Suzan-Lori Parks's *Venus, In the Blood*, and *Fucking A*," *Comparative Drama*, 42 (Summer 2008): 181.
69 David Krasner, "*In the Blood* (review)", *Theatre Journal*, Vol. 52.4 (Dec. 2000): 565.
70 James C. Taylor, "Theatre Talk on KCRW (National Public Radio-Southern California)" July 26, 2003.
71 Ibid.
72 Christine Woodworth, "Parks and the Traumas of Childhood," in Philip C. Kolin, ed. *Suzan-Lori Parks: Essays on the Plays and Other Works* (Jefferson, NC: McFarland, 2010): 147.
73 Sova, 32.
74 See Harvey Young, "Choral Compassion: *In the Blood* and *Venus*," in Kevin J. Wetmore and Alycia Smith-Howard, eds., *Suzan-Lori Parks: A Casebook* (London: Routledge, 2007), 36.
75 Schafer, 192.
76 Kia Corthron, Rebecca Gilman, Kenneth Lonergan, and Suzan-Lori Parks, "Talking Shop (Which Takes in the Whole World")," *New York Times*, Feb. 25, 2001: 6.
77 Hilton Als, "Grace Under Pressure," *The New Yorker*, March 29, 2010: 102.
78 Ben Brantley, "A Family Triangle of Archetypes Amid the Sandbags of America," *New York Times*, March 18, 2010.
79 Ben Brantley, "A New Storm's Brewing on Catfish Row," *New York Times*, January 12, 2012. http://theater.nytimes.com/2012/01/13/theater/reviews/audra-mcdonald-in-the-gershwins-porgy-and-bess-review.html?_r=0.

80 David Cote, "Time Out Theater Review: *Porgy and Bess*," NY1.com, Jan. 13, 2012.

81 Quoted in Hilton Als, "A Man and A Woman," *The New Yorker*, Sept. 26, 2011.

82 Quoted in Patrick Healy, "It Ain't Necessarily 'Porgy,'" *New York Times*, Aug. 5, 2011, AR1

83 Melanie N. Lee, nytheatre.com review of *The Gershwins' Porgy and Bess*, January 18, 2012 (http://nytheatre.com/Review/melanie-n-lee-2012-1-18-the-gershwins-porgy-and-bess).

84 Quoted in Healy, AR1.

85 David Rooney, "The Gershwin's Porgy and Bess," *The Hollywood Reporter*, January 12, 2012.

86 Quoted in Healy, AR1.

87 Ibid.

88 Mark Kennedy, "A Reworked *Porgy and Bess* is Rich and Lucious," *Huffington Post*, January 12, 2012, n.p.

89 Richard Zoglin, "Loves You, Porgy," *Time*, September 12, 2011, 62.

90 Ed Siegel, "New *Porgy and Bess* Improves on Original," WBUR (Boston NPR), September 2, 2011 (www.wbur.org/2011/09/02/porgy-review).

91 Scott Brown, "The Gershwins' *Porgy and Bess* and the Weight of History," *Vulture*, January 12, 2012, www.vulture.com/2012/01/theater-review-porgy-and-bess.html.

92 *New York Times*, "Stephen Sondheim Takes Issue With Plan for Revamped 'Porgy and Bess'," August 10, 2011.

93 Kennedy, n.p.

94 Joseph Roach, "Interview with Suzan-Lori Parks and Bonnie Metzgar." Published in this collection, 118–119.

95 Wetmore, 136.

PART I

Interviews

1

THEATER'S VIBRANT NEW VOICE

Suzan-Lori Parks Puts Dreams into Words—and Invents a New Language for the Stage

Patti Hartigan

Boston Globe, February 14, 1992

She saw the title on the bedroom wall. That's right. Playwright Suzan-Lori Parks opened her eyes one morning, and while languishing in that trancey stage between consciousness and sleep, she saw the words: The Death of the Last Negro in the Whole Entire World.

"I jumped up and said, 'I want black,' because of the rhythm," remembers Parks. Equipped with the working title, she then wrote "The Death of the Last Black Man in the Whole Entire World," a dreamy play that cuts across the width and breadth of African and African-American history and creates a new theatrical language. The play, which is being performed through March 7 as part of Winterfest at Yale Repertory Theater, presents characters (Parks calls them figures) like Queen-Then-Pharaoh Hatshepsut, Lots of Grease and Lots of Pork, Black Man with Watermelon.

This is not kitchen-sink drama, nor is it agitprop.

"I don't write headlines," says the 28-year-old playwright. "Some people do that and they're very good at it. That's not what I'm about."

What she is about is language, the sheer sensuality and physicality of words. There are no stage directions in Parks' script; she says she writes the movements into the dialogue so that actors inherently know what to do while speaking. "Language is about breathing. It's about teeth and mouth and spit in your mouth and how your jaw works and what your hands are doing. It's all there. It's in the lines and the actors can pick it up and do something with it," she says.

Parks won the 1990 Obie award, the off-Broadway equivalent of the Tony, for her play "Imperceptible Mutabilities in the Third Kingdom." The titles alone are pregnant with potential, and the work makes it clear that Parks is a rare talent about to knock the socks off contemporary theater. She uses words in a way that makes you feel like you've discovered a new language. Encountering Parks for the first time inspires one of those "Eureka!" reactions that occur so rarely in contemporary theater.

Consider riding along in a train, reading this speech from "Entire World" about the birth of a race: "Wassername she finally gave intuh It and tugether they broughted forth uh wildish one called simply Yo… . Yes Suh Mistuh Suh breeded with hisself n gived us Wassername (thuh 2nd), and Wassernickname (2 twins in birth joindid at thuh lip)."

The train might just as well stop in its tracks.

Parks has already caused a stir in funky New York theaters, and now she is about to emerge as a voice to be reckoned with at the big-time regional theaters. She knows it: "I'm not a kid anymore," she says. The Yale production is not only significant because the 650-seat theater is about six times bigger than any theater Parks has worked in to date. It's significant because her work is now being done at one of the most acclaimed regional theaters in the country. And her play "Devotees in the Garden of Love" premieres this month at the prestigious new play festival at the Actors Theater of Louisville.

Stan Wojewodski, the new artistic director of Yale Rep and dean of the Yale School of Drama, had never seen Parks' work before inviting her to participate in Winterfest, Yale's annual festival of new theater. But after reading her plays, he knew he was in the presence of a major new voice, a cutting-edge writer. He says, "She is an extraordinary poet for the stage. I had a sense of productions thundering under the surface of her writing," says Wojewodski, who has redefined Winterfest, the brainchild of former dean Lloyd Richards, to include plays that aren't brand-new but that push the form forward. "When you read the play, there seems to be no story. The narrative doesn't seem logical. But suddenly, there is this very clear story that couldn't be told any other way. It's the moment when content becomes form."

The story is, in fact, about the death of the last black man in the whole entire world. (The black woman asks him, "Where you gonna go now now that you done dieded?") But Parks resists being categorized as a "black woman playwright" who only writes about the suffering of her race. It's an assumption too many people make about her without even seeing the work, she says. "I don't mind the label, but I do mind what happens next: Black woman playwright equals some sort of play. People say the black experience is X, and usually the X is the sorrows and frustrations and angers of people who have been wronged. That's all we get to write about. That's the black experience. Well, that's very important, but it's not my thing," she says.

Her thing is time. She wants her plays to be suspended in time, like a lemon liquid floating in clear fluid in a test tube. "My plays are like suspension, hanging and slowly drifting down," she says, sculpting shapes in the air as she moves her hand downward. "Floating, floating, floating, until…" She snaps her fingers. "It's over. The spell is broken."

During a recent interview at Yale, Parks illustrates her points with physical movements. She does push-ups while discussing her literary influences:

Gertrude Stein, James Joyce, William Faulkner, Samuel Beckett. She drapes herself over a bench, hand brushing her brow in an oh-my-God-you-make-my-knees-weak pose while explaining how she writes love scenes.

"Her work has the sense of the sheer pleasure of sound. Everything has meaning. Nothing is gratuitous," says director Liz Diamond, Parks' longtime collaborator, who won an Obie for her production of "Imperceptible Mutabilities." "The script is all gorgeous and dense and poetic. It's almost like jazz. If you follow the punctuation, it's written like a musical score."

Every word has meaning and more meaning. History becomes his story. Remember, in this play, becomes literally re-member, like Isis putting together the limbs of Osiris, like a slave collecting the pieces of her slain husband, remembering and re-membering.

Parks recalls writing short stories, poems, even novels as a little girl. The middle child of an Army colonel, she grew up in the world's cradle, moving from place to place, country to country. That provided her with large cardboard moving boxes that became puppet theaters for the talented youngster.

She is hardly a disenchanted Army child, not this woman. She remembers a charming and happy childhood full of rich experiences. "I've heard horrible stories about 12-step groups for Army people. But I had a great childhood. My parents were really into experiencing the places we lived," she says. In Germany, the family lived in a little hamlet with goats and pigs. Parks and her younger brother and older sister attended German schools and became fluent in the language.

She felt the muse early on, but it wasn't until she was a student at Hampshire College and took a writing course with James Baldwin that she decided to write for the theater. "He might say, 'You should write it down and hide it under a rock,'" she says, quoting a line from "Entire World." "That's a completely outrageous thing to say, just as outrageous as 'You should write plays.' Who are you? What do you know about me? But I went ahead and did it anyway. Why not?"

She then decided it was more important to study acting than playwriting and spent a year at the Drama Studio in London. "It really made a difference in my writing. It dawned on me that a lot of people write with ideas in mind. So I've got an idea – a gggrreat idea for a play," she says, jumping up and down in her demonstrative way. "But I never really have ideas, per se. I have these movements, these gestures. Then I figure out how to put those gestures into words."

She sees the work as an organic blend of physical and intellectual communication. She likens it to the Seido karate lessons she began taking a few years ago: The body and the mind are one, like "Zen in motion." She first imagines what her characters are doing, then writes the words to fit the motion. She illustrates: First she sits up straight, then slumps, then leans forward, using a different tone of voice to match each pose.

She's used that writing technique for all of her work, which in addition to the Obie-winning play includes "Betting on the Dust" and "The America Play," along with a film, radio productions and television spots. There have been two grants from the National Endowment for the Arts and several fellowships. She's currently writer-in-residence at the New School for Social Research in Manhattan, where she makes her home.

The plays, she allows, are conversations with herself. "You will write it down," a character in "Entire World" says repeatedly. "You will write it down." But while the playwright's vocation is evident in the play, Parks says the work must be more than a private meditation. "Art is about having a conversation with yourself. But if it doesn't at some point connect with other people, then it's drivel," she says.

The connection, however, has more to do with mood than message. Parks says she values the collaboration with Diamond because the director and close friend doesn't "turn up the message dial." The playwright wants the audience to experience the play on several levels. "The black man has a line: 'Aint eatable so I out in out ought not aint be eatin it aint that right.' You put the language in your head and your heart and you feel it," she says. "The form is important. I can say a lot more through language instead of 'OK, it's message time.'" Parks wants her plays to work on the audience like complex carbohydrates: "You eat them and they stay with you for longer than a headline. Or bang – like sugar or a candy bar. What did it say? A minute later, you don't know."

And she knows she's taking on Big Themes and new forms in the work. "It's a big story. It's epic," she says of "Entire World." "It's bigger than a naturalistic play about Sally and Jeff in their apartment in New York. That's a cool thing to write about if that's what you're into, but that's not what I'm into."

Just as she resists labels, this rare talent resists being pinned down on What It All Means. "The message of this play isn't that black people have been treated badly, even though they have been. There are things that the spirits in the play tell you to do, like you should write things down. But I don't know if that's the message," she says, grinning as she comes up with a summation that is both factual and enigmatic. "The message of the play is: This happened once. That's all."

2

THE NEXT STAGE

Is Playwright Suzan-Lori Parks the Voice of the Future?

Erika Munk

The Washington Post, February 28, 1993

"Her voice has already made a difference on our stage," says Arena Stage's Laurence Maslon, speaking of playwright Suzan-Lori Parks. "By the end of the decade, everyone will be doing her." He adds, "If we can't hear her, there's nothing wrong with her voice, just something wrong with our ears."

Of course, the theater world – from the avant-garde to Broadway – is full of hype. But hype can be, after all, a form of hope. American theater is always looking for someone to pull it out of the doldrums, or maybe the abyss. And some think that Parks, whose startling *The America Play* is being performed as a workshop production at Arena through tonight, just may be that someone.

At 29, Parks has been praised in publications ranging from the *Village Voice* to the *New Republic*. *New York Times* critic Mel Gussow called her *Imperceptible Mutabilities of the Third Kingdom* one of the 10 best plays of 1989 and Parks that year's most promising new playwright. Peter Wallace, who directed *The America Play* workshop at Arena in anticipation of staging a larger production, says: "Suzan's writing is unique, but she's not set in some little niche on the far side of the mainstream. This is what the mainstream will be if we continue doing theater."

Why all the excitement? Because of Parks's poetic language, her stagecraft, her humor; because she's writing about American and African American history in all its varieties of loss and survival. Realism has dominated our stage from O'Neill to Miller to August Wilson. Parks writes about reality too, but doesn't reach her truth by mimicking the kind of plots, dialogue or characters you can find on TV.

Her originality lies not just in words but in images. Consider this from *Death of the Last Black Man in the Whole Entire World*, staged at Yale Rep last winter: A black man hangs from a noose over a stage on which another black man stands, rope around his neck, among a litter of watermelons, surrounded by characters called Before Columbus, Queen-then-Pharoah Hatshepsut, Lots of Grease and Lots of Pork, Old Man River and Ham.

The America Play is about a black man named the Foundling Father, who says that he "was told that he bore a strong resemblance to Abraham Lincoln. He was tall and thinly built just like the Great Man. His legs were the longer part just like the Great Man's legs. ... He was a Digger by trade. Dug graves."

Possessed by his likeness to Lincoln, he leaves his family, digs a "great hole of history," opens up a booth at its bottom, gets a stock of cap guns and invites the public to shoot him: He's narrating our American drama from below.

In the second act, his wife and son, hearing that the Foundling Father is dead, come searching for his body. But instead of finding his bones, they find "Wonders": George Washington's wooden teeth, peace pacts, emancipation papers, bills of sale, and medals for honesty, croquet, bowing and scraping, and fakery. Throughout the act, the assassin's gunshot echoes. The play ends with the Barnumesque exclamation: "Ho! Wonder! Ho! ... note thuh hole thuh fatal bullet bored. ... And how this great head is bleedin. ... Note: thuh last words. ... and thuh last breaths. ... And how thuh nation mourns... ."

"I'm filling gaps," Parks explains. "My history is a gesture toward the untold story, a different kind of archaeology." Doug Wager, Arena's artistic director, says Parks's digging fits perfectly into his own goal of "working toward the creation of a new American myth."

In *The America Play*, shared myth is centered on the African American experience, but the play is outside what Parks describes as "dramas that tell audiences, 'Oh, black people were doing all these things we don't know about, or showing how oppressed we are by white people and how we triumph over oppression and how, by extension, we're obsessed.' I don't want to create an audience in which the black people just feel good and the white people are just 'mea culpa-ing.'"

Not that Parks's language – and her view of black history – have met with universal praise. Says critic Margot Jefferson, who is black, "What I like best is that she's quirky, and I never know what's going to come out next. But I'm afraid that the strength of her instinct to get into language and emotion can lead into a kind of incantatory indulgence in the word. I sense a struggle between her particular expression of black life and a declamation of it."

Parks was born in 1963 at Fort Knox, KY. Her father is an Army officer, her mother's a teacher, and she had the unsettled childhood of an Army brat, but within the safety of a close family. A stint in Germany left Parks with a good grip on the language, so when she entered Mount Holyoke – "the first place I lived for a continuous four years" – she took a double major in English and German.

"In my junior year I took a short story class taught by James Baldwin, and you had to read your work out loud," Parks remembers. "I got so deep into it, really acting out my stories, moving around the room, that he said, 'Why don't you start writing plays?' And one day I walked past my professor Mary

McHenry and without a word she just handed me Adrienne Kennedy's great play *Funnyhouse of a Negro*."

McHenry remembers Parks as "taking everything in, like a giant sponge. As someone who had lived abroad and had a second language, she was already the sum total of a long list of experiences, a surprise to all those who assume that black people all come out of the same experience. She was quite wild intellectually, had a wonderful fire to her, but she was not an undergraduate eccentric. Many people have a vision – she has a vision and does her work."

Parks directed a production of Ntozake Shange's *For Colored Girls...* in her senior year, despite the fact that "theater people made me nervous because they dressed funny and had this attitude, so much affect." Still, after college she studied acting for a year in London, "because I knew that to be a good writer I had to know about acting. I learned how to make sounds. And now I have such a respect for training." In 1986 she moved to New York, where she became a writer-in-residence at the New School and her plays began to be seen off-off-Broadway.

Countering stereotypes is a large part of Parks's work and life. "I'm trying to explode the myth that women writers are boring," she says. "Serious writers can wear eyeliner." Or as Liz Diamond, who has directed five projects with Parks, puts it, "I've directed many plays by women – you know, ipso dipso, you're a woman, you can do that – but hers are different. They are full of feminist content – inside her primary concern with blackness." On this issue Parks simply says, "I was black before I was born; the woman thing will take longer to figure out."

Diamond, who is white, met Parks at a coffee shop in 1988. "We hit it off like a house on fire," she says. "We had a lot in common – a passion for Faulkner, hatred of smarmy psychological realism, love of high theatricality and the sound of words in actors' mouths."

Parks's dialogue, which can look formidably opaque on the page, is absolutely clear when spoken because it comes from a precise effort to capture African American sound and patterns. When she started out, Parks says, she'd get "weird letters" from theater directors saying things "like, 'you are obviously not writing plays! It really doesn't make any difference, all your little spellings, it just makes it so hard to read' – and this from someone who'd read Joyce." The problem wasn't Parks's "difficulty," it was that making the effort to really hear what she had written meant entering an area of difference that even avant-garde theater managers didn't find worthwhile.

Laurence Maslon says of Parks: "She exercises the muscles of African American actors, allowing them to do what Sam Shepard allowed white actors to do 20 years ago – be musical and non-natural without losing the gutsiness of the characters. They have to dive into the 20- foot-deep end of the pool – she writes the riff and they have to rise to it."

During the workshop performances of *The America Play*, the crew would watch the play and later talk about its passions and ideas – not a common event. Like that crew, audiences can get deeply involved in smart, brave, complicated theater. This is, after all, a complicated and emotional moment in American life. But most producers are too timid to do these plays and nourish these audiences.

They fall back on standard entertainment instead. But they'd be wise to remember that Lincoln, when he went to Ford's Theater, was looking for a lightweight night out. He went to see a pop comedy, *Our American Cousin*, a play so predictable that Booth knew in advance exactly what line would get a loud enough laugh to cover the sound of his shot. Conventional theater just covers up the sound of history. Parks lets us hear it, if we'll let ourselves hear her.

3

SUZAN-LORI PARKS

Han Ong
BOMB, Spring 1994

The quality of Suzan-Lori Parks' imagination is unassailable. Her plays provide ample proof: *Imperceptible Mutabilities in the Third Kingdom*, *The Death of the Last Black Man in the Whole Entire World*, *Devotees in the Garden of Love*, and *The America Play*. Through them she reaches an articulation she doesn't quite approximate in real life, a great horn sound, drunken and lucid at the same time, and they in turn speak very well of her.

There is nothing like reading Suzan-Lori's work. Actually there is nothing like hearing Suzan-Lori read them. Picking at them for yourself, you hear horns. In her voice, the words take on the quality of bells, still low, but with an extra ping of recognition arching between phrases.

She sits somewhere in the fifth ring, all alone amongst her generation, peerless. Her back is ramrod straight. She is alone. She is always alone, although, intermittently, critical Christmas lights snake their way to her feet, knowing someone for whom to illuminate, to gift with the company of praise.

OCTOBER 1993

Han Ong: I want to talk about the physical world of writing. Are you aware of how you sit on your chair when you write?

Suzan-Lori Parks: I usually don't write sitting down. To me, language is a physical act. I do this with my own writing and I try to get my students to do this when they write—to move around, so that they are focusing on the breath of the characters, on the physical life of the character, and are putting themselves in an approximation of that character's physical experience. That's where the words come from: movement. I dance around, dance around, dance around, and then I know what the character's saying. I act it out, then I get it in my body, and then I take it up and get it in my head… then I sit down and go, "Oh yeah, right…"

HO: Playing the secular piano.

SLP: The chair is just there so I can rest my ass somewhere when I do sit down.

HO: It's the middleman.

SLP: Right. I figured out part of *The America Play* the other day just by putting on Rickie Lee Jones' "Tigers." I worked it out by moving through it, not by sitting down and thinking it through.

HO: It's evident to me that your writing is a kind of music. Let's talk about the correlation between playing music while you write and the words evolving.

SLP: It's a different music for each play. For *The Death of the Last Black Man in the Whole Entire World*, it was a lot of jazz. I listened to Ornette Coleman practically all the time when I was writing that play. The play moves like that.

HO: It's ornery. And for *The America Play*?

SLP: It took me so long to write that play. I started in 1990, and here it is 1993 and I just figured out what happens at the end. It's taken me about a year to figure out the final moment, the last breath. Working on it, I listened to a lot of different stuff. Opera, opera, opera—I love it. The basic shape of each sound, of each line, is operatic, but then I had to cut underneath which is why now I've gone back to Rickie Lee Jones. She's way out there, and also she's very much along the ground. I needed to come back from the spheres and hit the last footprint.

HO: What propels you to variegate your musical inspiration?

SLP: There are aspects of music that I borrow and use in my work: repetition and revision. A big part of jazz is repeat and revise, and repeat and revise. That's what my work is all about. But similarly, you can get the same idea in Wagner or Mozart. *Don Giovanni*'s motifs are played over and over.

HO: What you see as music, I see as architecture—scaffolding. You can go back and do other things, like take longeurs from the main narrative, and still take comfort because there is an inherent structure.

SLP: Right, and all music has that. It's really the height of the ceiling or width of the building. Opera is a very high ceiling, and with jazz, the interior of the building looks different. That's really why I go to different types of music. The feelings I want to evoke are different.

HO: When the characters come to you and into your body, do you lose yourself in them or is there still a sense of self?

SLP: That depends on how you define "you," and "self," and "them." Because they are me, and I am them. It's just more of me. When they come up, when they appear or speak to me or however you want to put it, it's not that I'm losing myself into them. It's that I'm hooking up to more of me.

HO: You're just accessing you? Just going deeper…?

SLP: Or further, or wider, or opening that door. I don't feel that I lose myself so much, because I don't really know who I am. I know that what I am is not just this person in this outfit, or even the name, the social security number, I know that I'm something else…

HO: Let's talk about how you put 12 characters' bodies on stage. How you make them stand or sit or carry a watermelon. How do you put one body in relation to another?

SLP: Well, I leave that mostly to the director. And I like working with directors.

HO: Do you see their bodies when you write?

SLP: I feel their bodies, I know what their bodies are going to be doing. 95 percent of the action, in all of my plays, is in the line of text. So you don't get a lot of parenthetical stage direction. I've written, within the text, specific directions to them, to guide their breathing, to guide the way they walk, whether or not they walk, whether or not they walk with a limp, whatever. They know what to do from what they say and how they say it. The specifics of it are left up to the actor and the director. The internals are in the line, the externals are left up to them.

HO: It helps people to hear this because I think a lot of critics write out of ignorance…

SLP: I think what happens is when you're new, you're weird. And as we grow as playwrights, so do our critics grow in their understanding of our work. That's really how it should work. They educate us through their writing about theater, and we educate them through our view of the world and our writing. They are learning how to look at us. The problem these days is that they have not yet figured out the words with which they can talk about what we're doing. I see it in so many articles now, people are actually struggling to find the words to talk about my work. It's evolving from talk of "black" and "race" to, "Look what she's doing with non-linear time." "Look what she's doing with the whole idea of the structure of a play." It's all about the structure of the play!

HO: Let's talk about why you write plays…

SLP: I've said I write plays because I love black people. I just figured it out fairly recently. Not that I had any other reason before that, but I realized why I want black people on stage—because I love them. And it probably sounds very vague, but it's true.

HO: That's why you get paid the big bucks.

SLP: No, I get paid the big bucks because I am vague and yet, everyone understands. That's poetry, see. I'm a poet. I'm not a journalist. I'm vague but you know exactly what I mean. I write because I love black people. I don't know, that in itself will take me a long way.

HO: What do you want out of all this?

SLP: All I want to do is be able to write the next play or the next book or the next screenplay—that's all I want, It's really all I want. I realized that this summer when I was in a rough spot writing. Everyone says I'm the witchcraft genius or the hot new thing and I say, I'm just a playwright who wants to write her next play. That's it. That's all I am. And then in the life front meet the man who takes me to the moon. Rocket scientist, you know what that means? That's double entendre, baby. Maybe, if he likes to dance that's good too. That's a very good sign. And he has to be able to have a conversation and talk about his feelings. Oh baby, baby.

JANUARY 1994

HO: When you read a piece of work, there are what I call emanations. There are vapors coming from it. Your vapors seem to me to be so strongly about joy.

SLP: Right, and not about, "Oh my God, I'm a black woman and I'm having a hard time." John Wideman had an essay in the *New York Times* a while ago where he was talking about the black writer and the magic of the word: that when faced with problems of the English language, African Americans manifest this drama in two ways, complete fluency or complete silence. The second thing that he said was that in African American life and writing, the yoke becomes a joke. I'm paraphrasing, but that relationship, that love of play, we are encouraged to forget.

HO: Because serious art…

SLP: Serious art is more about issues and messages and subjects. If you're a serious artist, you deal with issues. Because of the history of African Americans in America, or Africans in America, however you want to say it, a lot of great writing has been done in that vein. But we forgot that we are also people who love the relationships between yoke and joke. To me, that's the whole. That's it. That's everything.

HO: Maybe it's also because people feel that joy or levity is a violation of the memories of suffering.

SLP: Actually, humor is the only way to remember, because the relationship between throwing up and laughing is so close [*laughter*]. Humor crosses that gap between what you know and what you think, what you know and what you don't know. Laughter and that joke crosses that gap. That's the way I work; other people work in different ways. Part of it is working with the director, Liz Diamond. She has helped me develop my sense of humor, to put it lightly. We both love the dumb gag, the knee slapper. There's a lot of power in that, and there's a lot of really serious stuff going on in *The America Play*, but I swear, I can only think of the jokes. The jokes led me to write *America*. The relationship between "nigger" and "digger" was the whole play for me. When I could allow myself to have a little chuckle about "nigger" and "digger," I knew who those people were in the play.

HO: That play is the distance between nigger and digger. I don't mean to pat you on the back, or via you, me, but when you're an ethnic writer writing in the theater, what people expect of you is an exploration of ideas racially linked in terms of oppression or marginalization. What they don't expect, in fact, what they don't want you to do because it fucks up their perception, is formal experimentation.

SLP: I honestly believe that form and content are the same thing. In stepping out of the, "I'm a black person, I'm oppressed, and when I represent myself on stage, I'm going to represent an oppressed person," you are also stepping outside of a particular form. To explore the form is to explore "digger" and "nigger," and to explore where that's going to take you. It's all linked.

HO: These issues of marginalization have become so internalized that they have stopped becoming abstract groupings; they've become felt things. Marginalization is present not as an illustration of whitey beating down a black person, but Woman with Fried Drumstick trying to get Black Man with Watermelon to eat in *Last Black Man*. It's about the idea of the black man having his mind so much elsewhere that he needs somebody to remind him to eat. That thing that takes up his mind might not necessarily be oppression, but ultimately it's linked to that.

SLP: But what is it that he's thinking about? He's thinking "Who am I? Where am I? What is this thing in my lap? I don't feel very good right now. Is this melon a part of my body? You know what, wife? I think you should dig me a hole." In *Last Black Man*, the black man keeps saying, "Make me a space six feet by six feet by six." Dig me a hole, woman.

HO: He knows it's a grave?

SLP: Oh, yes, because he has to. He's got to lie down, but what's funny is that *Last Black Man* is about the creation of the hole and then *The America Play* takes place in a huge hole, an excavation.

HO: You had to deal with the aftermath of digging the hole.

SLP: Yes. *The America Play* is like *Last Black Man*. He says "dig me a hole." Now we have a hole, so what are we going to do with it? You spend some time in it and then you leave [*laughter*]. That's so funny.

HO: But that's so telling. Maybe that's the journey that you've taken, or that I've taken. Okay, I'll cop to it. I want a hole dug, which is to say, I want to show you what this country is doing to me. I dig a hole. I put myself there. I've spent time in it. Now I want out. I want alternatives to the hole. What is the antithesis to the hole? It's humor.

SLP: It's both sides. The joke with the hole is that it's not only h-o-l-e, but it's w-h-o-l-e. I want everything. I want the whole thing, the whole hole. It's not just that the hole represents what this country is doing to me and all that. I don't even think that. I think the black man wants a hole, because he wants to rest.

HO: I'm saying that the realm of ideas can be so internalized, that it doesn't flick up the writing. A lot of people allow their ideas to exist on the level of journalism. It's not only easily gettable, but it is stated as such, without the leavening of rhythm or poetry.

SLP: But, I've always been sort of relaxed about what other people do. Certain people have certain needs, and those needs are met by certain kinds of plays. In our first rehearsal for *The America Play*, after a cold reading, one of the actors pointed to the play and said, "This is for us." I had forgotten that, of course, it is for him. It's exactly for him. I have to feel I'm fulfilling a need. The need sucks hard—like a black hole—and that's why I write the way I do. If there weren't the need, I wouldn't write this way. I wouldn't be sucked into it.

HO: You need the play.

SLP: Well, who am I? It's the question at the very center of every one of my plays. Who am I? Am I Black Man with Watermelon? Well, I don't know. Yeah, sometimes.

HO: That's a distinct thing. I know who I am. That's where my plays proceed from. I am all of my characters.

SLP: I'm not saying that I'm some of my characters and not others. I'm saying that the question at the center of my play is: Who are we, where are we?

HO: We. Who's we?

SLP: Well, that's it. It takes a suspension of ego. In the old days, it was, "willingly suspend your disbelief" But now it's, for me, "get out of the way." It's Zen. Suspend your ego long enough to ask the question, who am I, really? I write for me. Well, who am I? I'm not just Suzan-Lori Parks, thirty years old, whatever. It's all those who came before me, because my family comes from all over. I don't take any of those things for granted, none of them. I think that's why I tend to write the way I do.

HO: There are phrases in the plays that I read, or hear, that stick with me, that stand out like a thumb, like hitchhiking. One line that thumbed a ride with me was, "If you don't write it down.." [from *Last Black Man*].

SLP: "... then we will come along and tell the future that we did not exist." Right, right.

HO: That's one of the most political statements I've ever heard, at least in the theater. I was about to say radical, but it's not radical, it's simply true. It doesn't have to shake up any of the old structures. It just reminds us. You're witnessing.

SLP: That's the perfect word. I'm witnessing. I'm not judging. I'm not proclaiming. I'm not messaging. I'm just saying, "Here it is."

HO: And don't let them tell you that we were not here, because it invalidates…

SLP: Not even that. We were here. We are here. Every play I write is like a religious pageant. In Oberammergau, Germany, they have that reenactment of the Passion of Christ. They rehearse for ten years. Someone plays Mary, and someone plays Jesus. My plays are like these passion plays where the community comes together to reenact the passion of whomever. They're like a guide book to who we were, or how we are, or what we should be. When the actor on the first day of rehearsal said, "This is for us, this is us, this is us!" Up until then, perhaps, he had felt that he hadn't one of those kinds of characters to play, and suddenly there it was for him, and he could be this person.

HO: Your plays are very present tense.

SLP: Actors have told me that my plays require them to be there moment to moment. They can't start at the beginning of a scene, and say, "My character's angry in this scene and I'm going to play the whole scene angry." It won't wash. They have to say, "I'm angry here. Oh, this word, I'm mad. This word, I'm really happy. This word, I'm fuckin' pissed off." They have to do it word by word. It's a challenge because it requires them to be completely present. I do play with time, but it's because it's all happening right at once for me. Everything that ever happened, it's all happening right now.

HO: Somebody told you they saw *The Death of the Last Black Man* and did not understand a single word.

SLP: It was a young guy, and I told him it was okay that he didn't understand a single word, and it was really great that he could stand up in a room full of people and say that to me.

HO: I also felt that one of the reasons he brought that out was that he hoped you would explain it to him.

SLP: I can't because I don't understand all of it. I just know that it's something that happened and that I'm witnessing. It's like Revelations. Someone just wrote it down. Then the biblical scholars throughout the ages explained it to us. I'm not a theater scholar. I'm a theater writer, so I just write it down. But it was nice that man did that. That took a lot of courage. He stood up and said, "I didn't understand one word" [*laughter*].

HO: One of the things that I interpret as a clue to how your brain engages words and transfigures them is when we were just lounging around, and you were reading the Oxford English Dictionary, looking up a certain word. And indulging the wordness of the word. I think that comes from a love. Or pathology. Or both.

SLP: It's both. Words are charms. Spelling is like a magic.

HO: Words to me are like little plants. I touch them and they move this way.

SLP: It's different. It's not outside of me. I ingest them and digest them, and they move me literally in my bowels.

HO: So they're food?

SLP: It's like food. It's very religious. Christ is the wafer and you eat him.

HO: I don't believe that the wafer is the body of Christ. What I believe in is the ideal. I need to be in love with the idea of transubstantiation, because it's magic.

SLP: What's interesting is that at a very early age I learned that I, to survive, had to make everything my own. That's why I can love the idea and the "reality" of transubstantiation, because right from the get go, I made things mine. They made sense to me. Words make sense to me. Me! They're mine. They're not the property of Catholicism. I don't go to church; I think Cardinal O'Connor is full of shit and the Pope is tired, but the idea of ascending into Heaven, and sitting at the right hand of the Father is some of the best poetry that I've ever read. You get a church full of Catholics and the big high ceiling and everybody saying, "Our Father." You get eight hundred Catholics in a room mumbling that. That's deep shit, man.

HO: Besides a pageant, is it fair to say that another analogy to draw, in terms of your plays, is attending mass.

SLP: That's what I did as a child, and I found it, not moving, but it was a great show! The guy is in those robes, man. It was like James Brown and Elvis, and he was turning around, ding-a-ling-a-ling. The bells in *Last Black Man* are Roman Catholic Church right down the line.

HO: Did I tell you I used to be an altar boy?

SLP: [*Laughter*] You were an altar boy? Figures.

HO: Another line of yours that hitches a ride with me is from *Last Black Man*. "You, I waved at you, and you waved at me, and I haven't seen you since."

SLP: The Queen is over on the African coast and she's saying to the others, "I saw Columbus comin' over to meet you. 'To borrow a cup of sugar,' so he said. But,"— and I'm paraphrasing— "I knew better. I waved my hands in warning. You thought I was just saying, 'Hey.' You waved back, and that's the last I saw of you."

HO: Politics resides so plainly in your work. It's almost subliminal, like in that line, "Write it down and hide it under a rock."

SLP: I read the play to a good friend of my mom's, the anthropologist John Langston Gwaltney, who used to teach at Syracuse. He's blind, actually. It was great to read a play to a man who would never see the play. But after I was finished, we talked a lot, and then he sang this song, "I went to the rock to hide my face, the rock said to me, 'No hiding place.'" That was his take on "Hide it under a rock." I don't know. *Last Black Man* is such a double-edged sword. The end of it is, "Hold it, hold it, hold it," which means "Embrace," and "Wait a minute," at the same time. It's both of those motions at once. I'm not sure what I meant by, "Hide it under a rock." It could mean hide it under a rock for safe-keeping.

HO: That's what the strongest reading is.

SLP: Hide it under a rock so people won't see it. Hide it under a rock, as opposed to hiding it under something that's less [*grunt*], you know, less strong. Maybe they'll never think to look under a rock. That is something that is also in the experience of English as second language. I know English is one of your many languages, but for me the joke is that English is my second language.

HO: What is your first language? Is it the language of your plays?

SLP: Probably, but behind that there is a language that I speak that's probably the root of the language in *Last Black Man*. It really makes no sense, and I climb out of that onto the rock, and make a little bit of sense, which is a play. Then there's standard English, which I speak. But something else goes on. There's the yoke/joke thing, and there's a third thing, which is the veil. Language as a veil, and that may be where "hide it under a rock" comes from. Part of it is, "the truth will set you free," and part of it is, "maybe we're not ready to be free yet, because we've been in chains for nine million years." It's a veil because it is not our first language.

HO: What do think about the state of American theater? This is coming from somebody who is really in the thick of things.

SLP: Right, I'm in the thick of American theater [*laughter*]. I'm in the thick of theater, thick. You thick of theater?

HO: Are you sick of theater?

SLP: I got into theater because there are things about theater that I love, and that I can do. You sit down. You write. You think about how a play has to work to be effective. That's what makes it the most difficult form. Plays have to be soft and loose and completely flexible and completely taut, to withstand the minds, and hearts, and souls of thousands of hundreds of people, and actors getting in there and saying, "What's my motivation?" And directors going, "What are we going to do at this moment?" Think of Shakespeare. He was such a good writer because he was a playwright.

HO: I'm completely blind to whether or not it's the hardest form, because I think it's the one form for which I have a natural fluency and a gift. Even though it might be harder than some novel writing, I sit down and the plays come out of me.

SLP: I'm not saying they're hard to write. I'm saying it demands the most of a writer, because it's not just, "Is it a nice story?" It's not just, "Do the words rock and roll?" It is not just interesting message. It's not just clear point. In playwriting, it has to really work night after night and you have to be able to interpret anew every night, every minute, every day. It's like someone who's practiced Yoga for nine million years. They're incredibly strong and incredibly flexible at the same time. That's what a play has to be. I'm talking about a kind of playwriting that really demands something of itself, too.

HO: By virtue of your gift, this could legitimately be called the Suzan-Lori Parks era.

SLP: [*Laughter*] I don't care about that.

HO: Bullshit. Yes you do.

SLP: No. I don't have to claim that. I honestly don't. I do care about writing as well as I possibly can.

HO: Are you writing the best you possibly can right now?

SLP: Right now, I'm writing better than I possibly can. I spend three years on a play, and I look at it and can't believe I wrote it. I wonder where it came from. I feel like I'm writing beyond myself.

4

ALIEN NATION

An Interview with the Playwright

Michelle Pearce

American Theatre, March 1994

Playwright Suzan-Lori Parks has been writing plays for 11 years. Her latest play, *The America Play*, investigates the ideas of history, greatness and costume by using the image of Abraham Lincoln. She is interested in musical forms and uses musical terminology in her scripts, such as the word 'rest' to signify a pause within a character's lines. Parks believes that plays should also be both literary and historical rather than merely dramatic.

Michelle Pearce: Is this a play about Lincoln?

Suzan-Lori Parks: No, it's not. Well, not really. I think it has more to do with greatness and costume, actually. You could look at Lincoln and see him as the sum of his outfit. You know, his beard (actually he had lots of different kinds of beards) and his hat, coat, vest and shoes.

MP: What inspired you to write this play?

SLP: I wanted to write about a hole. You can riff on that word, you can think about that word and what it means and where it takes you (or where it took me, anyway). You think of h-o-l-e and then w-h-o-l-e and then black hole, and then you think of time and space, and when you think of time and space you think of history, and suddenly all these things are swirling around and things start attaching themselves to each other and suddenly you have two characters sitting in a hole digging and a guy who looks like Abraham Lincoln appears. And, "Wow, that's interesting."

MP: What is the significance of the John Locke quote?

SLP: Putting it at the beginning of the play and also in the program notes may encourage people to think about the idea of America in addition to the actual day-to-day reality of America. "In the beginning all the world was America." All the world was an uncharted place, a blank slate, and since

FIGURE 2 *The America Play* by Suzan-Lori Parks, directed by Liz Diamond, Yale Repertory Theatre, 1994. Michael Potts (Brazil) and Reg Montgomery (The Foundling Father). Photo by T. Charles Erikson. Courtesy of the photographer.

that beginning everyone's been filling it with tshatshkes, which we who come next receive and must do something with.

MP: In an interview a few years ago you said that people not from the dominant culture are the people who can challenge the form of things…

SLP: Well, everybody can. There are people who challenge the form who are trying to make a splash, you know. And if you want to be weird, I suppose that's one reason to do things that are nontraditional. But if you feel that the traditional shape of things doesn't accommodate what you are doing, then it's a more organic and natural process. Suddenly you find yourself doing something else. So yeah, a person from a nondominant whatever—a person like me—might realize that more quickly. But there's a tradition of white guys—white, weird, cool, straight guys—doing that. Like Sam Shepard's early stuff. Obviously the well-made play wasn't suiting him at all.

MP: Do you think the same thing is true if you look at history, as you do in this play, that you're going to maybe look at it differently—

SLP: If you're from—

MP: If you're from a nondominant—

SLP: If you're from Mars? I think that's the word we should use, Mars. Capital "MARS" or maybe a lowercase "m" to stand for that thing. The other. The alien. I take issue with history because it doesn't serve me—it doesn't serve me because there isn't enough of it. In this play, I am simply asking, "Where is history?" because I don't see it. I don't see any history out there, so I've made some up.

MP: Well, in the play it's a theme park.

SLP: Right, it's a theme park and the characters pass by and they wave. That's what it is to me. I can get more out of history if I joke with it than if I shake my finger at it and stomp my feet. The approach you take toward your subject really determines what you're going to get. So I say to history, "Anything you want. It's okay, you can laugh."

MP: Do you see any kind of change in your playwriting since you started?

SLP: Yeah, yeah. The subjects have changed. But there are some things that are similar. I tend to still be interested in musical forms because they offer greater, infinite, incredible possibilities—whereas traditional dramatic forms are not as interesting. Or, to say it a different way, traditional dramatic forms are, I think, more interesting when they are informed by music. That's what I've been interested in for years. This is my 11th year writing plays.

MP: And you're how old?

SLP: I'm old enough to be writing plays. But I think I've gotten better. And I still like putting footnotes on plays.

MP: I associate footnotes with a kind of academic writing.

SLP: But I love them, they're so great! It's not like, "so you'll understand this play you have to read this line." Most of them are totally made up and ridiculous. One of them talks about some of the Foundling Father's unpublished works. One of them talks about what Mary Todd might have said on the night her husband died. It's playing, again, with the form and the idea of a footnote.

But you haven't asked me about those extra character names in the text.

MP: You did that on purpose?

SLP: The word "pause" does not equal "LINCOLN. BOOTH. LINCOLN. BOOTH." It doesn't. Imagine, you go down the page and you read "LINCOLN. BOOTH. LINCOLN. BOOTH. LINCOLN. BOOTH. LINCOLN. BOOTH. Thus to the tyrants." It's very different if you read "Long Pause. Thus to the tyrants." "Long Pause"—what is that? It's garbage, you know what I mean?

MP: So what's the difference between a "Rest" and seeing the character's name?

SLP: Well, "Rest" is actually a great word. It's musical. And having the word "rest" over and over and over to indicate every single place where the character takes a little break in between paragraphs of speech is perfect. See, the words I write down on the page are the words that I want you to take inside your head. Every word you put in a play should be like this guy [picking up a volume of Joyce]. Playwrights should get tough and write literature instead of just writing a show. You shouldn't just plop some language together and get people to cry. It should be literature, a show and some sort of historical document—which is what a play is. Why not do all three?

5

MAKING HISTORY

Suzan-Lori Parks: The Shape of the Past

Tom Sellar

TheatreForum, Summer/Fall 1996

Tom Sellar: How did you hear about the Hottentot Venus?

Suzan-Lori Parks: I overheard some people talking about her, I think it was at a party. They were discussing her, this woman with a big butt. And I thought, "oooh. She's going to be a character in one of my plays." At the time I was writing a play called *Everything*, which had a lot of historical characters in it. So I decided to include her in the play, and then *Everything* became *Venus*.

TS: So you went and read all the historical documentation about her?

SLP: It took me a while to figure out what I wanted to do with it. What did I want to do with an autopsy report? There were a couple of drawings, a sketchy account of where she came from and where she died. Bits and pieces of things. What do you do with the fact that her labia were kept in a jar in the back room of the Musée de l'Homme in Paris? You have to draw on that.

   In 1994 I went to the Villa Serbelom in Italy on a Rockefeller grant – you live in a villa for a month while you try to finish your work. And I was at the point where I thought, "If I don't get to the heart of this play, I'll lose my mind." I had many drafts, and I knew that they were not quite right. I had lots of notes and things – and after years of work, I suddenly wrote it in a week or two. It was hard. I had to find Venus, I had to make contact with her.

TS: Did the story of the Hottentot Venus suggest the shape and structure of the play to you?

SLP: We mostly only know that Saartjie Baartman was born in Southern Africa, went to England, and died in France. So I've filled a lot in between those events. There are people I've added, like the Mother Showman, who's sort of a cross between P.T. Barnum and Mother Courage.

I've left some things out, and I've included other things. Most of it's fabricated, it's questioning the history of history. The play doesn't just swallow the story whole and regurgitate it onto the stage. It embraces the unrecorded truth.

TS: I want to ask you about form, because in some ways *Venus* is very different from your other plays. It has a sort of linear spine to it, with scenes going back and forth from there, but always returning to the narrative. In the past you've talked about your writing as "repetition and revision." Is Venus written as "rep and rev" too, or is it something else to you, something different?

SLP: It is, it's just on another level, the next level maybe. For example, in *The America Play*, you had the Father, who looked like Abraham Lincoln, and then in the second act he was repeated, he was followed by a young man (his son), who behaved a lot like he did. So that was another way of doing repetition and revision. Not just in words, but in actual characters on stage.

In *Venus*, The Man is later The Docteur. The Brother later becomes the Mother Showman and then The Grade School Chum. And The Resurrectionist turns into a watchman at the jail cell. So there's a lot of repeating of faces. But also of words and phrases. Every time Venus has a big decision to make she says "do I have a choice?" – or someone says, "just say yes, just say yes." Same thing, same situation, again and again and again, but it's always different. You're revisiting it each time.

TS: That reminds me of something you said in an essay you wrote for Grand Street, and about how Josephine Baker was "improvising her life" in a sense, always revising it as she retold it. It's like "rep and rev" as a way of creating your life. Is Venus like that? Is she in that position?

SLP: She is, she is. She's got to make her life up out of lots of little bits and pieces. But Baker would tell her life story to fit her present moment. When Baker was a star, she would tell her rags-to-riches story – even though that wasn't her true story – whatever the truth was, if there was one.

Whereas there's lots of different people telling the Venus story at once. We have The Docteur giving a lecture many years later, at a conference in Tübingen. His mind wanders and comes back, so he's telling the story as a sort of "dis-re-memberment." And The Resurrectionist is telling the story too, as a sort of re-memberment of the story: "the year was 1810…" And then you have Venus telling her own story, just by being present. By the end, she has a speech: "I was born near the coast…" and so on. So you have these three people trying to tell the story, and it goes backwards and forwards. It also has a play-within-the-play, since – among many other things – it's about show business, showing yourself, being in a show.

It's a much more traditional structure than what people are used to getting from me. But even though you can say it's more linear and traditional, it still confounds people!

TS: Tell me how you hooked up with Richard [Foreman].

SLP: I've been a fan of his work ever since I moved to New York. Liz Diamond and I have made a lot of theatre together, and there's nothing bad in that relationship at all. Liz is one of my best friends. But I knew that if I really wanted to grow; I was going to have to work with someone new. I really wanted to work with someone who had a *lot* more experience than I do. Just to see how I would change, what I would learn. Because you can start getting very comfortable in your work – it can be very good work, but you get comfortable and wonder, "am I not learning things that I should be learning? Who else is out there who would make me write on my feet?" – which Richard does. We'll make a cut or something, and Richard will say, "we seem to need something else here now." I usually don't write in rehearsal.

TS: Richard has a very strong, very specific formal sense. He asks actors to move at certain kinds of angles, he wants to use head mics a certain way, he knows what the lettering should look like, what the total visual landscape is. What do you think you've gotten out of working with a director who has such a strong sense of form?

SLP: It makes my job easier. It's like being a dead playwright. Really! That's the real test, to see if your plays are any good. Can it be done without me? That's why sometimes I don't come to rehearsal. To see: is the writing good enough, is it strong enough, are the characters interesting enough to hold up to someone's ideas?

TS: Have you ever thought about directing your own stuff?

SLP: I haven't. I haven't.

TS: Running your own theatre?

SLP: Never, never. Directing, maybe someday, but I like writing so much. And I want to be able to write everything I want to.

TS: Have you found anything out about the play in rehearsal that you didn't think you would? Any surprises?

SLP: I knew it was funny. I knew it was sad. But that was without Richard. I knew it was weird and unseemly – and he definitely brought that out. That's a very difficult thing to embrace. It's not a feel-good play. It's not a "politically correct" play, and that is very important. It's not the story of a black woman who's victimized. It's not that simple.

TS: It's more about the currents in these people's lives, the way all these things circulate – great love, chocolate, race, history, bodies – constantly circulating.

SLP: Like the Milky Way, a galaxy of all these things going around! Yeah, exactly.

TS: I want to ask you about a specific line, "the Venus Hottentot iz dead, there wont b inny show tonite." It's repeated over and over in the prologue and epilogue, and the actors and I were discussing it the other day. It's kind of saying "she's dead, she's dead, don't get inside her head,

don't feel sorry for her, don't psychologize her, 'cause she's not here."
Also – because the play begins with her death, tells her life story, and
then ends with her death again – it makes the whole evening a kind of
resurrection that these twelve people create every night. A resurrection
of Saartjie Baartman on stage.

SLP: Yeah, that makes sense. I've done a resurrection in so many of my
plays. In *Death of the Last Black Man*, the line that's repeated is the
announcement, along the same lines, "this is the death of the last black
man in the whole entire world." In effect it's saying, this is what it is, this
is what we're doing. There's a gravedigger at the center of *The America
Play*. I'm obsessed with resurrecting, with bringing up the dead. Every
night the dead rise.

TS: Do you ever think of yourself as a kind of playwright-resurrectionist?
Digging around in the Great Whole of History for the voices?

SLP: Oh, totally. Or letting them in the house when they knock on the door.
You know, sometimes you dig, and sometimes you just open the door.
Which is what eavesdropping is, hearing stories as they come into my
head. That's why theatre for me is important and exciting. I'm creating a
kind of history.

   When I did *The America Play* – which is about this man who looks like
Abraham Lincoln, who goes out West and performs – people said "did it
really happen?" and I could say "yeah, it happens every night." That's as
real as anything else. That's why theatre's interesting to me because you
can insert it into real life and sort of make history.

TS: And history's a show too?

SLP: Exactly, floats go by: Napoleon, Queen Elizabeth…

TS: It seems like you come back to the nineteenth century a lot. Is there
something appealing about that time to you? Big ideas, intellectual
currents, or a certain look?

SLP: My last two plays have dealt with the nineteenth century somehow. But
any period appeals to me really. Anything that's big, that throws a lot of
shade, is exciting to me, whether it's the nineteenth century, or B.C.
time. But it has to be big.

TS: In your play *Devotees in the Garden of Love*, there's this expectant bride –
George-then-Patty – who finally wins her suitor after making sacrifice
after sacrifice. Is she like Venus? Is there any connection between these
characters who sacrifice for this ideal?

SLP: I think Joseph Campbell may have spoken of "the three faces of God."" In
Venus there are three faces of love. Venus, the love-object; the unloved
(who is the Bride-To-Be in the play-within-the-play); and the lover,
who has two faces, as the dis-rememberer (The Docteur), and as the
re-memberer (The Resurrectionist). I don't think that at the beginning
of the play Venus wants love. I think she wants money, and she wants to
come back home after a couple of years and be rich. But as she goes out

into this world and realizes that she is not loved, then she wants love, she wants comfort. So when The Docteur comes in, he's like her knight in shining armor. By the end all she says is "love me, love me, love me."

TS: And a lot awful things happen to Venus, which she's told are because of "love." The Chorus of Spectators maul her because the public "loves" and "adores" her and The Docteur tells her that the anatomists at the academy "love" her.

SLP: "Love" is a word that is used so casually, I know what you mean. Richard often says that good art tries to circumscribe, to circle around what it can't quite comprehend, that nameless thing. And I think that's what I'm doing. "Love" is what I'm circling around.

TS: Is your process of circling around, searching for what's present, one reason you have the "spells" – where sometimes you simply list a character's name in the script, but don't include any dialogue for that line?

SLP: No, those are when I'm really on to the character, but what's being experienced has no words. I want a sense of "there is a moment here" so the reader actually can see something on the page. Like the scene where Venus is being persuaded to go to England. She asks, "do I have a choice?" and these two guys are saying "think it over, think it all over," and on the page you see "THE BROTHER. VENUS. THE MAN. THE BROTHER. VENUS. THE MAN." I know exactly what they're doing, but they're not talking, they're just being who they are, emanating their energy.

TS: Did Richard need guidance from you to find that kind of thing? How did you work together?

SLP: I told him what they were. But he needed very little guidance, and that's why I enjoyed working with him so much. I got the sense from the first couple of meetings we had that he really understood the play. There were a couple of things he didn't get, like The Mother in the play-within-the-play is the mother of The Young Man, not of The-Bride-To-Be. Technical stuff. But he completely got the humor, the sadness, and the unseemliness. We'd talked a lot about the play while we were casting it, and we were on the same wavelength from then on. Of course, Richard has his own thing going, too. But it wasn't at the expense of my play.

TS: Has working with Richard changed the way you think about your future work at all?

SLP: I'd like the work always to be this good. I'll see you in the year 2001 – it takes me 5 years a play!

TS: You've just finished your first feature-length screenplay, *Girl 6*, which Spike Lee directed. And what's next? You're writing a new play and some more screenplays.

SLP: There's a play at the back of my mind, called *Deluxe*. It's big, I'm thinking big. I'm doing a novel, well, three novels actually. We'll see what they turn out to be. It's very hard, because you have to write all the way across the page!

And I've written another screenplay since *Girl 6*, called *Gal*. It's an adaptation of a novel that came out a couple of years ago, by Ruthie Bolton. And I'm about to start two more. One's an adaptation of *The America Play*, called *Road to Reno*. It's very different from the play. They're in Reno, in the West. The Dad is a stand-up comedian, he does "historical comedy" but he's not that successful, and the mother and the girl drive a 1962 model Hearse.

TS: It's an American movie, there's gotta be a car and a shot of the road.

SLP: A road, a road and a big Hearse moooooving down the road.

TS: What about the play, *Deluxe*?

SLP: Well, there's lots of death in it, of course.

TS: And love?

SLP: At this point there's just a bed scene. It's kind of a myth, it takes place in a town. Basically, it's to answer a question I asked myself: what would it be like if five Greek plays were running simultaneously in your head? It's going to be lots of fun.

TS: Formally, is it similar to *Venus*?

SLP: Maybe. Have you ever done any martial arts? I have. *Venus* is kind of like getting your black belt. After years of study and hard work, you complete an arduous task and reach a new level. And on this level, there all these things that you don't recognize, and you have to learn all over again. And that's why I'm doing these novels, these movies, this new play that I don't really know about.

TS: You have to learn the moves…

SLP: Yes! I have to learn new moves. I have no idea what kind of writer I am. I don't. I find out with every play.

6

FOR POSTERIOR'S SAKE

Una Chaudhuri

Public Access, May 1996

The Program of the Joseph Papp Public Theater/New York Shakespeare Festival

The verbal fireworks of Suzan-Lori Parks' plays invariably dispel the gloom that could otherwise engulf some of her main subjects: lies, loss, death. Her confident ear for the undaunted, unstoppable poetry that lies beneath the cruelest fates makes her plays resonate far beyond their singular subjects. In her hands, language becomes an alchemical crucible, transforming lies into nourishing myths, loss into discovery, and death into a rehearsal for living better. Hers are quintessentially America Plays (as her last play was entitled)—as lively and eloquent a record as any of the liabilities and liberties involved in closing out the so-called "American Century." Shortly before her new play *Venus* went into rehearsal at the Public, she talked about it with Una Chaudhuri.

Una Chaudhuri: This is a fantastic subject; not only is the story amazing in itself—an African woman brought to Europe and exhibited as a freak and imprisoned and studied by doctors and finally dissected and her sexual parts preserved in a museum where they remain to this day!—but it opens too many issues of concern today, such as the complex connection between race and gender. How did you come to *Venus*?

Suzan-Lori Parks: I overheard [director and frequent Parks collaborator] Liz Diamond—this was years ago—talking with someone, and she said 'this woman with a big butt.' And the bell went off in my head and I thought—hmm… that's a subject for a play. I didn't know anything about her and I had to go to the library and dig and dig and dig.

UC: So what was it about the big butt?

SLP: Oh, well, the butt is the past, the posterior: posterity. She's a woman with a past, with a big past—History.

UC: You wrote once that you think of the theater as an incubator for the creation of historical events. Why is that creation important to you?

SLP: Well, I don't see history as some great and beautiful Persian carpet that's been Unrolled Across the Floor of Eternity so that all its Splendors are Revealed. There are so many blank spaces. There's a line in Virginia Woolf's *Between The Acts*, which is one of my favorite books, "'You don't believe in history,' said William." I've put that above my desk. Because I really don't [believe in history]. I know that things happened in the past, but I do think that how they happened is more up for grabs than we are often led to believe.

UC: The idea of using theater as a vessel of remembering has a special poignancy here, because you are remembering someone who was both literally dismembered but also taken apart in terms of her meaning— dispersed among many medical and legal and anthropological and literary texts, excerpts of which are quoted in the play. Was part of your idea to find out what had not been captured in that way?

SLP: Yes, the play itself is that: it's what didn't get used up or chopped up. I'm not condemning the guys who cut her up—I mean, quite frankly if they hadn't cut her up I never would have heard of her—what I'm saying is that it could have happened this way. For me the play came out of something beyond those discourses, something about her. I was drawn to her as a subject because of her name, Venus, love, and I write a lot about love in my work. There was also the idea of someone getting up on stage pretending they are someone that they are not. And that can be so much fun—and so I wanted to give these actors the opportunity to play lots of characters and change roles a lot. Because it's all about the Show.

UC: Isn't there a dark side to that theatricalization though? The Hottentot Venus was on stage, but she was also in a cage. She was dehumanized as a freak to be gaped at. When working on this story is there a danger of repeating the original violation?

SLP: I was trying—really hard!—I was trying to make it all all right somehow. I didn't want to make her a victim. And yes, it was horrible that they looked at her, and everything else was horrible, horrible. And it was so very hard to write it, I just couldn't finish. And then at some point I had the feeling that she herself, Venus, would say to me: "Sometimes telling the story is the only thing that makes it all right." I know that sounds smarmy and sentimental, but *putting it out there* can make it O.K. It's like in my play *The Death of the Last Black Man*—we see him die several times, and he comes out with a rope around his neck, and it's all really horrible, but it's a play, a kind of play that's more like a religious experience, you know, like at Oberammergau where they parade a Christ through the streets and they reenact his story. So it's more like a miracle play than: Look at her, she's a black woman with a big butt.

UC: The other danger is that one can wind up retelling the debilitating story of oppression and victimization?

SLP: Yes, that's why it took me forever to find her voice and her attitude. I had to find the balance, where she really was. I wanted to give her scenes so that we could really hook up with her and find out that: yes, she's very intelligent, yes, she had a hand in her own destruction, and she wasn't just some dummy or some opinionated loud-mouth. So I tried to give her little things—she can count, and she can wheel and deal, and later, when things are a bit better for her—I just love that scene—how she enjoys showing herself off, how she's so thrilled with herself.

UC: How consciously did you engage the big social and political issues—gender, race, the myths and legends of colonialism—embedded in this story?

SLP: I have the sense that people—not just men, people across the board—don't like women, and also that people, not just white people, but people across the board—don't like black people, and being 'fascinated' with a black person or a woman can be a part of that. But I'm not raising a banner, or trying to Tell the World that this exists. My main commitment is to the characters in the play, to Venus and the Negro Resurrectionist and the Mother Showman (she might be my favorite character, she's really *evil*, really bad!)—and when people like that come into the play, even the Doctor: sure he's a white guy and he's had advantages but he still comes into the play, comes into the room or the space in my brain wanting to be in the play, willing to join in the effort to tell the story—that's what I'm committed to. The 'issues'—I leave those to other people who are more qualified to discuss them.

UC: Speaking of legends, this is your first time working with Richard Foreman. I can think of so many places where your two theatrical universes might overlap—they are both 'architectural,' highly structured and stylized, both deeply engaged with language. But I can see some obvious differences too: Your fascination with facts, for instance, versus his almost hermetic mysticism. What happens when a dramatic vision as singular as yours meets a theatrical universe as distinctive as his?

SLP: I love that question because it reminds me of this physics question I remember from when I wanted to be a scientist: what happens when the immovable object meets an irresistible force? The answer is: everything. That's my answer, just the beauty of the word—everything happens. There is no limit. Richard is fearless, both with his own plays and also in the production of plays he hasn't written. Fearless, with a will of iron, but also incredibly kind. And he has a really good understanding of the play. So there is no limit to what can happen.

7

ADRIENNE KENNEDY

Suzan-Lori Parks

BOMB, Winter 1996

Adrienne Kennedy is one of the greats of contemporary playwriting. A few years ago at the L.A. Theater Festival I had the good fortune to meet her. We hung out, walked along the ocean and talked about everything. Her plays are a passionate odyssey into the psyche of post-African America. "Spider webs strung on little stars," says Wally Shawn. No fooling. Besides her two Rockefeller grants, she is the recipient of the Lila Wallace Reader's Digest Award, a Guggenheim Award and, in 1994, an award from the American Academy of Arts and Letters. Published works: her autobiography, *People Who Led to My Plays* and her collected plays, *Adrienne Kennedy in One Act* and *Intersecting Boundaries*; and her first play written in 1964, *Funnyhouse of a Negro* received an OBIE. In other words, her work has been totally cool for years, cool enough to make her one of the only five playwrights that are included in the *Norton Anthology of Literature*. Her plays are currently being produced by Signature Theater Company at The Public Theater in "A Season of Adrienne Kennedy." This past October we sat down to chat for *BOMB*.

Suzan-Lori Parks: Signature Theater is doing all of your plays this year. How did you all meet up?

Adrienne Kennedy: Edward Albee, who was the first producer of *Funnyhouse of a Negro*, gave it to James Houghton who called me up last spring and told me that he'd been reading my plays for the first time. Jim asked where I lived, would I be interested in doing something… They don't like to do people who live out of town, they want you to be involved in it. So he said, "We're thinking about this." But I got awfully, awfully excited. And he called me two or three weeks later with a formal proposal—by that time I had become glad thinking it wasn't going to happen, because I'm really frightened of productions.

SLP: Why?

AK: I've had a lot of experiences that weren't up to my expectations. Very often I'm not in New York for the production period. I wasn't here when Joe Papp did my plays, I came for the last week. I was living in London. And when Ellen Stewart did my plays I never went to rehearsals. Seth Allen didn't even want me to come—I worked a lot with Joe Chaikin when we first did *A Movie Star Has to Star in Black and White*, but most often I go to colleges to see my plays… I'm really not a part of it. I love being a writer—but I can't say I love being a playwright.

SLP: Why?

AK: I feel that God gave me a gift to create what I call "little scenes," I really mean that, I'm not trying to denigrate them. I can create little scenes on paper. But I've always found getting involved in a production very difficult and often a tremendous let down.

SLP: Being in rehearsals isn't my favorite thing either. I'm not a "theater person." Some people love it, but…

AK: That's exactly how I feel. I took a lot of writing courses when I was in my twenties: novels, stories, poems. I worked very hard at all of them— but it just so happened that it was my plays that got the most praise. In any case, Signature is an excellent, dedicated team of young people. Several years ago James Houghton had this very powerful idea of doing a season of one person's plays and apparently it's won them a multitude of awards and prizes. But even though I consider it a blessing to have four plays done back to back, I find it very fearsome, and frankly I'll be happy when it's over. I have a feeling of foreboding because I don't know what's going to happen between now and the time that it is over.

SLP: Bad review-wise, or production-wise?

AK: Some reversal. I've become secure with these academics, who for 20 years or more have been xeroxing my old plays and teaching them to their students in universities. For better or worse—that suits me better, temperamentally, than facing the New York critics. Maybe I'll go to one production at Stanford or something, and I have made peace with that. I really owe whatever career I have to these loyal academics who have always been producing my work in the universities.

SLP: Like Johnny Appleseed, they've taken your work out into the world and introduced a lot of young people and theater companies to it.

AK: Yes. And also it doesn't have the same element of the unknown to it, all the variables one encounters in having the plays done in New York.

SLP: It was an academic who introduced me to your work—Mary McHenry at Mount Holyoke College. I was walking down the hall and she came out of her office and held out her arm as if I were a train and she held a mail bag and I just walked by and took from her hand a copy of *Funnyhouse of a Negro* and just kept walking and I thought, *Funnyhouse of a Negro*, what the hell is this anyway?

(From Funnyhouse of a Negro.*) … When they first married they lived in New York. Then they went to Africa where my mother fell out of love with my father. She didn't want him to save the black race and spent her days combing her hair. She would not let him touch her in their wedding bed and called him black. He is black of skin with dark eyes and a great dark square brow. Then in Africa he started to drink and came home drunk one night and raped my mother. I clung to my mother. Long after she went to the asylum I wove long dreams of her beauty, her straight hair and fair skin and grey eyes, so identical to mine. How it anguished him. I turned from him, nailing him on the cross, he said, dragging him through grass and nailing him on a cross until he bled. He pleaded with me to help him find Genesis, search for Genesis in the midst of golden savannas, nim and white frankopenny trees and white stallions roaming under a blue sky, help him search for the white doves, he wanted the black man to make a pure statement, he wanted the black man to rise from colonialism. But I sat in the room with my mother, sat by her bedside and helped her comb her straight black hair and wove long dreams of her beauty. She had long since begun to curse the place and spoke of herself trapped in blackness. She preferred the company of night owls. Only at night did she rise, walking in the garden among the trees with the owls. When I spoke to her she saw I was a black man's child and she preferred speaking to owls. Nights my father came home from his school in the village struggling to embrace me. But I fled and hid under my mother's bed while she screamed of remorse. Her hair was falling badly and after a while we had to return to this country.*

SLP: A person who's new to theater can read your work and think: I can do anything I want. That's what your plays did for me. I can do with theater what I think needs to be done—it's liberating. It's a profound experience. Why did you start writing plays?

AK: I always wrote plays of sorts, little scenes about what was happening. I basically picked on my family, what was happening in school. I saw our house as a stage. When we'd have dinner, I'd go upstairs and write what we said. And then I saw *The Glass Menagerie* when I was about 15. It was at the beginning of the summer, and I came home from *The Glass Menagerie* and started to write a play about our family. I have no idea what it was about, I threw it away. But in the meantime, coincidentally, my high school homeroom was the drama room—it had all the Samuel French editions, and a stage. So I decided to take a drama course. The drama teacher, Eugene C. Davis, used to go to New York every summer for two weeks, and he would come back to tell us all about the plays. He would say things like, "One day I saw Tallulah Bankhead walking down Fifth Avenue," and we were just, Ahh! You know, this is Cleveland—this is Ohio.

SLP: Right.

AK: And I was quite taken with it. Even when I was in high school I wrote stories and sent them off to *Seventeen* magazine. When I came to New

York with my husband, he was a student at Columbia and busy all the time, we were always meeting people who were doing interesting things… I decided I would take a course in playwrighting. And my drama teacher at The New School told the class I'd written the best play. There were about 100 people in the class, and she said that I'd written the best play. That played a huge role.

SLP: What keeps you going? You talk about the professors, the academics around the country who introduce students to your work…

AK: Oh, I am just compelled to write scenes about what I think is going on in life. That's all. I'm just compelled to do it. I teach, that's how I earn my living, so my writing—other than grants—doesn't make me money. Apparently, I just love to do this.

SLP: You said the first plays you wrote were about your family. You took advantage of them…

AK: You shouldn't say I took advantage of them. You can say I was engrossed by my family.

SLP: You were engrossed by them and engrossed them into your plays.

AK: My mother was very pretty and she and my father were very dramatic. They always said that I was dramatic. They always said that. So the forces all came together. They were so intriguing—I was captivated by their friends and their stories, by the towns they came from in Georgia, and by the fact that they all went to school in Atlanta. I was mesmerized by them. And I still admire—I have a feeling I like people from that generation better than my generation. I love to hear my father tell stories about Morehouse, my mother's stories about Atlanta University. I visited their home town every summer of my life, Montezuma—

SLP: That's a beautiful name.

AK: That town has a mythic quality to it. It has that red sand and the cornfields, all those white buildings.

SLP: I had the chance to see the two plays, *Funnyhouse of a Negro* and *A Movie Star Has to Star in Black and White*, by Signature, and I was impressed and struck by your use of biography. I'm interested in how history spews out biography. You use the idea of life story. But I'm also aware that life story, or biography, means different things to different people, it's not a clear cut, easily defined thing. And I wondered how…

AK: How I use biography?

SLP: Well, telling a story of someone's life, or telling the story of your own life, your autobiography.

AK: Suzan-Lori, I have to totally credit that to my mother. There were two children. I was the only girl. And she just always talked to me. She would tell me things that happened to her… her dreams, her past… it's like the monologues in my plays, it really is. Because her stories were loaded with imagery and tragedy, darkness and sarcasm and humor. She could describe a day when she was sitting on her porch in Georgia and what

happened… and my father always gave speeches about the cause, the Negro cause. So, there is no doubt in my mind that I try to merge those two things. I'm genuinely fascinated and I will always be—by that pool of stories I heard when I was growing up.

SLP: But supposedly black people don't *tell* things. I'm fascinated by the tension: the pool of stories, and yet all those things that *aren't* told. All those things that aren't talked about…

AK: The secrets.

SLP: Because we could set the race back 10 years or something or we don't want to admit that that kind of thing went on in our family too, there are people who just aren't spoken about completely. I'm fascinated by that tension.

(From *A Movie Star has to Star in Black and White.*) *JEAN PETERS. When my brother was in the army in Germany, he was involved in a prank and was court-martialled. He won't talk about it. I went to visit him in the stockade. It was in a Quonset hut in New Jersey. His head was shaven and he didn't have on any shoes. He has a vein that runs down his forehead and large brown eyes. When he was in high school he was in All City track in the 22 dash. We all thought he was going to be a great athlete. His dream was the Olympics. After high school he went to several colleges and left them; Morehouse (where my father went), Ohio State (where I went), and Western Reserve. I'm a failure he said. I can't make it in those schools. I'm tired. He suddenly joined the army. After Wally left the army he worked nights as an orderly in hospitals; he liked the mental wards. For a few years every fall he started to school but dropped out after a few months. He and his wife married right before he was sent to Germany. He met her at Western Reserve and she graduated cum laude while he was a prisoner in the stockade.*

AK: Obviously, there's a lot of fiction, because there has to be. There's a lot of fiction in everything I write in order to make it compelling. Very often I buoy up the secrets, like most writers. I loved nothing better than to hear my mother on the telephone, voice dropped to a whisper…

SLP: Right, right.

AK: And sometimes she would tell me what the whisper was about. And I became truly fascinated by what our community was always whispering about. These were all civic leaders, or teachers, a rather stable group of people who my parents knew since about 1935—so I definitely became fascinated by all their secrets. And very often my mother would tell them to me.

SLP: You have your immediate family, and then you have what I call your extended family, in Hollywood—the Hollywood stars. Their ghosts are still out there. A lot of them are on hiatus but…

AK: They haven't been in a movie in a while…

SLP: I remember, I loved when we met in California.

AK: I was so happy.

SLP: We went to Universal Studios. That was so much fun for me, to watch *you* interact with these…

AK: These ghosts.

SLP: Yes. These ghosts of Hollywood.

AK: I have no idea why I fell so in love with the movies. I guess it was so common. All of my childhood friends were in love with them, we'd see the double feature on Saturdays. I could spend days being a character. And then my mother was crazy about them. She took drama lessons when she was at Atlanta University and she always talked about that so fondly. She was so enamored with all those people: Joan Crawford, Bette Davis, Ginger Rogers. If I'd had my druthers, I would have loved to have been a movie star, a '40s movie star!

SLP: They had the best clothes.

AK: Their outfits! Thulani Davis and I were talking and she said, "They got to wear cocktail dresses in the daytime."

SLP: And those shoes, their hair! But at the same time, there weren't any black movie stars… I mean, to fall in love with being a '40s movie star is to fall in love with something that didn't include who you are.

AK: As a child, I was blinded to that.

SLP: I think it's puberty or adolescence when you realize, my hair!

AK: I was blinded to that, too. But I'm still totally crazy about that particular period.

(From *A Movie Star has to Star in Black and White*.) SCENE I *Movie music. On the deck of the ocean liner from Now Voyager are BETTE DAVIS and PAUL HENREID. They sit at a table slightly off stage center. BETTE DAVIS has on a large white summer hat and PAUL HENREID a dark summer suit. The light is romantic and glamorous. Beyond backstage left are deck chairs. It is bright sunlight on the deck. BETTE DAVIS. (To Paul). June 1955. When I have the baby I wonder will I turn into a river of blood and die? My mother almost died when I was born. I've always felt sad that I couldn't have been an angel of mercy to my father and mother and saved them from their torment. I used to hope when I was a little girl that one day I would rise above them, an angel with glowing wings and cover them with peace. But I failed. When I came among them it seems to me I did not bring them peace… but made them more disconsolate. The crosses they bore always made me sad. The one reality I wanted never came true… to be their angel of mercy to unite them. I keep remembering the time my mother threatened to kill my father with the shotgun. I keep remembering my father's going away to marry a girl who talked to willow trees.*

SLP: You were saying that you don't have friends in the theater because…

AK: Well no, I never had a lot of friends in the theater even though I've lived basically in New York since 1955. I was always home taking care of the kids, staying up late at night writing, trying to balance all these things:

going to the supermarket, cooking dinner, and writing… So I never had a chance to go to all the events. I would submit my things to people, and then I started to teach. It was so hard for me to learn to teach. My plays seem to be more like poems, they have a following—but there's never been any real income in them so I had to learn how to teach. And I was such a *quiet* person, to learn how to do that was very, very difficult. I feel like I've always been under a lot of pressure. But I don't know what an alternative would have been. I didn't even start to teach until I was 42, 43. And at that time, a lot of the students were my older son Joe's age. So, very often I enjoyed the fact that I was in his world. I was learning about his world quite a bit.

SLP: Did you write a play recently about him?

AK: That's Adam.

SLP: So you have Joe and Adam. The play's *Sleep Deprivation Chamber*. That's a beautiful title. What's it about?

AK: This is the day of the O.J. Simpson verdict, so this seems strange—but Adam was beat up by a policeman about four years ago. He had a tail light out on his car. So we got mixed up with the criminal justice system, I don't even want to talk about it. But that's what the play is about. We based it on his case. And of course fictionalized it. He was in his own front yard and the policeman beat him up and then charged him with assault and battery. Which is very common. They do that all the time.

SLP: They charge you with something because they have to charge you with *something*.

AK: Yes. So the play is… that's what it's about.

SLP: [*Pause*] I could ask about O.J. now.

AK: Well… I feel that O.J. was madly in love with Nicole and she was getting away from him and he killed her. I do believe that. I would love it if a person like that would say, "Yes, I was madly in love, and I killed her," and go to an institution for five or six years on the grounds of insanity… He still has to face his children. He has to, somehow, face his children. He had so many dark, so many other personalities. Very smart man, very successful man.

SLP: A *very* smart man.

AK: But I felt sorry for his mother. I always feel sorry for the mothers.

SLP: You're two completely different people. You've got an L.A. persona and a New York City persona. How come?

AK: [*Laughter*] Oh *those* two different people…

SLP: Yes—what other people are there?

AK: I thought you meant I was the quiet person who doesn't say much, and then the person who writes these plays.

SLP: Well that's true…

AK: People told me when I was teaching at Berkeley, that I was so much more relaxed. I wore light-colored clothes, I always went out to lunch and dinner with people. And people said, "You should live here." I taught at Berkeley off and on for a long time. I always think I might go back to Berkeley, maybe in several years. But I couldn't *write* there. I was totally relaxed there and I'm seldom relaxed in New York. Are you relaxed in New York?

SLP: I'm able to write in New York. I'm not relaxed when I'm away from home. I'm *never* relaxed. But I can flip into this mode of calm… I can get by.

AK: See, I felt relaxed in California. I used to daydream about living in Santa Monica. This is a long time before it was chic, or expensive. When I was in California my asthma went away, I didn't have high blood pressure. But yet, I can't *write* in California.

SLP: One needs a certain amount of excitement or dramatic tension. Jell-O doesn't hold together for no reason. It's like surface tension on a lake. Electricity and all those things are happening.

AK: Well, no matter how many places I've gone to live, I return to the Upper West Side. I particularly love the winter light. I'm able to really write there. And I love the architecture of New York in general. The architecture. I feel I'm immersed in… really profound history. It inspires me. There's this tremendous body of artists who have lived here.

SLP: And what are you working on now?

AK: I'm just working on some stories, some stories.

8

INTERVIEW WITH
SUZAN-LORI PARKS

Shelby Jiggetts

Callaloo, Spring 1996

Shelby Jiggetts: Who are some of the people who have influenced you?

Suzan-Lori Parks: Well, James Baldwin is one because he told me that I should try writing theater. He told me to go down that road. I was at Mount Holyoke College at the time, and he was a visiting professor at New Hampshire College. He was teaching at Hampshire around 1983, I think. And it was a course in short-story writing. In that class, I was really animated, and he asked after a class reading, "Why don't you try writing plays; have you ever thought about writing plays?" And being that I was very impressionable, I tried just that. These days I'm not impressionable at all. I've become hard. Back then, I was like a piece of wax. Another writer who has had an influence on me was Tennessee Williams. I remember I read one of his plays. I mean, it was the kind of play that people, you know, the cool people, were calling dumb theater, but it was theater that I liked. I'm a big fan of bad theater. Tennessee Williams is not an example of bad theater, but it could be compared to "serious theater." I went to see *Amadeus* in Philadelphia, and I loved the people in costumes runnin' around. I just saw them runnin' around and I was thinking, damn, that is the coolest thing I've ever seen! Look at 'em—runnin'! And they had wings on and stuff. It was great! What the play is about… I had no idea. And I didn't care. Musicals like *The Sound of Music* or *Oklahoma,* you can't beat them. I mean, just the idea of people, you know, in costumes. You know those nuns and the cowboys—I mean in the separate musicals. The nuns and their costumes—I love that whole thing.

SJ: What does play writing mean to you?

SLP: The more I think about plays, I think plays are about space. Plays are about space to me. Plays are about space, and, say, fiction is about place. I think that one of the things that led me to writing plays is the understanding I have inside about space, because I moved around so much when I was younger. And I think somehow that sort of helped along that process. Maybe it's just the pageant of people through my life. You know, all the strange people not connected to any one backdrop.

SJ: What does moving around mean, and did that influence your writing?

SLP: My dad was an officer in the army, and we moved around everywhere— well, I mean it seems like we lived everywhere. We lived in Germany for a while. We lived in Kentucky, we lived in Texas, we lived in California and North Carolina, and Maryland and Vermont, and all over Germany when we were there. And some other places that I can't remember. At one time we were moving every year. I think moving around had an influence on my writing.

SJ: You talk about people who encouraged you: were there people who tried to discourage you from play writing?

SLP: I was being discouraged from studying English literature by my teacher in high school and discouraged from writing plays by some of my teachers in college. Those two things together, there's nothing like it! There's nothing like rejection to make you strong!

SJ: In what ways were you discouraged?

SLP: Well, my teacher in high school said that I shouldn't write because I couldn't spell. She told me that if I studied anything, don't study English. I was very good at chemistry. Actually, I wanted to become a scientist, so I was very good in those two subjects; I thought, oh, I'll be a rocket scientist. But then I read Virginia Woolf—ah, Virginia Woolf, *To the Lighthouse.* That novel pulled me from the science lab into the literature lab. I said good-bye to physics. Then I wrote my first play in college; and in the English Department most of the professors were really nice, but the professors from the Theater Department didn't think I knew anything about theater because I hadn't taken a class or anything. I was just writing plays for an honors project. And they sort of gave me the old thumbs-down. I have to admit, the play I wrote wasn't a good play. It was badly written; it was a first try at writing. But it had all of the things in it that I'm obsessed with now. Like memory and family and history and the past. And the play had a lot of dirt on stage which was being dug at.

SJ: A recurring motif.

SLP: Exactly. The digger motif. And the Theater Department guy, whom I will not name, said, "You can't have dirt on stage. That's not a play." You know, not having read Beckett's *Happy Days,* I hadn't even seen the Morca plays where they put sand all over the stage. For some reason, I didn't really like theater. Theater was where a lot of people with too much attitude wore funny clothes and funny little costumes, and they talked with funny voices even though they were from, like, New York and New Jersey. And I didn't respect that. And then there was this woman, this professor, a great professor, Mary McHenry, who was an English professor, still at Mount Holyoke. When I didn't get honors, I felt totally dejected. But she made me understand that I can do anything I want. After seeing her, I was just, like, "Ah, forget it. I can do anything. I'll just be, like, crazy, you know."

SJ: Ah, how liberating.

SLP: Yeah, she's great. You know there are some people who come into your life and save your life. Meaning they do what you need. But I still couldn't stand theater. I thought theater was dumb. Why would I want to do that? I liked fiction writers. Theater people to me were the actors. I didn't know any playwrights. Or actually people at Hampshire who wrote plays were really, really cool, and they were really exclusive, and, of course, I would try to make friends, but they didn't want anything to do with me because I was really dorky. I didn't know anything about theater. I was pretty ignorant. I read a few plays. Actually, I read Shakespeare because I was an English/German major.

SJ: Let's talk about your linguistic word play. I love the way you play the language. And that dialect that you use in your work recurs. I think now when people talk about your voice, it is that very American dialect that has a voice in the characters. Where did that come from? What's the earliest that you recall using it? Was it in that first play?

SLP: Was it in the [*Sinner's Place*]? [*Sinner's*] *Place* was the first play. Two girls are growing up, and one moves away and one stays home. Then the one that stays away comes back, so there's all this tension. You know, memory and history. And these two people who are a lot alike are now different. So I think there might have been word play in that, because they spoke differently although they had lived in the same place. But I don't know where it actually started. It probably started when it was most visible. And it was most visible in *Imperceptible Mutabilities* because it looked so strange, and that is one of the reasons why people found the play, or rather still find the play, difficult to read because, basically, it's just an attempt to get things on the page how I think they sound to me. For example, it's some letters together S-S-S-N-U-C-H. I remembered that because it was the only thing on *The America Play*. And I was just sniffing because I had allergies, and I'm sitting here thinking, that's an S? Well, actually it's like a series of Cs and Hs. So, it's an attempt to get, you know, the sounds on the page and the fun that I had with that. Sometimes it depends on who they are talking to. Sometimes it depends on what they are trying to say. Sometimes people say, "o.k." Sometimes people say, "k." And it's fun to write. So, I just was trying to get more specific because, if someone says, "I'm going with you, 'k?" that's different from, "I'm going with you, o.k?" It's different, it's a different thing going on. It's "the" sometimes, and sometimes it's "thee." It's a recording of, not only the way words sound, but what that means. The difference between "k" and "o.k." is not just what one might call black English versus standard English, for example. Or black English versus mid-Atlantic English. It's not that, so much as it's an attempt: I am trying to be very specific in what's going on emotionally with the character. Because if you just try out, "I'm going with you, O.K," "I'm going with you, 'K," it's a different thing going on. If you jump to that word faster, if you put your words together in a different order, you're feeling something differently, and it's just an attempt to try to be more specific so that I don't have to write in all these parenthetical things. It's a Shakespearean thing, and it's a Greek thing. They did it in their time with things like the line, and things like that. It's just getting more specific, letting the words hold the emotion. Instead of some parenthetical stage direction.

SJ: There is such emotion attached to the way language falls that it's more than oral. There is an emotional resonance too?

SLP: Exactly. See, I write from the gut, or the balls. I don't have balls, but I know someone who does. That's tacky, I know, but I write from the gut. I think theater should come from there. Especially because it's life and, you know, you gotta infect people with language—it comes from the gut. If you sit around and try to infect people with some kind of idea that you have that's not grounded in your gut, they're not going to feel anything with their gut. They're going to walk out of the theater maybe with some great ideas, but they are not going to feel it. Your whole body should be involved in the whole experience.

SJ: You do not provide the map in your writing; you give us a lot and you give us this language, but just looking at two very different directors and their approaches to the same play provided a more emotional experience, the other a more sort of engaging intellectual experience.

SLP: Well, I think I provide the map, but I think the map is the map of—you know—I'm not going to say the map of the world, but the map of, say, New Jersey. I mean it's the map of a piece of land. And what I try to do is say there are 10 roads, 20, 50 roads—take one. I get a kick out of just seeing what people do. I think that the playwright provides the map. But I think a bad play only has a one-way road. Yes, I think the bad play has one road; one idea, one message, one way of doing it. It's so much about one thing. And everybody walks out of the theater going, "Yeah, homelessness is bad," for example. That's not a map; I don't know what it is. It's bad art.

SJ: So you're not disappointed when people come away with an intellectual experience rather than an emotional one?

SLP: I'm not disappointed. I'm saying what I enjoy. What I think theater or a play should do is provide the opportunity to feel it in your gut. It's in what a director chooses. What's a great scene from a play? I think the writer of *Oedipus* provides the opportunity for a gut-wrenching experience. But, then, each production has the freedom to do what it wants to do. And sometimes the people, the very talented team, only has the means—the economic means or the emotional means really—to go so far to understand it in such a way, and sometimes they have the means to understand it another way, and it just depends on the production. I'm not disappointed. When the director does a great job, I try not to get involved. And that's what I love.

SJ: People in your plays tend to observe other people, like the naturalistic surveys.

SLP: Ah, like the Founding Fathers observing themselves.

SJ: Foundling Fathers observing themselves and talking about themselves.

SLP: Yes, there is a lot of watching going on. I like to watch. When I lived in London years ago, someone said to me that the most exciting thing about *Hamlet* is that it's about theater. I thought that was so interesting. Then as I wrote my plays, I thought the most exciting thing about theater is that it's about theater. The most exciting thing about watching theater is that people are watching, and I think that's fascinating. That's why I get nervous when I go outside. There's so much watching going on. People are watching you, you are watching people. It's like over-stimulation. I think that is what theater's all about. It's about one person looking at somebody else. What's really exciting is that people who are watching are dressed up in costumes and pretending they are not who they really are, and that's really fun to me. Yes, there's a lot of watching in *Venus*. In *Venus,* the doctor is watching Venus, and the Resurrectionist is watching everybody. Then actually at the end he becomes the watch, the death watch on Venus. So, it's all this kind of looking. There's a whole lot of looking going on.

SJ: You think that's culturally based in the black community?

SLP: I'm sure, I'm sure there's something there that's about that. Remember, we lived in Vermont in the early 1970s. It always happens wherever you are. Vermont in the early 1970s, Germany in the 1970s. I think it's a byproduct of being different from other people. I think it's culturally based, and it's also what the forum of theater is all about.

SJ: Do you think that, as black people, we are watched more?

SLP: Yes, I think so.

SJ: That's the sort of a scenario you put in plays. Venus is being watched by Europeans. It seems that so many things led up to The Hottentot Venus being a topic of interest for you. A black woman who is watched by European society.

SLP: In *Devotees* [*in the Garden of Love*] black people are watching something we never see. We can assume that it's just a bunch of black people having war. We can assume that by extension because we never see the war. We are told about it but we are never told, but the two black women on the hilltop are watching the war. So yes, I always think it's culturally based. But there's always something else going on. There are riches on the medium in which it is working and something personal which is of course connected to the cultural experience but also to something else. Which I'm sure I'm defining as I go along because I'm not sure. You write your own story and then you don't know really what it is. The watching really works in the plays because theater is about watching. I think that if theater weren't about watching, I would think it would be some comment on what Europeans are doing to us.

SJ: Yes, but the other thing too is that the watchers provide a kind of guide. For example, the Resurrectionist is our host, and this is the story of a woman's life.

SLP: Exactly. So now put that into the equation—those are two black men. The Foundling Father and the Resurrectionist who are diggers, by trade. They are both diggers who are watching the whole business. Basically, if you stretch it… you… I mean, yes, the doctor is watching Venus, but who is watching the doctor? The Resurrectionist—the black man is watching the doctor. So what really is going on there? I'm not sure. The Founding Fathers watching the Foundling Father whose name he never reveals, but who else is he also watching? He's got one eye on Lincoln. Lincoln is not watching him even though Lincoln is behind him. Lincoln can't see him, so he is somehow behind Lincoln.

SJ: We can talk about that question, too, when we talk about your art. I mean we've talked about how preoccupied black people are about race, and what's exciting about your work is that you have black people preoccupied with each other. In really wonderful ways, history is there. History obsesses them, but not a "this one did this to me" kind of history. I think about the way that you talk about slavery and the way slavery is used in your *Imperceptible Mutabilities*.

SLP: It looks at the bigger picture. It's not only trying to tell the story of your people, or put the blame on somebody. I think that is what some artists do. Their art says, "If I could just put this heavy weight on somebody, I would feel a hell of a lot better." Which is true, but I think they, over time, learn that the important thing is to solve the riddle of the universe instead of just putting the blame on somebody else. That's really the question. For example, it's black out there, so that's like a black hole. It becomes more of a powerful thing than putting the blame on somebody else. Because if you think about the history of humankind, it's relatively short compared to the history of the universe. These bigger things resonate on our daily lives like quantum theory. That resonates—the atomic theory and all that—resonates in our daily lives, as does "The Big Bang Theory." So it's the bigger thing that makes for more interesting relationships between things.

SJ: Who are some of the dramatic writers you admire?

SLP: I like Adrienne Kennedy because she made me feel like I could do anything at that moment. I admire the hell out of her as a person, as a courageous person. We were on a panel together, and someone was telling us that we should all call ourselves feminists. They were asking me, "Do you call yourself a feminist?" And I said, "I call myself Suzan-Lori." And they asked Adrienne, "Why don't you call yourself a feminist?" and Adrienne said, "I reserve the right to call myself whatever I choose to call myself." Lorraine Hansberry, I admire, again, right along there with Tennessee Williams. Unfortunately, she didn't get to write as many plays as she wanted to, but something like *A Raisin in the Sun* or *To Be Young, Gifted and Black* is incredibly inspiring and beautiful. I don't want to write plays like August Wilson because he is writing them. You know we only need one August Wilson, as we only need one Suzan-Lori Parks. I do admire what he and Lloyd Richards together have managed to do with the American theater scene because it is hard out there, and they managed to get out there and make wonderful theater. You got to stay on your toes in this business.

SJ: Does staying on your toes mean that you read your reviews?

SLP: I used to, but I haven't read one since 1990. I have had one read to me since then. But I get really nervous when people I don't like talk about my work. I sort of create this thing of anonymity, and I don't like to talk—it makes me very uncomfortable. So when people talk about my work, I kind of don't really pay attention to them. Not because they don't have anything to say, but because it makes me very nervous.

SJ: So you've never really heard anything about yourself that really seemed wrong or true?

SLP: Some people have said, "She's some kind of witchcraft genius." But would you let that really sink into your head?

SJ: If form and content are inseparable, where do you begin? If you wanted to tell the story of African-American history—strange sons, love, or an African woman displayed as a novelty for the king, or the death of the last black man—how does the play begin?

SLP: A play begins with characters. It never starts with an idea. I think some people say, "Oh, I have a great idea; I want to talk about the homeless problem." And then they write a play about homelessness. But my plays never start with an idea about anything, and it is only way, way late in the game that I figure out the question: So what's the play about? And not even then. I'm still thinking about what *The America Play* is about. So it's very late in the game. I always start with characters, sometimes a word. *Death of the Last Black Man* started with the words on the wall, the writing on the wall.

SJ: Do you think that it started when you got an idea that was on the wall and the phrase lingered with you? Do you think something could be built around that?

SLP: Yes, some characters, some things out there give up themselves and allow themselves to be turned into characters and plays. Then some things don't—they want to rock and roll. It is not as if they wanted to take journeys and conflict—they just wanted to rock.

SJ: What about the influence of music on your writing? Your writings vary, you know, the use of the refrain, the use of circular and motion. It is very musical.

SLP: I listen to a lot of music, different kinds of music for each piece. *The Last Black Man* was jazz. I listened to it a lot before I wrote the piece. That was basically just sound, and I put it together to make a story or melody. Yes, you can kind of pat your foot to it. For *Venus,* it was definitely opera. I can't remember what it was for *The America Play.* The other play might have been opera, too.

SJ: How does music feed you during your writing? Does opera give you that sense of space that you were talking about? Or pageantry?

SLP: It does give me a sense of space and pageantry. Yes, and a story on the grand scale is pageantry. An epic, sort of complicated in a way that is not difficult to understand. Opera is complex, but it is not obscure. It is driven by nothing but human emotion, tragedy. There are so many things going on. But also jazz in a different way. When I was having such a hard time finishing *Venus* last year, it was John Coletrane's "Blues Train" that totally got me through that experience. I listened to that so many times. I must have listened to it a million times. Then it was also the "Goldberg Variations," because Bach is like jazz. I don't mean to say it that way, but the "Goldberg Variations" are so great. It does feed. It's faith, structure. Sometimes if you have nothing else to balance you, you have to create a surface like a painter would. A surface on which you can build the foundation of the play. Some people use an idea, which I think is a false surface. I think you need some sort of structure like the "Goldberg Variations." How many are there, 24, 27? Then the end, and it's like great. What a nice structure, how easy. So you have that surface, and you just do your thing. The same thing with Ornette Coleman. There he goes down the road, and then they all sort of come back together; and they might do something weird at the end, but it's structure. It's a kind of structure, so it sort of creates a surface. That is why I steal from them all. I do. I steal a lot from those musicians because they have a great structure.

SJ: Like every good writer, you do your homework in every play that you write. Unlike every good writer, your homework finds itself in the play. When I first asked you about the play within a play in *Venus,* do you remember what your answer was? You said because it was a real play.

SLP: It was there actually. It was actually a play like it was actually happening when she was alive. Bad answer, but I was stalling big time. I knew there was an answer; I knew it had to be there, and I wasn't sure why.

SJ: Word play.

SLP: And word play, and black people on display, and womanly parts, and plain parts. The quotation is: "Who in the performance of his manly

FIGURE 3 *Venus* by Suzan-Lori Parks, directed by Beth Schachter, Muhlenberg College, 2008. Scene 24, The MotherShowman (Holly Cate) calls out to spectators to come and see the Venus Hottentot (Catherine Davidson) in her cage: "What a bucket!/What a bum!/What a spanker!" Costumes by Liz Covey. Scenery by Robin Vest and lights by Sarah Jakaubasz. Photo by Joe Edelman. Courtesy of the photographer.

part does not wish to get claps," which I have changed a little bit. It was actually said in the late 1700s. It works, and it makes the scene good because it makes it so that we see the chum. The School Chum is so bad that he's great. It picks the doctor up a little bit, and they see that he actually feels bad. But he's one of those people who feels guilty, and that's enough.

SJ: What draws the need to put in the information? In a way, it's so incredibly smug because you give us all these wonderful guides to how your mind works and to the larger world that has influenced the mind of the characters, which is really exciting. Just facts and the way they work their way into the plays. So I was going to ask you about its relationship to history because, to me, so many of these plays are about history. The footnotes all seem to play with the notion of history, because when you share something you found in a book—is that history? History incorporated in dramatic writing? Is it still history? It seems to be part of the joke.

SLP: It is part of the joke, I think. And I think because theater—or as I see it or as I want to use it—can make history. It is sort of the reverse of, "Don't believe everything you read." I'd say: Believe it, because it is true. Or: Don't believe everything you see. I think because if you looked back into the past or looked up onto a screen, a film screen, or looked in a show, or looked on the shelf in the library, you don't see enough of you. Or even if you do see enough of you, I do think you have the right to put some of you up there by any means necessary. If that means putting some of you into the 20th century, into the 1990s, and you want to be a poet, or a novelist, or a rap star, or basketball player—do it that way. If that means inserting some of you back in the early 1800s, why not? I think it is just as valid as what we are told happened back then. I think it has an equal weight. It should not be viewed as, "Oh yes, this is some historical document." But rather, "Oh yes, this is an account, not of what happened but of what was. Or an account of what is." Faulkner has this great thing: he talks about is and was, or was and is. History is not "was," history is "is." It's present, so if you believe that history is in the present, you can also believe that the present is in the past. It's mostly directional.

SJ: In what way are you writing this? Is it multidirectional?

SLP: Exactly, so you can fill in the blanks. You can do it now by inserting yourself into the present. You can do it for back then, too.

9

LOVE AND WAR SEEN IN BLACK AND WHITE

Ronni Gordon

Union-News (Springfield, MA), April 10, 1997

In *Devotees in the Garden of Love*, a mother and daughter sit on a hilltop as a war is being waged, down below, over the daughter's hand.

In keeping with the modern age, they watch the war on TV. They wait a long time for it to end. In the process, they give up everything they own.

The play, by Mount Holyoke College alumna Suzan-Lori Parks, will be performed at the college in South Hadley tonight through Sunday, in a production directed by the author.

A 1985 graduate and two-time Obie Award winner, Parks talked earlier this week about her work, which has attracted a lot of attention to the 33-year-old writer.

Her plays often spring from characters who take her and, she hopes, the audience, on a journey.

"I'm not an issues playwright. The characters will lead you to all sorts of places."

She is interested in certain themes, she said, such as time and history, and the tension between the past and the future.

In *Devotees*, the characters are three women: the mother, daughter and a reporter who gives them progress reports on the war.

She got the idea for the play after David Henry Hwang, the author of *M. Butterfly*, got a commission from the Actors Theatre of Louisville to work with a younger playwright. His assignment was to find someone to write a companion piece to a one-act of his.

Parks said he came to her and said, "My one-act is about interracial relationships."

She got back to him with this seed for *Devotees*, her one-act: She envisioned black women in white wedding dresses.

"It's the black–white conflict," she said, laughing.

Hwang said that was fine. The two plays were produced in 1992, but because Parks was busy writing, she never did get down to see it.

When Mount Holyoke asked her to come work on a play, she thought *Devotees* would work well because of its three-woman cast. Also, she said, "I thought, 'What a great way to see what it looks like.'"

She said she's been enjoying her work with the students and trying to make sure that they have fun, while at the same time encouraging them to give their all.

She resists reducing her plays to a "soundbite," but she can talk about certain themes in *Devotees*, she said.

"It's all about getting married, being married, waiting to be married, looking pretty," she said. It's about "how much hope they have, how disappointed they get, how they carry on."

As time passes, the women give up all sorts of things in order [to] get by. Whatever they have gets transformed "into service for the war machine," she said.

Still, they talk about love through the whole play, she said.

In the end, the daughter makes the best of what she has.

She said the play has been called a "dramedy" – part drama, part comedy.

Parks'[s] other plays include *The Death of the Last Black Man in the Whole Entire World*, *The Sinner's Place*, *Betting on the Dust Commander*, and *The America Play*. Her play *Imperceptible Mutabilities in the Third Kingdom* won an Obie in 1990 for Best New American Play. Her newest play, *Venus*, which premiered last year at the Public Theatre in New York, won Parks her second Obie.

Parks said her style is totally different from that of Wendy Wasserstein, another well-known playwright who graduated from Mount Holyoke.

There isn't anything particular in the school's curriculum or in the water that might help nurture playwrights, she said, except that, "A woman's college is a good place to develop strong women."

10

SUZAN-LORI PARKS

David Savran

June 20, 1997

From *The Playwright's Voice: American Dramatists on Memory, Writing and the Politics of Culture*

[*The following is an edited version of the originally published interview.*]
Suzan-Lori Parks's apartment, Brooklyn, New York

David Savran: What got you interested in writing?

Suzan-Lori Parks: I used to write as a kid. I thought all kids were writers. That's kind of how my mind works, I guess. And the more I read, the more I loved to write. When I was in high school my English teacher said, "Whatever you do, don't major in English in college," because I was a poor speller, a phonetic speller. I still am but I'm getting better because I figured out that spelling is more visual than aural. It's pictures. You just take pictures with your head. So, I was a chemistry major at Mount Holyoke College for the first year. I always like science. But then I took a class in which we read Virginia Woolf and I loved *To the Lighthouse*. And I thought, "I really want to write." So it was that book and other books that got me back into writing.

DS: When you started writing in the eighties, what theatrical work particularly interested you? Or other kinds of writing?

SLP: When I was in college it was more that I loved literature. Virginia Woolf. I didn't read Faulkner, Joyce or Proust until long after I graduated from college. Or much of Baldwin's work. Or the Greeks. It was more writing itself, not necessarily a specific book I'd read or a play I'd seen. Theatre made me very nervous. When I was in college, it was populated by students who wore funny clothes and had a lot of attitude. Men and women alike. And that put me off. I didn't feel comfortable around them. Not that I felt more comfortable around English majors because they had another kind of thing going on. I used to say that theatre's full of people with funny hats. So I didn't really go to plays at all. The first real time I spent in the theatre at Mount Holyoke was when I went up there in March [1997] to direct *Devotees in the Garden of Love* [1991]. I studied some theatre at Hampshire College because you could take courses there. I remember I read *for colored girls* and directed it in college – but not in the theatre. We just brought some people together and put on a show. I remember I liked Edward Albee and thought, that's cool, funny, weird. I had a real thing for Faulkner.

DS: I find it interesting that many of the writers you name, like Faulkner and Joyce, are in part writing about writing.

SLP: Right.

DS: Writers for whom the materiality of the text itself is so important. Because that's so important for your work, too.

SLP: It is because those writers, like Toni Morrison, trace the human mind. There are things going on in the world, like in *To the Lighthouse* the war happens and people die and in *Beloved* the war happens and people die. And slavery happens. But you're tracing the fine lines of the human mind. It's that kind of writing I love. It's not less concerned with things going on outside but I use them to understand what's going on inside. And it is a lot about the text. With Faulkner, the text and the story are equal. For writers I'm not interested in, the text is just a way to tell the story. And even in some plays, the story is the most important thing and the ways it's communicated, the text of it, the form, is secondary. But the thing I like about Faulkner is that they're equal.

DS: What about Adrienne Kennedy?

SLP: I'm a fan of hers. I remember a teacher of mine in the English Department at Mount Holyoke. I was walking down the hall one day and she saw me coming and ran in her office and came back out with a book and kind of held it out like I was a train and she had the mailbag and I just took it and kept walking, and I got to the end of the hall and it was *Funnyhouse of a Negro*. So I read it and reread it and reread it and reread it. It also had a hand in shaping what I do. I thought anything is possible. I could do what I wanted to do instead of what I felt I had to do. I was having some problems because the first play I wrote was for my senior thesis and it wasn't well received. My first bad review. But I had a problem with the set. I wanted lots of dirt and digging and stuff like that. And one of the guys on the committee said, "We don't have dirt on stage." And knowing nothing about theatre – because I didn't go to theatre – I said, "Oh, okay, guess not." And then I found all these plays, like *Happy Days* and *Bury the Dead*, with dirt on the stage but I didn't know enough to defend myself. So I said, "I just wrote it, I don't know. You guys don't like it, that's alright." I think she gave me Adrienne Kennedy to encourage me to do what I thought I had to do instead of what people expected.

DS: When did you come to New York?

SLP: In '86. I graduated in '85 and went to London for a year and studied acting because I thought I was going to be a writer. I had the confidence but not the ambition. That's why I look at kids – I call them kids, but college students, younger people whom I teach – it's like they have amazing amounts of ambition and less confidence. But I had a lot of confidence for someone who had just been thrown on the trash pile by the English department. James Baldwin had been very kind and I had great private moments as a writer, times when you really feel, Wow, I'm in that other world, writing, and this is great. So I had a lot of confidence. So I said if I'm going to do this playwriting thing which I enjoy, I should study acting. I didn't want to study writing because I didn't think it was going to help me – I'd already gotten burned. So I went to London. Then, because my parents live in Syracuse, New York, I moved back there and within a month or two I moved to New York. I didn't know where else to go. I knew one person, Laurie Carlos, whom I met in Texas at summer theatre. She let me stay in part of her huge apartment on Riverside Drive as one of her several roommates. That was in '86. So I've been here eleven years which is longer than I've lived anyplace because my dad was in the army and we moved around.

DS: When I saw *Imperceptible Mutabilities*, I was really struck by its relationship to a lot of New York experimental work: Richard Foreman, the Wooster Group, Lee Breuer. When you were here in the late eighties, did you see much of that work?

SLP: I think at that time, to be honest, I was ignorant of it. I moved to New York and got a job as a paralegal because I had to make money. I'm very good at typing and office work and shuffling papers around. So I got a job and I hung out around the Poetry Project because Laurie taught there and she invited me to take part in her class. And she helped me get started. But I was really ignorant. I didn't know what an OBIE was until I'd won one. I wasn't one of those people who read the *Village Voice* or went to see Richard Foreman. I worked from nine to five every day and would show up at the Poetry Project in these little kilts and tights because I'd come from the office, and try to mix in, and people would make all these comments that I wasn't cool, that I was just this goofy kid. And I still had this funny feeling about theatre people. It's just a different vibe that makes me uncomfortable.

DS: Still?

SLP: Sometimes, yeah. I don't go out very much. I haven't seen ninety-nine percent of the shows in a given season. So I hadn't seen all these fabulous people. I forget what was the first Wooster Group or Foreman show I saw. I was decidedly uncool. I just didn't know. Didn't see anything on Broadway, of course. I went to poetry readings.

DS: Which is perhaps one reason why language is always foregrounded in your plays. I've noticed the lack of stage directions and I know that that's frustrating sometimes for my students. I don't find it so, but I've seen several of your plays performed. Why do you use so few stage directions?

SLP: There are two answers. The first is that the Greek guys and Shakespeare didn't use many stage directions. In *Medea*, Creon, I think, says something like, because she's begging him, "Get off your knees and let go of my robe." And there's no parenthetical thing, there's only Creon's line, which I always thought was really weird and interesting. Suddenly the actions were coming from the guts of the people. I was taught that anything in parentheses you could do without. So if you put the action in the guts, in the stomach, in the bodies of the characters instead of in the parenthetical thing hanging on the side, it's more integral. That seemed to make sense to me. It seemed to make sense to them. It seemed to make the language more exciting. Too many plays are full of lines like, "So it must be very hard for you. (*She picks up her glass and holds it to her lips.*)" And he says, "You know it is." That bores me, I sit there and think, "Live! Do something!" Not that what I write is more realistic but most of the action is in the lines. The Foundling Father, for example, will say, "A nod to the president's bust." And that's exactly what he does. Sometimes it's in parentheses because he doesn't always say it. For a long time people thought I didn't know what I wanted. Someone told me about an article in the *Times* last year that came out after reviews of *Venus* that said, "Obviously she's too wishy-washy to have told Mr. Foreman what she wanted." People always assume that I don't know what I want. The reality is that I do know and I put it in the line. When I can't get it in the line, I put it in a stage direction. And when I truly don't care or want to see what the director comes up with I won't put in anything. Because it could be anything. I'll put in something like, "He's in the big hole which is an exact replica of the Great Hole of History." I want to see what the director says. And the director's going to say, "It's a museum, it's a black hole, it's a fishbowl." That is a magical to me, when people think for themselves. It's not when I have to write down every single little thing.

DS: So your plays demand that actors, directors, readers take a more active role, unlike contemporary naturalism where everything tends to be spelled out. There, it's just a matter of illustrating the text. But to read your work, to understand it, you have to take possession of it. Most people are not used to playing such an active role.

SLP: Right.

DS: But that's also related to the content of your work. In the essays in your book of plays, you write about your concept of repetition and revision which makes me think of Henry Louis Gates's theorization of Signifyin(g): repeating, transforming, displacing. In your work I see

FIGURE 4 *Venus* by Suzan-Lori Parks, directed by Beth Schachter, Muhlenberg College, 2008. Scene 12, the Chorus of Anatomists (from the left, Daniel Ryan, Robert Grimm, Wilma Cespedes Rivera, Kate Franklin, Teddy Lytle) practice measuring on the Venus. The Negro Resurrectionist (Anthony Franqui) explains to the audience how anatomists dissolve the flesh of a corpse to better measure the skeleton. Costumes by Liz Covey. Scenery by Robin Vest and lights by Sarah Jakaubasz. Photo by Joe Edelman. Courtesy of the photographer.

people, through repetition and revision, taking possession and changing their relationship to the past, to each other.

SLP: I spend years writing a play but I never think it out like that. So when someone says something like that to me, my mind scrambles to understand the play in those terms. For example, I got *The Signifying Monkey* years ago when it came out and though I've read snatches of it, I still haven't finished it. And after I wrote *The America Play* I was flipping through it – because every once in a while I like to flip through that book – and I read something about a gap: in the identity there is a gap, a hole, or a chasm, something like that. And I thought, "Ah , interesting." Because I wasn't thinking about the chasm of identity when I wrote *The America Play*. I know what you're talking about but I can't say that.

DS: So you don't sit down consciously to use or to write about these things.

SLP: Some people do. I've heard some people talk about their plays, or some visual artists say, "I'm going to do X, Y, and Z," and you see it and it's pretty much what they said.

DS: And the figure of the chasm is repeated and revised in many of your plays. Isn't The Third Kingdom section of *Imperceptible Mutabilities* – middle passage, being torn away from Africa – also about a chasm?

SLP: Right. That's a wet chasm. In *The America Play*, it's a very dry chasm. In *Venus* there's a chasm that is filled with a speech: the intermission. And we put something there, right between the butt crack. In *Imperceptible Mutabilities in the Third Kingdom*, there was no Third Kingdom. And Liz [Diamond], who would always tell me about people I didn't know like Robert Wilson, told me about his *Knee Plays*. And she asked for something in the middle that would connect the parts. Or you can look at it as something that goes on while we change the scenery. Anyway, that was the chasm.

After I wrote the plays, I was trying to help people find their way into them so I wrote the essays. If someone in the play repeats something, they repeat it because they have to but I don't necessarily know why they say it so many times. Because it sounds right, they have to say it. In *The America Play*, there are lots of echoes: the bust, the cut-out, the Foundling Father, the memory, the son who comes and follows in his father's footsteps.

DS: But as lines and actions are repeated, the meaning changes. I'm thinking, for example, of the multiple assassinations of the Foundling Father.

SLP: Right. I took that from the jazz thing of repetition/revision. Jazz musicians were the first people I knew who did that, but then later on I found Bach. *The Goldberg Variations* is one of my favorite examples. Pop music does it. Everything does it. First, I heard someone talking about it in terms of jazz and how you can repeat a phrase and then change it. A piece that has a beginning, middle and end structured by repetition makes more sense to me than on structure by a lead-up, climax and resolution. Because for me plays are more like religious experiences than secular ones. The excitement in a play doesn't come from wanting to find out who did it? Who killed him? Or will they stay together? Or will they get divorced? The excitement comes from watching happen what I already know is going to happen. Like the Greek plays. They knew all the stories. They knew Oedipus. The thrill is to see him crumble. So it's more like a religious pageant. That's much more exciting to me.

DS: That's why there's so much in your plays that can be understood as ritual. Ritual repetition. And you also write about spells and possession – both of which are also connected to ritual.

SLP: Theatre makes more sense to me like that, and not because of any historical link to Greek plays or anything. I was thinking about that even before I'd read a Greek play. My family is Roman Catholic. And there's a lot of drama – holding things up, and bells are ringing, and holding something else up, and the bells go off again. It makes much more sense to me that that's what theatre really is, rather than a whole bunch of people pretending to be people they aren't. The audience and the players are involved in this recreation of something that could have happened, didn't happen, will happen, is happening right as they're creating it.

FIGURE 5 *The America Play* by Suzan-Lori Parks, directed by Liz Diamond, Yale Repertory Theatre, 1994. Reg Montgomery (The Foundling Father) and Gail Grate (Lucy). Photo by T. Charles Erikson. Courtesy of the photographer.

That's why repetition makes sense to me, why I keep employing it. I just finished the first draft of my first novel and it's the same thing. It's a circle book. Not that they start where they end, but it's like *The Goldberg Variations*. Or like Ornette Coleman. You play the beginning and then you don't know where he is and you're getting nervous and just when you think you're lost in the wilderness, there's the reprise, there's the aria, or there's Coleman playing the end of the song which is sort of like the beginning. And you go, "Wow, I was there all the time, just for a moment it looked mysterious."

DS: Was Gertrude Stein and her use of repetition an influence? Or the way that some of her works take apart the distinction between narrative and dramatic forms?

SLP: I'm a big fan of Gertrude Stein. I've read her work and I used to teach *Ida* in one of my classes. But I haven't read her or Faulkner in a long time. I never read critical analysis of her work, so I don't really understand it except that it sounds good. It feels right. Maybe I don't read her so much anymore because I'm more interested in character. It's not an idea or concept or message or place. They might start with any of those elements but what they really start with is character. With *The America Play*, there were two people looking for another person. With *Imperceptible Mutabilities*, it was the three women together in the apartment with the roach problem. Who were they? *Venus* – of course she's the center of that play. I'm really much more interested in characters than I am in language. Language is just something that comes out of the people. I say certain things in certain ways. Like if I vomited right now all of a sudden, the vomit, I think, would be a lot less interesting than me, who I am and why I threw up. So, too, it's who these people are. In *Last Black Man* [*The Death of the Last Black Man in the Whole Entire World*, 1990], who are they? They talk funny because they're in a really funny place. They're walking a line between the living and the dead, or he is anyway. Most of the people in the play are dead. They really don't make sense a lot of the time because they're dead. It's not anything more than that. And the woman, his wife, just wants him to eat, because she's alive: "Eat, just eat, that's what we do when we're alive. And we try to figure things out. We sit here wondering, where were you? Why are you dressed like that? What's your problem?"

When you came in today I was talking to a film person. The first thing I said was, "I figured out who these people are. We can't go forward until you hear who these people are." The story, who cares? The message – concerns about the race issue, the women issue, all these issues – I don't care. Once I figure out who these people are, then I can figure out what happens. Because the characters talk to you. I don't, like, decide it's going to be about something. Once you lock in on a character then the character, or that part of your psyche, or that character who is part of you, will dictate what it is about. And you just have to listen.

DS: So then you, as a playwright, become possessed when you're writing?

SLP: When the going is good. As I wrote in the essay, it's not a voodoo priestess kind of thing – I wish it were that exciting, but it's not. It's more like a Zen thing where you just have to remove yourself from the path. I'm in the way of the play, I have to remove my Self so that the play can be what it wants to be. It's like that, which is very hard, because you have all these things that you want it to be about, or that it should be about. You have to just let it do its thing. And it's always interesting, a nice little story.

DS: Do you write many drafts?

SLP: I did lots of drafts of *Venus* over five years or something. They were all just really bad. And then I got a fellowship to Bellagio – it's very beautiful, very inspiring, magical. But it wasn't magical when I was there, it was horrible. I was trying to finish this play there and it took me two weeks of flipping out and then finally the stone just rolled away from the tomb and I wrote a whole draft in less than a week. And the language was totally different. The same thing with *The America Play*. What was going on in the second act is exactly what I was doing. Two people were looking for this man while I was looking for him. Who is he? Where is he? We don't know. We have these pieces of things. And then suddenly, there he was. Then the first part of it was easy: he's in a sideshow. Clean up the edges and there it is. Sometimes I wish I could talk about my work more theoretically. I listen to Richard Foreman talking about his work and he uses all these impressive words and I think, "Dang, I might think about doing that." Then I think about my characters and think, "No, they don't need me to talk like that about them." That's not who they are.

DS: What makes a good production of one of your plays?

SLP: If it's imaginative. There are good productions that I have been involved with and others when I haven't. I once saw a very good reading of my work at the University of Chicago. The Onyx Theatre did a reading of *The America Play*. Great job, totally different from what Liz [Diamond] and I had done. It was the gut bucket version. It was funny. It was like black funny. And I thought, "Dang, this is real like, sideslappin' play." Marcus Stern did a really great job with *The America Play* at A.R.T. that I wasn't involved in which was bizarre, very imaginative. The productions I've done with Liz have been great and incredibly imaginative because the director works with the play. She doesn't do a number on the play. That means like a bowel movement on the play. Because you're looking at the bowel movement and not the play. I guess that's fine if the play is well known like *Hamlet*. Then you do it in a bizarre way and that's fine. But newer plays should be seen in an imaginative way, in a way that makes them pop, but not in a way that obscures them. Because then you're just watching the window dressing, which I don't think is a good idea. Because then the audience is not enjoying the play. They're just watching things that obscure the play. And I think that life is difficult enough. And challenging theatre is challenging enough without having it made more challenging by some stuff that a director or a playwright wants to put in the play to make it more interesting. Playwrights do that, too, and I am getting to be a very good editor of my own work. I always cut so much it scares people. I'll go in to production and say, "Let's cut that scene, it's not necessary. It's a lovely scene but it makes five layers instead of three." The people who have trouble are the people who think it's got to be weird and avant-garde and abstract. When I directed *Devotees in the Garden of Love* up at Mount Holyoke, people up there were just beside themselves. They kept saying, "I can't believe it's just this straightforward." I said, "Look, two women on a hilltop, what do you want? We're gonna put them on a hill." "Are you sure you want to put them on a hill? Shouldn't we put something up there?" "Why put something up there? They're on a hill. In wedding dresses. Watching a war. Just like it says. And every once in a while that third woman runs her mouth." They couldn't believe it. They were just beside themselves. It was a great experience and I couldn't get over it. I thought, this is telling me something. We had a beautiful green hill, kind of flat on the top, enough room for the wheelchair. It went around and around.

DS: And it was peaceful?

SLP: Except that we had an underlying soundtrack of war which would come up and go down at certain times. I'm sure *Last Black Man* is hard because you're thinking, "What am I doing with all of those people? Where do they go? Where do they move?" if all else fails, let them stand still. Why do you need stage business? I think whoever invented it is just goofy. Because I think that ruins lots of or really great plays. You can have people standing there, just talking. If it gets a little bit like a chorus or a concert, so? They can stand and be still for a minute and just speak. They don't have to be lifting up glasses and adjusting their bifocals.

A lot of people I've never met have done wonderful productions because I don't go around the country and see my plays. People get mad at me or they think I have an attitude. If I write a play, say, in 1986, like *Imperceptible Mutabilities* and some wonderful person does it in '96, great, I'm so happy they're doing the play. But I'm in the middle of writing my novel.

DS: I ask this not to be voyeuristic but in part because I understand that your work, like *Girl 6* (1996), is a critique of voyeurism. I know that all writers' works are autobiographical in some ways. They use elements from their own lives. I know, for example, that you grew up in a military family....

SLP: My dad was in the military. A military family: we all packed guns and did drills.

DS: So I think of that when I read "Greeks" [part four of *Imperceptible Mutabilities*]. But can you talk more generally about the autobiographical element in your work?

SLP: Looking back, there are a couple of different things I'm interested in. One is the question, Who am I? And that has a lot of answers. I was talking to a friend of Liz Diamond, this East German guy and I'd ask, "How can you be sure of that simple thing, who the hell am I?" And he'd say, "You're you, you're Suzan-Lori Parks, you're a writer." So that's the jumping off point for all these plays. That's why I gravitate most to character and why I don't write poetry. Because I often think, "I could be anybody." I really believe that. But after "Greeks" people would say, "Gee, your dad got his legs shot off in the war?" and I'd laugh. Even *The America Play*. Someone was interviewing me and really kept pressing, "So, this is really the story of your family?" Every time I would try to answer, she would come back to it as if I were avoiding the subject. I finally said, "My dad abandoned our family when I was very young and went off to play Lincoln." And she said, "Really?!?"

But the question in these plays is, "Who am I?" I could be anybody. I'm reading all these books on yoga or Zen or Jung, and I'm carrying around the *Portable Jung* and he talks about the collective unconscious (and I'm paraphrasing), that primitive consciousness, that under consciousness, that bedrock. That's the territory I explore. The story of the Foundling Father, Abraham Lincoln, that's me. I feel like I'm as much him as I am Brazil or I am the Black Man with Watermelon. A lot of people will ask, "Why do you write all these men in your plays?" Well, I don't know. Or they'd think *Venus* is more autobiographical. You have to talk about love. People kept saying, "I see so much of you in that play." I would laugh. I mean, I'm everywhere, we all are. And that is what's so difficult to believe. We are everybody. Everybody is us. We are all one person. I don't think I'll ever write a play about the years I went to a German school. But who knows? I'm growing, I'm changing. I might.

DS: And it may be that your experience in German schools has filtered into your writing in terms of your use of English.

SLP: Exactly. I think the problem I have with the question about autobiography is that some people assume that the line between the writers and the material is a straight line. Sometimes it is, especially these days when everybody seems to be writing a memoir. I heard it called a me-moir – me, me, me. If I were a housewife who had a drunk husband and lived in Iowa for ten years, maybe I'd write about it. But unfortunately fiction writers and people who concoct stories are getting pushed aside in favor of real stories. You see the ad for COURT TV: no scripts, no actors, it's all real. Or *Rescue 911* or *Cops* or any of those shows that focus on real people doing real things. The space left for imagination and fiction is getting smaller and smaller and the imagination is being de-emphasized in favor of real life, which I think is not good because what's under the surface?... I mean reality is very fleeting and, I don't know, I can't describe it. The spirit and the soul of people reside in the imagination, not in the stories that fill up the six o'clock news. "One man Shot in Harlem." "Two Boys Mutilated Downtown." What is that? That's just like fuzz, it's interference.

DS: As I was reading your plays, I was thinking about how frequently TVs appear, as a sign perhaps of realness and banality, and how important it is for you keep them if not in the foreground, at least in the background.

SLP: There are a lot of TVs, aren't there? Even in this novel, lots of different characters are referring to the television a lot and how, "He was just like on TV" – how we're beginning to imitate this constructed thing. In *Imperceptible Mutabilities*, a horrible thing is happening on television, as opposed to the horrible thing that's happening in the women's own living room. Or in *The America Play,* dad is suddenly on TV. And in *Devotees* too:

"The modern-day bride ought to be adequately accoutrementalized for the modern age" by watching the war on TV! It's not an evil thing. I enjoy television. There's lots of great shows, lots of great shows, lots of movies I wasn't old enough to see when they came out, and an overwhelming amount of garbage.

DS: What do you see as the main differences between theatre and film or television? Theatre, of course, caters to a very small, selective audience.

SLP: I think theatre's best when it's like church. And I think it's the worst when it's like TV, or like a movie. I saw that *ER*, one of the hot shows, wants to film it live like they used to. Some sitcoms are live now. TV used to be live – I think it probably was much more interesting. It had that life in it that film doesn't have. And I like movies, and not just arty ones. There are plenty of popular movies that I just love, but movies are dead, I think. That's the difference. Theatre's alive. People are living, they're right there doing what they're doing in front of you. The people in movies could be dead, might be dead, are often dead. It's a different kind of experience. I think theatre's much more interesting when it's a religious kind of thing.

DS: Do you think that has to do with the nature of spectatorship and the fact that the theatre audience is more of a real community, they're more participants, more active than a film audience?

SLP: I talk to the television. A friend still remembers when George Bush was giving a speech about something or other and I was over at her house watching. And she keeps reminding me that I just kept talking to George Bush: "I think you're so stupid!" I was yelling at this man as if he were in my living room. And I've been in movie theatres where people talk to the screen. Mostly black people for movies that have lots of black characters. Or anybody can be on the screen and they'll talk, "Watch it!" or "He's stupid!" They'll yell things out. So movies and TV can be active in that way. There's call and response there too.

Theatre's the only place where the people on stage know that you're watching them and that's the difference. When you're on stage and you look out there, you know that somebody's looking at you and that, to me, is weird. In *Mutabilities*, when they realize they're being watched, they-be-gin-to-talk-like-this-because-he's-watch-ing-us-it-all-be-comes-ver-y-con-trolled. It's a strange moment. Venus is being looked at. The guy in *The America Play* is there for you to look at and interact with and kill. That's what it is in theatre, it's not so much that the audience is shouting or watching but that the people on stage are parading themselves and enjoying being involved in this kind of thing – look at me, look at me, look at me – which is kind of creepy.

DS: So then one of the most important moves in your plays, as in the first scene in *Mutabilities*, is the change from subject to object, to being looked at.

SLP: Right.

DS: But I also get a clear sense in your plays of the violence that accompanies that process. "Marlin Perkinssgot uh gun." Looking can be a kind of violence.

SLP: It's sort of like the jungle, stalking – you know how cats do it, they watch, they look, they get you in their sights. But it's not something that's conscious. It's just what happens with these people. The women on the hill in *Devotees* are watching. Their stuff gets taken, or they're encouraged to give things away, and they're watching something that's very violent. But that's very much a cultural thing. I love to sit and watch people watch violent things. There's a fight going on and people are standing around. I love to watch the people watching the fight. I don't know what that's about. Bad things happen in my plays because unfortunately that's what happens to the characters. But they're also independent of each other. In *Last Black Man*, there's no one really watching but there's such a difference between the living and the dead. The watching thing is independent. People are being watched because it's theatre. And that's what theatre's all about – watching. In the novel nobody's really watching anybody. People are just talking, they're telling a story.

DS: You also use that in *Girl 6*, to show what happens when she's auditioning, the violence of the look of the director.

SLP: In plays I have more or less total control but in that screenplay, Spike [Lee] added stuff. I didn't like that part where she takes off her clothes and exposes her breasts. I didn't want it in there, I didn't write it, and I told him. He wanted that because it said some things he wanted to say. It was his baby so you just let it go and don't worry about it. That movie to me had more to do with the question of identity. She's everybody. "Who am I? Who do you want me to be? You want me to be blond, I'm blonde. I'm brunette, I'm Asian too." So that is really how it lines up with the rest of my work, how the self is malleable.

DS: She's constantly changing, with all the wigs....

SLP: All the costume changes. That's what I love about that. The same with *The America Play*. Who is he? *The Last Black Man*. Where is he, who is he, what is he? Is he alive or dead? He doesn't know. He's both, he's neither. All those people, they could be anybody. All those Third Kingdom people.

DS: Are these questions specifically linked to your ideas of African-American identity?

SLP: Maybe. I don't know. I'll make it a funny answer: it could be, but because I believe in the universal consciousness, no. I think that everybody, if they're able to let go, just for a moment, of the person they assume themselves to be, will realize that they are anybody. On the surface, it's tied into the African-American experience because that's who I am. But one step back, it's part of that big, primordial soup.

DS: I don't know whether this is related to your answer, but I've noticed that in addition to the lack of stage directions, you don't often specify the race of your characters. And Liz Diamond's production of *Imperceptible Mutabilities* used a white actor to play a black character in part four. Alisa Solomon wrote about the confusion that choice engendered for at least one spectator at a post-play discussion.

SLP: Because the boy was white, they thought the mother had cheated. That was the first and last time I yelled at someone in the audience. I said, "How stupid are you?" for a while, I didn't do post-play discussions. But I have learned to turn any question from the audience into a good question. It's a real feeling of power, that you can take something incredibly ridiculous and say, "That's a really good question." And then you talk about whatever you want. And the person in the audience says, "Thanks." Yeah, the race of the characters. I guess I don't specify. Maybe I should so that everyone will know they're black. But in other people's plays, they don't say they're white. Sam Shepard [she picks up *Seven Plays*]...let's see, he's a damn good writer. "Dodge, in his sixties. Hallie, his wife, mid-sixties. Tilden, their oldest son." The problem is that the years go by, people will continue to assume that these people are white and assume that my people are whatever they want them to be – a lot of lightening up as the time passes, or whitening out. Just one more thing I haven't thought about. Some people say, "Anybody could play the Foundling Father as Abraham Lincoln." And I say, "Anybody can play it but I don't necessarily have to watch every production of this play." Or *Devotees in the Garden of Love*. They could be three white women. There's nothing especially in that play, or in *The America Play* that requires the characters to be black. Not like *Death of the Last Black Man*. Black Man with Watermelon. Black Woman with Fried Drumstick. The rest of the people, who knows? In those plays, the characters could be anybody. And that's fine. But I guess I want to see...I have my preference, everybody else doesn't have to share that preference. People can do whatever they want, but I don't necessarily have to go to opening night of their production.

DS: On the other hand, your use of black vernacular makes it pretty unmistakable for an attentive reader.

SLP: Sometimes. But again, with *Devotees* or *The America Play*, not necessarily. And I think of my use of black vernacular as a sort of borrowing, like I borrow from everybody. Black slang is changing so rapidly and I really am not up on it. I work with kids in Harlem during the school year, young kids, and we get together and play on computers. And every once in a while I pick up some words from them that I've never heard before and don't even understand. Black vernacular is like a place where you can go and borrow from. Some people read Mac Wellman's work and think he's black. I don't know what he's borrowing from. I know he doesn't' speak the way his characters do, but I don't know if he's borrowing from black vernacular or Midwestern-speak. There's a kind of joy with language shared by a lot of black people I know and a lot of words and the sound of words. It's not black or white, it just a love of saying things and saying something twice if it sounds really good. But I started by talking about the Self, and if that's an African-American thing. I think it's more of a human thing.

DS: When, in "An Equation for Black People Onstage" you write, "Within the subject is its other," it leads me to think that the different identities that characters take on are in part fantasies – a racial identity, a gendered identity. Do you think of them as fantasies? Although I realize that just because they're fantasies doesn't mean they don't produce real effects.

SLP: I don't know if it's fantasy. I think it's more that that's the way it works on this planet. That's how we live. To play a part in a play and be on stage is a fantasy because you know as you are doing it that it has its limits. The phone sex thing, that's a fantasy. You know when you're engaging in it that it's a fantasy. You know that you're not really there. But I don't think race or gender is a fantasy. Gender is a reality but I don't think it's the be-all and end-all reality. There are other things beneath the surface that are also important, that are also present.

DS: And you point out that identities are not homogeneous. There's not only one kind of blackness or femininity.

SLP: Right. I think it's different now but there are what I call the black police, which are not black police officers but the people who are making sure that you're black enough. I guess other groups have these police, too. People who are making sure that your writing is black enough, who you're dating is black enough, and what comes out of your mouth is black enough, and what you wear is black enough. There are some people in the community and it's their job to monitor others, making sure you're up to snuff. That essay was more talking to those people who would ask, "Why don't your plays deal with real issues?" And on the other side, there are the people who are not part of the community, white people and other folks, who think that black plays should only deal with certain issues. Like every black play should be another *Raisin in the Sun* or another *Fences*. They should deal with the struggle, uplift the race, in a kind of basic, twelve-step way. There's a light at the end of the tunnel and we are walking toward it. I don't know about that. I haven't really looked too hard but I haven't seen that kind of policing going on in other groups as much. It seems to me that others have more flexibility or allow their members to do lots of various things.

DS: Why do you think the black police are so stringent?

SLP: I think there's more at stake in keeping black people contained. It's a question of international security. Because once the whole group realizes that they're actually free, wonderful things could happen. And I think that things would change in a way that a lot of people don't want them to. Because the accepted roles of black people are so entertaining and stimulating. The fascination with basketball players, the way that people on the golf course bow and scrape before Tiger Woods. I watch that and go, "This is a weird country." Other people in other groups have a little more room. Everybody knows about the policing of black people by white people, but the other side of it is equal and strange. 'Cause once anybody jumps out of their skin, of their identity, and swims in the underground sea of the unconscious where everybody is and it doesn't really matter who you are and everything is mythic and strange and large – I don't know, I'm not sure what would happen. That would be the end of the world.

DS: How do you see your relationship to feminism? Because all of your plays have what I would call feminist content. *Devotees*, for example, seems so clearly a critique of a kind of masculine aggression.

SLP: Perhaps to a theatre scholar. But it isn't necessarily for me. I get funny when I hear that language. I don't think that way. To me it's not a critique; it's a show. In my plays most of the time everybody's bad. And everybody's good. *Venus* is bad and good. The women in *Devotees* are just as bad as they are good. And the men you don't see are just as stupid as they are interesting and brave and doing what society says they should do. People say I wrote *Venus* because I'm really interested in colonialism and the objectification of the female body. And it was none of those things. I wrote it because I wanted to give this great character two hours of a play with her name on it. And I wanted to give a black actress a chance to play a really cool part and be the star of the show.

So, feminism – I don't really have any language to talk about it. I like to see strong women characters because stupid women characters bore me. I like to see strong male characters – stupid men, on stage and off, bore me. I like to see characters who are complex, black or white, Asian or Native American, or whatever. Well drawn and multifaceted. Clichés are dumb. And I don't think that's feminism, that's just intelligence. I don't like being Afrocentric, it's being smart. I also don't like to see female or black characters more intelligent than they should be because the playwright is using the character as a mouthpiece. They have faults. It's Venus who says yes to going to England. Granted, she's in a tough place. But she wants to make a mint. She thinks she can win. She is no more intelligent than she needs to be. I wanted to see a black woman on stage with a really cool part. Or three black women in *Devotees*. Or sure, they could be white women. White women need good parts, too, where they don't have to take off their clothes. Boy, if I see another woman take off her clothes, I'll scream – or fall asleep. My boyfriend Dave and I have a game that we play with movies. When the movie starts we ask, "So who's going to be the titty girl? Who's going to show her breasts?"

We'll guess and invariably it's one of the ones we expect. I think people deserve better than that – audiences, writers, actresses, actors alike. More than just violent black men on TV or in the movies. Or sympathetic black women.

DS: Your talking about stereotypical representations of African-Americans leads me to think about your use of history. All your plays are really history plays. But your idea of history is very different from what we see on TV, for example, with its fixation on celebrity, on the clash of personalities, all told with strings of depthless images. You're so attentive to historical struggle and the violence in history, whether it's the offstage war in *Devotees* or the murder of Lincoln or lynching in *The Last Black Man*. Your work is so steeped in the violence of history.

SLP: Violence is what happens in plays. If I model my plays after anything, it's Greek plays, where he's stabbing his eyes out, she's put the poisoned dress on and the horses jump off the cliff. Sure, it's linked to African-American history but it's also borrowed from the Greeks. All these *Wild Kingdom*-type activities would be the center of the play rather than psychological dramas. I can watch them but I don't understand them in a way that allows me to write them. I don't get it. *The America Play* was so much about Lincoln having been shot while watching a play so you have to put it on stage because that's just fun. And the *Devotees* thing is so Greek. The action is off stage. And *The Last Black Man* is Stations of the Cross. There's Jesus going through his changes. That's where the interest in violence comes from.

DS: So history functions for you the way that myth did for the Greeks.

SLP: Right.

DS: You know that your audience knows it, so you can present it in a different way. It's repetition and revision again.

SLP: And if they don't know, I'll tell them. When I was a kid I used to love to read Greek myths. That was my favorite thing. My parents got me all these illustrated books – I love books that are illustrated. And then biblical stories – Jesus doing things and Moses doing something else. Larger-than-life people doing very basic things, but almost childlike in their simplicity. Or fantastic – there's Persephone minding her own business and the world opens up and this guy comes out and drags her down to hell. That's a good story.

Why do I like history? It sounds sappy: to give voice to people who are voiceless. I don't know about that because all these characters are parts of me. I think we're all one person. History, I don't know. Why is *Devotees* what it is? David Hwang wanted me to write a play about interracial relationships to be a companion piece to a play he was writing for the Humana Festival. I said, "Okay, let me go home and think about it." And we hung out for a little while and he asked, "So what have you got?" And I said, "I've got three black women in white wedding dresses.

And that's interracial, right?" And he said, "Sort of …" So we went ahead. But I wrote that play because I wanted to give black actresses a chance to wear pretty dresses, wedding dresses. When I did it at Mount Holyoke – and this is a women's college, with women scholars very serious about their work – I had forgotten why I wrote this play. We went costume shopping and the designer took us to a bridal salon with racks and racks of bridal dresses. You should have seen those three actresses! They were ecstatic! I remember seeing them try on those dresses and seeing their faces light up. I want dresses with trains going down the block! So the plays have all these weird reasons. It's not so much that I have an agenda as I want to see women in pretty dresses. I want to see a black guy dress up like Abraham Lincoln because I think that would be really funny. There he is walking around having a good time. I'm not thinking so much about history. He is though, about the past and how the past is behind you. How you follow in someone's footsteps and how that doesn't make any sense because they're actually behind you. So you're walking the wrong way. But that's really the drama of being alive. It's passing through time. That's what we do. That's what people do when they're watching a play. They pass through a certain amount of time together.

DS: I see your plays as rituals of remembrance, bearing in mind, of course, that re-membering is always a function of dis-membering. You must dis-member in order to re-member. As in *Imperceptible Mutabilities*: "A mine is a thing that dismembers/remembers."

SLP: That's what it is. You put things back together. People say, what's *The Death of the Last Black Man* about? It's about these people who come together and remember him. They gather together and put on a play and every night they remember the last black man. That's like church: "This is my body, this is my blood. Do this in memory of me." And *Venus* is very much a re-membering and dis-membering. The dis-memberment happens right in the middle. The intermission speech is called "The Dis(-re-)memberment of the Venus Hottentot. And he does her autopsy. That's the lecture that he gives, right in the crack of the play. So he cuts it. Basically, re-membering is putting things together that don't always perfectly fit. For example, the re-membering of Lincoln and his story by The Foundling Father who embodies him and puts him back together, and also by the son and mother who look for both of them and re-member them. And at the end, when everything is together, there's a huge (w)hole inside a huge hole. There's the hole in the guy's head while he's sitting in a replica of The Great Hole of History. So it's not neat and tidy.

DS: Because history is not a seamless narrative, it's a hole, an abyss – and a whole.

SLP: Right.

DS: In *The America Play*, The Foundling Father talks about history "as it used to be," in which everything is "by the book" and nothing is "excessive." Yet all of your plays tell a different kind of history: history as excess, the history we don't know what to do with. There's either a vacancy, a hole – or there's too much of it.

SLP: That's funny. I forgot about that line. It's history that you don't know what to do with or history that's hiding in the shadows or is being pushed to the edges, or it's in the margins, the gaps, the crevices. It's not the big story, it's the fringe stuff. Particles of things. Writing for me is so much like archaeology. That's why I like *The America Play* so much. The whole action of the play is exactly like what writing it was. Brazil is digging because I was digging. They put things together as I was putting things together.

DS: So the play is also about the act of writing.

SLP: Yes. History is not just the Great Wall of China, the Pyramids of Egypt, the Neuschwanstein Castle, Stonehenge. It's all the little bits and scraps. That's how narrative seems to be working for me. With my novel, there's a narrative but it's not just someone telling you a story. It's all this little garbage and little pieces of dirt and dust that just kind of fall on the page. It tells a story but it's just remnants, and the little things that people throw away if they could. Or that you did throw away. Or saved too long. As you can tell, I have all kinds of weird stuff, like pieces of my hair when I had red dreadlocks. I love characters from the big History, like Lincoln. What a costume! I'm working on something I'll probably never finish because it's one of nine million things I'm writing, but it has Napoleon in it. Why? Another great outfit. I don't know anything about Napoleon except he was French – which is another obsession of mine. *Venus* speaks French, and the ladies do in *Devotees*. So I love building a play. You start with a character, then you hollow him out, then you fill him with all the knick-knacks that surround him, all this stuff, and make him walk and talk, make him black. They don't start as history plays but history kind of creeps in and lies there and takes over. But writing movies is different because most of the stuff I've written thus far has been assignment, which I actually prefer because then I'm just doing a job and can write my own thing on my own time.

DS: So they give you a story?

SLP: I'll give you an example. Someone hired me to do an adaptation of this book called *Gal* by Ruthie Bolton which came out three or four years ago. You read and reread the book and then you do something with it. People call me up when they want good characters. So I figure out what the characters are doing. At least they don't call me up for car chases.

DS: And you're working on your novel.

SLP: I am. And I have a couple of commissions, one from the Wilma Theater of Philadelphia and one from the Public. I don't know what they're about yet. But I'm most excited about the novel now because I've always loved novels more. That's what I read most. And while I know I'm going to write several of them, I'm not going to stop writing plays.

DS: How long does it take you to write a play?

SLP: It depends. I started *Venus* in 1990 and I finished it in '95. Then we did it in '96. It takes about five years. A screenplay takes less time because the form is not up for grabs. But plays take so much longer because I have no idea what it's going to look like. Not what it would look like on stage but what the shape of the play is, which means what it is about – the two are connected. *Venus* will have more stage directions than the other plays. I like writing stage directions like, "She's pregnant." "She's pregnant again." Things like that are really fun to put in the margin because they're not simply telling you what's going on on stage. The writing is very clean so I put things off to the side. And some things I want to happen and I don't want them talking while they happen. So I just wrote them down. Someone saw *Imperceptible Mutabilities* and then *The Last Black Man* and said, "You're writing is changing." And I think that's a good thing. I keep retracing the same steps or the same themes or the same interests but I do it in different shoes. The tracks look completely different from one play to another. It's all about, "Who am I?"

DS: As you know the American Theatre is not in very good shape right now, despite the fact that there are many different theatres in this country. How do you feel about that? Do you feel that you're writing for a dying art? You're lucky in that you're getting your work produced.

SLP: I guess if I didn't get produced I would still write. But when did it start dying? I guess it's been dying since I started writing plays so I haven't really noticed. Although they take funding away here, there and everywhere, which I think accelerates the dying.

DS: One thing that I find so interesting about your theatre is that it's almost as though it's about the state of theatre itself. Yours is a haunted stage. You have all these characters who have come back from the dead. That's an important way of remembering.

SLP: And if theatre's dead, it won't be possible to remember in this way anymore.

DS: All the playwrights I've interviewed thus far have written plays about haunting.

SLP: What does that say about you?

DS: I'm really fascinated with thinking about theatre as a site for remembering, for bringing back the dead, for staging the past, for coming to terms with loss.

SLP: I think it's because theatre is so close to religion. I don't know all religions but I have a feeling they are bridges between the Self and the people you're not, or the people in your past. It's natural to have plays that are haunted. It's part of the hard wiring of theatre and that's what theatre's for. *Hamlet*'s about a ghost. And the more we can do to capitalize on what theatre's for, the more theatre has a chance of surviving. The more we put on plays that look like movies or TV shows –

DS: Why not just watch TV then?

SLP: It's a lot cheaper. People are writing plays that should be movies or TV to try to get a leap into Hollywood. That's not helping either. I'm most concerned with the death of the imagination. Because if that goes, I'll really be sunk.

11

A BETTER MIRROR

An Interview with the Playwright

Kathy Sova
American Theatre, March 2000

Always considered an eclectic and youthful voice of the American theatre, Suzan-Lori Parks has now moved into the role of mentor and teacher as she prepares to head the new A.S.K. Theater Project's Writing for Performance Program at CalArts. She also has three new plays under her belt: *Fucking A*, which debuted last month under her direction at Houston's DiverseWorks, in conjunction with Infernal Bridegroom Productions; *Topdog/Underdog*, scheduled in the fall at New York's Public Theater; and *In the Blood*, published here for the first time, following its critically acclaimed production at the Public.

Kathy Sova: You have said that, unlike writers who hold a mirror up to society, you write about what's not there, what we don't see. How do you go about that?

Suzan-Lori Parks: Some people think I am an issue-oriented writer, but I've never said to myself, "I'm going to write about such-and-such an issue"—that would make for incredibly boring writing, at least to my taste. Creating someone I don't know and her made-up world shows us more about who we are—is actually a better mirror—than if I were to parade in front of you an instantly recognizable person in an instantly recognizable situation. I'm not saying, "Let's make it all abstract and weird and difficult and thereby you will know more about yourself." My process is much more organic than that. In *Fucking A*, Hester Smith and her world are foreign to us, but when we meet her, she draws us like a magnet, and we learn a lot about our own world. The same for Hester La Negrita in *In the Blood*. If there is a great psychic distance to travel between an audience member's seat and the character on stage—and if the character is very rich when you meet her—then the trip is incredibly intense, very visceral.

The Greeks understood distance and the journey; their plays often include events that happen offstage and are retold to us later. In *Blood*, I use the confessions, the characters' interior monologues, to describe events that happened offstage. As we hear confession after confession, it occurs to us that so much is happening offstage that we must ask, "What is going to happen in front of us?"

KS: What is the connection between Hester La Negrita in *In the Blood* and Hester Smith in *Fucking A*?

SLP: In the middle of writing *Fucking A*, a riff on Hawthorne's *The Scarlet Letter*, I started another play, *In the Blood*. Though *Blood*, a more chamberlike play, grew out of *Fucking A*, the two are completely different. Hester La Negrita and Hester Smith are two separate characters, each in completely different worlds—they just share a name and a connection to the letter "A."

KS: The onstage murder in *In the Blood* is painful to watch. It seems that violence has become more overt in your later plays—why is that?

SLP: The first "real" piece I wrote in college [Mt. Holyoke] was a short story called "The Wedding Pig," about a school teacher in a small Texas town who attends a violent harvest ritual that goes dramatically awry. It was while writing this piece that I first knew I was going to be a writer, when I felt that whole big nonpersonal wave of psychic energy coursing through my veins. The story had elements of sex, love, violence, history and ritual, all connected—and all five of those elements have been around a long time in my work.

KS: In *The America Play* we see Abraham Lincoln get shot over and over again by Booth. In *Topdog* you've written a character who is an Abe Lincoln impersonator. You're not done with Lincoln, are you?

SLP: No, I'm not—or I should say, he's not done with me. Do you know that John Wilkes Booth was born on my birthday?

KS: What makes a perfect play?

SLP: I'm not interested in perfection, maybe because I don't know what that is. But I do know what a good ride is. So "perfect plays" could be plays that give me a really good ride. *Oedipus* is a really good ride. There are plays that I love—*The Glass Menagerie* is a great play. A lot of Shakespeare's plays are great, but none of them are perfect. A playwright friend refers to a good play as "actor proof," meaning that the playwright has done everything he or she can to ensure that the play doesn't fall apart from production to production, that the play's integrity remains intact.

KS: Your relationship to George C. Wolfe and the Public Theater is quite special in its length and depth of commitment.

SLP: Before he even had a theatre, George said he wanted to do my plays. He saw a production of *The Death of the Last Black Man in the Whole Entire World* at BACA Downtown in Brooklyn, and said, "I'm going to do your work." And he has. *In the Blood* was the third play produced by George (the Public also did *The America Play* and *Venus*). They have committed to my two-character *Topdog*, and they've commissioned me to write another play. Each time I have a production lined up with them, I'm as excited as if it were my first production ever. It's wonderful to be so supported.

KS: You have taught playwriting at Yale, and beginning this fall you will be heading the new A.S.K./CalArts writing program. If there is one lesson you'd like your students to take away from your courses, what would it be?

SLP: Discipline. The courage to think for themselves. And the passion to imagine what's not there.

12

AN INTERVIEW WITH
SUZAN-LORI PARKS AT CAL ARTS

Lisa Colletta

September 7, 2000

Lisa Colletta: The focus of this interview is finding out how you balance your life as a playwright and now a teacher. I was reading an interview with you in *American Theatre* and they had just published one of your plays, *In the Blood.* The writer describes you as eclectic, the youthful voice of the American theatre. And, basically, I wondered how you saw your role as a playwright complementing your role as a mentor and teacher?

Suzan-Lori Parks: I've been writing plays since 1983. No, 1982. While I did not go to a MFA program like the one I am heading here, I learned a lot along the way from the school of hard knocks, by just being out there and writing. I know I did a lot of things that were helpful, some of them weren't, but I guess I can pull from my career things that can help a student. For example, having them do movement and dance or having them do voice. In other programs they don't have to, as far as I know. I may be wrong. Other programs may change overnight. But as far as I know in talking with other students and having taught at Yale School of Drama among other places, students are not given this kind of training.

LC: It seems like the program here at CalArts is uniquely positioned in its disciplinary interest.

SLP: Yes. In their first year, students take a set group of classes. I tell them that there are no electives. But we did squeeze in one elective. We have two writers. Next year there will be two more and the next year there will be two more for a total of six at any one time in the three-year program. It's a very rigorous set schedule. As one of them said today, they looked at the schedule and listened to me talk about the importance of putting the writing first. "There are so many cool teachers. There are so many cool things to take." But it's important to focus on the writing for these three years, so when they come out they will have a certain number of scripts, a certain number of productions, a certain number of ideas for new plays. One of them said today, after looking at the schedule, "Oh, we're on a path," and I said "This is a path. This is not just a playwriting course." I really want to teach them discipline, the ability to stick with something when it's hard. If I can teach them that then they can go out into the world and be artists. Even if they choose to get into any kind of art, or maybe not even do art, or whatever they do in their life, I want to encourage them to learn how to stick with something when the going gets rough (which I think is the core of being an artist actually). I think all great artists can do that because it's usually not easy. Even when people are "Hooray, hooray, bravo your play!" or your beautiful painting or whatever, you still might go home to your desk, or to your studio or whatever, and find all your artistic wheels stuck in the mud and you have to really learn how to hunker down and stick with this project, writing, or whatever.

LC: There was a roundtable published in the *LA Times* two weeks ago where you commented on political theatre. You were talking about the idea of craft and that you're not interested in theatre that makes the play fit into an idea.

SLP: I believe in the mind behind the mind. It might sound airy, flaky, fuzzy, but it's actually just basic. We have our conscious brain, all this frontal brain activity. And then there's the mind in the back. If you want to bisect it mathematically, the mind is back here [*points to the back of her head*], which is the more primitive mind. And I believe in the mind behind the mind. I believe that this mind, the front mind, the conscious mind, the mind that we use for driving and balancing our check book and all that, is more limited when it comes to creating art. I really believe in the power of the mind behind the mind, the other mind, the subconscious, unconscious mind. To access it you can't just have an idea: "I'm going to write a play that says x, y, and z," and so you write your play and gosh darn if it doesn't just say x, y, z and nothing else. I was talking to Chris Barreca, who is the head of design, about that. Often when a playwright approaches writing a play in that way, the play is limited. It just says x, y, z; it may say x, y, z very well, but it says nothing else. What if a playwright approaches a play in a different way. I was interacting one day with Mary Lou Rosato, an acting teacher, and she made a beautiful gesture. I said, "Maybe there's a play in it." If you start from there with just a gut feeling of a gesture, that's very deep. That's where my plays come from.

LC: Unfortunately, they didn't pursue that train of thought in the *LA Times* article. What did you mean when you said that your plays are more organic? They grow out of something?

SLP: They grow out of something very deep and are initially completely mysterious: For example, why was I really fascinated, obsessed by Lincoln?

Someone could say, "Oh, slavery," but it's more interesting than just a piece of American history or African American history. It's something else. A combination of his height, the log cabin aspect, the fact that I was born in Kentucky, his costume, the fact that John Wilkes Booth was born on my birthday. All these amazing things. I didn't know anything about him when I started. I didn't know until last year when my fiancé told me, "You're born on John Wilkes Booth's birthday." And I just started laughing. But what was very uncanny was that there were two dates given for his birth. It was either May 10, which is my birth date, or August 26, which is my sister's birth date. It's that kind of stuff. It's not that I want to say something about slavery (certainly it was bad: it sucked, but it got us here) or that I want to say something about Lincoln. So it comes from those weird, deep places, deep inside the root of your spine or the back of your head. They call this part of your head the mouth of God. So organic. I can't judge and say that my play is more organic than hers. I know I get a lot of mileage by allowing the mystery to exist for a long period of time and being okay about being lost.

LC: How do you create that type of learning situation with your CalArts students?

SLP: Susan Solt wanted me to come here. Susan, Fran, and Steven Lavine, the president, they all wanted me to come to CalArts. Second of all, I chose my students, Patty Ketcherperil and Matthew Deegan, who both did undergrad theater stuff and have been doing theater outside of school for a little while. They're both very respectful of the process of the art form and very much interested in learning from me and from the institute. They're brave and intelligent. I planned to create an environment of support so they know that I am interested in what they do. I think they're wonderful writers already. I want them to tell me what the future of theater is, since it's in them and other people like them. I like them to tell me something about theater. I want them to write the plays that they are going to write, I don't want them to write like me. It's more like a support system. It's providing a supportive, loving environment with an iron rod of discipline. And they seem to be into it. In our playwriting classes I wanted to teach some yoga, but I'm not certified yet to do it to the whole institute. Still, I can teach it to them. I was going to do Suranga Yoga, which is like power yoga, but it's not power yoga: it's Suranga yoga. We are going to start practicing together.

LC: This idea works out nicely with your views on gestures, the mind–body connection.

SLP: The students are also taking voice with Fran Bennett. So they'll be working on their actual physical voice as well as their writer voice at the same time. The two are totally connected. They'll be doing movement, which is going to be great. They're going to be doing acting with Marissa

Chibas, which is fab, together with the MFA acting students. And they'll be doing writing with me [as well as] the Shakespeare read-through with me and a host of invited teachers. There's also the hand drumming course, the one elective which they are really looking forward to. I think that's pretty much it.

LC: Which play is opening this spring at the Public Theatre?

SLP: *Topdog/Underdog.*

LC: And who is going to be directing it?

SLP: Charles Dutton, which is really exciting. We're in the process of casting now. We have all these people interested in doing it, but there are always conflicts, and scheduling, and blah blah blah.

LC: What other productions are in the works?

SLP: I have several productions of *In the Blood* going up around the country. They're doing it at the Guthrie, at Woolly Mammoth, and Perseverance Theatre in Alaska. Those are the three that I'm in contact about. I think a couple of other places are doing it as well.

LC: One of them is in San Francisco, isn't it?

SLP: Maybe. I usually don't keep up with other productions of plays, but those three I know because I talked to directors about staging, etc.

LC: That's an amazing play. It exemplifies what you were saying earlier about Lincoln. There's obviously the political statement but there's also something deeply human, just so touching about that connection with American history through Hawthorne. Would you comment on *In the Blood* in connection with the ideas about creativity that you have been discussing?

SLP: I didn't set out to write a play about a homeless woman, or issues of homelessness. Writing that play was so difficult, mysterious, and weird because it came out of another play. All of a sudden that play jumped out, and then there were two plays. For a while I thought I'd throw that one away and I'd just write that one and then I wrote *In the Blood*. The two plays are completely different but both very disturbing. Next fall I'm going to direct *Fucking A* here. We premiered in Houston and were going to do it in New York but we're doing *Topdog* first. So I'm going to do *Topdog* out there in March and *Fucking A* here later.

LC: So you're going to direct it?

SLP: Yes, I'm going to direct it unless we find some incredible director that I just have to work with.

LC: You said *Fucking A* premiered in Houston?

SLP: Yes, it had its world premiere there. It's going to be done at the Public too. *Fucking A* has a cast of 11 and is set in a totally different time period from *In the Blood*. And in *Fucking A,* Hester with the A is an abortionist.

LC: To end on an Institute note, what about the A.S.K. Project? Being sponsored by A.S.K. [a philanthropic foundation supporting the performing arts], Richard Foreman will come here which is going to be very exciting. Was there anything you wanted to say about this new kind of theater and what role it might play in the future of American contemporary theater?

SLP: I thank Audrey Skirball-Kenis and the Foundation. It's so forward thinking. I want to turn out hardworking writers. I don't necessarily want to turn out hardworking form-breaker writers, those who set out with an idea or blurb in mind before they write a play. I never set out to break the form. I actually set out to write as close to the play as possible: It's already written so I just have to listen. I don't have a problem with the form; that's why I'm doing a Shakespeare read-through. I like the form. I think the form is cool. Sometimes it doesn't always hold what we want and so the form breaks because the stuff we are putting in it is just overwhelming. But I don't need to turn out any form-breakers and I also don't need to turn out any writers who write like me. I hope to turn out hardworking, disciplined writers who are respectful of the tradition and who are respectful of their own voices. I also want to teach them how to learn to listen to themselves, to their own thing. Yesterday, after the new students meeting, I had them hold onto their ear lobe. The top part, that is, the part that is hard, the cartilage part. You turn it down, kind of fold it in. And you just talk and your voice totally changes. Just try it, it's really cool.

LC: It sounds like it's coming from somebody else. Or somewhere else.

SLP: Exactly. This mike, this huge microphone all of sudden. Like a god mike in a theater when the director talks into the God mike. We did that. I said, "I really want you guys to listen to yourselves first and then learn to listen to your close friends who care about you and who care about your work." So that's the kind of, "Oh geez, we might not turn out trailblazers, yah," or be on the cover of *Trail Blazer* magazine, approach. Either way, if they are hardworking and respectful of the tradition, of each other, of themselves, they will create theater that is rich and strange (if it's rich, it's always strange). But you've got to dig deep, and I'll know when you're not. I want you to give me the shit, I don't want you to give me the bullshit. I know the difference, so be ready to dig deep. And so to be given this money from the Audrey Skirball-Kenis Foundation to do that, I think, is a wonderful opportunity.

13

THE MYTHOLOGY OF HISTORY, FAMILY AND PERFORMANCE

Rick DesRochers

Public Access, August 2001

The Program of the Joseph Papp Public Theater/New York Shakespeare Festival

Shortly before beginning rehearsals together for the Public's production of *Topdog/Underdog*, playwright Suzan-Lori Parks and director George C. Wolfe sat down to talk. Literary Manager Rick DesRochers joined in the discussion and recorded the conversation.

Rick DesRochers: On the surface, *Topdog/Underdog* is a seemingly simple play about sibling rivalry and a younger brother's attempt to get the same respect and success enjoyed by his older brother. Can you talk about how the play sheds new light on the age-old fraternal dynamic of having a shared history?

George C. Wolfe: I don't think I've ever worked on a two-character, one-room play in my entire life, but what is exciting to me is that once you get inside this play, you realize that the *whole world* is inside this room. The relationship between the two brothers is astoundingly real and astoundingly mythic at the same time. How does one negotiate a real relationship with one's history? Where do the facts end, and where does the imagination really take over? One's own history is comprised of what one remembers and what one imagines. When you have a fractured legacy, as most of us do, then invention is a necessity.

Suzan-Lori Parks: People like their history in different ways, and when you come into the theater, the fun for me is that you see these characters named Lincoln and Booth, and you see a handgun introduced early on in the play. The real fun for me becomes: How do you like your history? How do you want to see this played out? We know what happens to Lincoln and Booth in actual history, but what are the other possibilities on stage? Some people like it by the book, as it was; some like it as it *could* be. People may hope for the play to conclude in a particular way depending on how they like their history.

GCW: *Topdog* concerns the mythology of family. I find that in a lot of families the older brother tends to be attracted to the mythology and illusions of family and is invested in creating a scenario of the white picket fence and family picnics together, which has glimmers of truth, but is not necessarily grounded in truth. Whereas the younger brother tends to be totally invested in the phenomenon of overthrowing the older brother so as to claim enough space for himself. In addition to this dynamic, because the brothers, in the play, are abandoned, the symbiotic nature of their relationship is intensified, with Lincoln and Booth playing out the dynamics and roles of mother/father and husband/wife for each other.

RD: George, I know that you are interested in the notion of how people role-play in their everyday lives. How does this play itself out in *Topdog*?

GCW: Lincoln, as a three-card monte player, is used to performing, and revealing what needs to be revealed and concealing what needs to be concealed, as a good actor does. He works with the response of the crowd. Booth, by virtue of the fact that he is a thief, is used to performing actions that no one watches. One is used to having the reaction of other people, the other is most effective when nobody notices him. What's fascinating is what happens when Booth wants to be noticed and attempts to become a three-card dealer. Booth wants to live in the legacy that his brother has enjoyed and has had success with. Lincoln has retreated from performance, and is just trying to craft some level of equilibrium in his life.

RD: In effect, they have reversed positions and performance strategies. Is there something fun for you, Suzan-Lori, writing a play about two men and their masculine dynamics?

SLP: I don't think about "dynamics," *per se*. What's important to me is that, when I was writing the play, I was the two men I wrote about. And that applies to any characters that I write. I become the characters and let them speak. In this play, there is no escape for the two men, there is no escape from this one room that they share. In other plays, I can fan out and become other people and have multiple perspectives, but here I have to deal with what these guys are going through first hand. When they were together I was *both* of them. When one brother was gone, I was the other one waiting for him to return. Writing this play was unlike any other writing experience I've ever had.

GCW: Masculinity is the ultimate performance piece. And success as a male animal depends on how much they inhabit that role. It's about how many women they can attract, how much money they make, and how much power they can possess. The success of being a man depends on how successful they are in convincing others of their masculinity. But ultimately Lincoln and Booth, in addition to being brothers, are also male animals fighting for territory and dominance over their domain.

RD: Throughout the play, Lincoln and Booth keep returning to their room. What keeps them coming back, and why is this so important for them?

SLP: Lincoln doesn't have any other place to live. Some people just fall, and can't get it together. Some people fall and they don't get up. That's just the way it is. Lincoln has given up his place on top, and returns to what he knows. He comes home to Booth, who knows who Lincoln is, and more importantly who he *was*.

GCW: And how they are defined or redefined when they are in that room? When the brothers are out in the world they are defined by other people's perceptions of them. Inside the room they have to deal with their history as family and there is no escaping that. Nobody understands their complexities except each other. They become defined by their own history. Intimacy requires that you negotiate a moment-to-moment relationship with another person who knows you.

RD: They retreat into this world of the mythological family, which provides home, stability, and clearly defined roles that allow them to survive.

SLP: We all go through this to some extent, where we return home in order to rediscover who we are.

GCW: And where we go to get re-anchored is family.

RD: Suzan-Lori, the Lincoln assassination act from *The America Play* finds its way into *Topdog/Underdog*. What brings you back to the idea of a black man impersonating Lincoln? And how does this work for you in terms of your playwriting?

SLP: I was at a discussion of playwrights recently here at the Public, and I was impressed by the fact that some writers set themselves tasks of what kind of play they are going to write, and how big in scope it will be, and how many characters it will have, the themes, images, everything, and what it is going to be all about. But I don't work like that at all; I just let it come out. I just let the characters do the talking, and I'm right in the room with them, doing it all as they are doing it. I feel as if I'm writing less from a place of "consciousness," and more from a place of "super-consciousness."

RD: What's interesting about that is it becomes the same experience for the audience. The surprise of discovery of what these characters are going to do, and what will happen to them is the same for the audience as it was for you when you were writing it.

GCW: I have this theory about theater. I believe that the audience can tell when they are in the presence of a stale truth. When you are overly conscious of what you set out to create, or recreate an old truth, then the moment on stage becomes false, and audiences can sense that. This is what Suzan-Lori does so well; her work is honest and direct, not in a series of manufactured moments, and the audience can tell when they are in the presence of that truth. They can smell it.

14

A MOMENT WITH...
SUZAN-LORI PARKS,
PLAYWRIGHT

John Marshall

Seattle Post-Intelligencer, May 26, 2003

Suzan-Lori Parks won the Pulitzer Prize last year for her play *Topdog/Underdog* and became the first African American woman to garner that playwriting laurel. A year before, the Mount Holyoke graduate received a MacArthur Foundation "genius grant" that brought her $500,000. Now the multi-talented wordsmith is on a national book tour for her debut novel, *Getting Mother's Body* (Random House, 257 pages, $23.95), with a robust first printing of 100,000 copies.

All the honors have not produced an inflated ego for this engaging woman with an effervescent personality. A smile is seldom far from her face.

John Marshall: You recently turned 40. How did that affect you?

Suzan-Lori Parks: My husband called everyone we know and threw a big party at our house (in Venice, Calif.). It was great; I got presents, ate cake, drank champagne, ate more cake. I do have a game plan. I'm just starting to play guitar, and in another 40 years I may have the chops to be a really happenin' toothless hot mama blues musician. My husband, who used to play with Muddy Waters, is teaching me.

JM: What impact did winning the Pulitzer Prize have on you?

SLP: It required me to keep reminding myself not to take myself too seriously. One could blow up or trip on yourself because of something like the Pulitzer. But I'm not that kind of person. I gotta keep going on to the next thing. I've got to not be afraid to play the guitar or sing for people, or continuing to grow. I also want to learn to surf. One could get locked in by the Pulitzer, thinking this is who I am. Doors open with it, but doors in your mind could close.

JM: What is your strongest memory of winning?

SLP: I finished my novel on April 6th, my play opened on Broadway on April 7th and I won the Pulitzer on April 8th.

JM: What was the genesis of your novel?

SLP: It's a deep and reverent bow to William Faulkner's *As I Lay Dying*, which also has characters on a journey dealing with a dead relative. So many of my plays have been about the dead. But the novel was really born in the landscape of West Texas, where we spent time when my father was with the Army in Vietnam. I love the big sky and arid landscape of that place. The characters came out of that landscape and the story came out of those characters. Then there was Faulkner's novel, which I had read eight years before.

JM: What was it like taking a college class from James Baldwin?

SLP: He had faith in me long before I even had faith in me. That's the great gift that a writing teacher can give a young writer. You can't overestimate the value of hearing, "Hey, you're good." He was encouraging in a scary way, not a soft mushy way. He teaches you to be tough on yourself.

JM: Why is Suzan-Lori spelled with a "z"?

SLP: It was the result of a misprint. When I was doing one of my first plays in the East Village, we had fliers printed up and they spelled my name wrong. I was devastated. But the director said, "Just keep it, honey, and it will be fine." And it was.

15

AN INTERVIEW WITH SUZAN-LORI PARKS AND BONNIE METZGAR

Joseph Roach

World Performance Project at Yale University,
November 13, 2006

[*The following is an edited and transcribed version of a public interview with Suzan-Lori Parks and Bonnie Metzgar conducted by Joseph Roach at Yale. From the audience, Elinor Fuchs briefly joined the conversation.*]

Joseph Roach: We're here today to talk about the first seven days of *365* and the balance of *365*. This is a special event by any measure. I know everyone here is interested in the scope of the project. How you conceived it—imagining a play a day for a year which you wrote and then imagining a play a day for a year which will now be performed in six or seven-hundred theaters, Bonnie?

Bonnie Metzgar: I think it is approaching seven hundred. It's very hard to know exactly how many theaters. Every day, it's a little bit more. It's amazing. I would say somewhere between 650 and 700 theaters.

JR: And the way in which you imagined this cycle of plays in terms of the issues that come up—the ideas, the images, the gestures, the characters—there's a continuity, there's connection that occurs across the weeks and months ahead. Do you want to say something about that? What from the first seven days might we see again?

Suzan-Lori Parks: In terms of subject matter? In terms of subject matter, there are recurring characters throughout the year. There are recurring themes. There are what I call tribute plays.

When I woke up one morning—it happened many times throughout the year—a famous person had passed away, like Johnny Cash. I wrote a play for Johnny Cash. Or, George Plimpton and John Ritter passed away kinda near the same time so they appear in a play together. It's called *A Play for (George Plimpton) and (John Ritter)*. Those are tribute plays.

Or, what I call project plays. There's a play called *Project Macbeth*. There's a play called *Project Tempest*, which is sort of an urban take, if you will, on some of the classics. There's a series called *Father Comes Home from the Wars*. Not the same father. A different father, a different home, a different war. Repeated. Revisited throughout the year.

I would say that the through-line through the whole cycle is not the traditional through-line—we're taught to see a series of story points as the through-line—but from play to play to play. [...] The through-line through the whole cycle—instead of a series of story points—is the river of spirit or the river of the collective unconscious like Carl Jung spoke of. Every day, I had to, as I was writing this, as I was making this daily offering to theater; I had to ground myself, immerse myself in the river of spirit and it comes through to connect all of the plays and it comes through tonight when we see you all [Yale students] perform. The simple act of writing the play, organizing the festival, hooking up with Joe and Emily [Coates] and the World Performance Project [at Yale]. Without you all, we would not be here at this wonderful place, not just here at Yale tonight, but we wouldn't be the 365 National Festival as lovely and developed as we are. So, we really appreciate you guys. The whole thing of writing the plays, of coordinating this festival, or passing it off to the first leg of the Northeast network. You guys are the Northeast network?

JR: We are the Northeast network. The "hub."

SLP: The Northeast network, the hub, one of the hubs. That whole act is about immersing yourself in the river of spirit and letting it pass on. [...] It's about creating and letting go. You all have created and, at the end of the week, you will pass it on to the next group of people in your network. Other theaters all around the country and some internationally are passing it on to the next theater within their network.

JR: I heard you speak earlier about letting go of this project and your ambition to make this available to us, to those who wanted to put it on in a way that is not conventionally imagined in the way that we put on theater. Do you want to talk about inclusion? "Radical inclusion" is a phrase I remember you using.

SLP: I love saying that. It's a phrase that came to me after the writing of the plays but I'm very aware that it's something that I had to do in the writing of them. Talking earlier today, Bonnie and I used this phrase "radical inclusion." To write a play a day, you have to practice radical inclusion. You cannot have a bouncer on the doorway of your creative spirit. The bouncer has got to walk away. You include everybody. You welcome all comers. All ideas are welcome to the table. For the 365 National Festival, we practice something very simple, radical inclusion, we welcome all interested parties to participate.

JR: It leads me to a question that I wasn't sure that I was going to ask because it's a question on the kind of subject that we often don't think it's appropriate to ask. I want to ask about religion. In your language, in your poetry, in your way of thinking and approaching the world, in the voice of your words on the page, on the stage and now in your presence, there is a language and a spirit. Would you talk about that in the work, if you'd like?

SLP: The spirit and God are separate from religion. I know this is Yale but I'm making these things up kinda on the fly as I go about my business.

JR: For God, for Country, for… whatever [*laughter*].

SLP: No, no, no. I really feel that God is separate from religion, which seems like something organized and codified with structures and rules, whatnot. And God is, I believe, bigger than any rule or set of rulebooks that we can impose on him, her, it… what have you.

I was pointing to my arm because I get very excited. If any of you speak Sanskrit, pardon my accent or lack thereof, "îśvara-prañidhânâd vâ," which means, loosely translated, "Follow God, the inner guide": it's from Yoga Sutra's 1:2:3. I have it written twice on my arm. Once in small print and once in large print. In place of a watch. So, what time is it? It's time to follow god, the inner guide! [*laughter*] What do I do right now? Follow God, the inner guide. It's right here. It has taken on wonderful significance this week because there have been stressful times and there it is right there.

The spirit, for me, is… this great coursing thing through which the plays come, the novels that I write come, the songs, the screenplays, even, come from the spirit. No, really, they have to come from there.

JR: I wonder if you would want to say something about spells. That's a word in your practice that's always intrigued me and it brings me into your work. I have a visceral feeling. I wonder if you would talk about that as a matter of the spirit and as a matter of technique.

SLP: A spell is… you'll see a character's name repeated with no dialogue. Or, perhaps there'll be two characters. You'll see it [the names] repeated with no dialogue. There's a little guidebook at the start of the plays. You'll see it. It's this thing that I've been doing for years. I keep thinking that I will never do it again but it keeps [showing] up because I find that the more I write that my plays explode into silence. It's where a character experiences their true inner state so they have an incredibly large moment with themselves or, if it's a spell like:

Joe Roach
Suzan-Lori Parks
Joe Roach
Suzan-Lori Parks

JR: We're having a conversation without speaking.

SLP: We're having an exchange of energy.

JR: We're in touch.

SLP: And the director, of course, can shape [it] as she sees fit. But it is an exchange of energy. It often precedes an emotional turn, an emotional change-up. It is that incredible exchange of energy that explodes into the clearing and that's the spell where we are in our true mythic state. And these plays, while they are snapshot plays, they are very small, short little plays, they are [also] mythic plays. They are operas. They are huge and yet tiny at the same time. They're these mythic characters, dealing with these mythic issues.

JR: Bonnie, do you want to comment on that as a director? Looking at a script from a directorial point of view when you are given this richness of a spell, casting it in the theater?

BM: I love engaging in Suzan-Lori's text because it has these—I guess now they're these—symbolic road maps for you to find. It was really interesting for us because there was a little while where the style sheet, which is this front matter that tells you what some of these symbols mean, wasn't available to some of our participants. What I got were all these e-mails from people taking a stab at what those spells really meant, different directors from around the country. Because I myself have been involved with Suzan-Lori's work for so long, I have, probably similar to you Joe, developed a relationship with when they come, the different flavors of spells, but it was really interesting to receive these e-mails from people with their own interpretations.

The interesting kind of questions are: Is it that they're sustaining the moment? Is it the two actors, as if the language continued, and they are still connected? Or, is it a frozen moment, which I think is a little bit different in terms of stage time. Is there something locked between them or do they coast closer together? I would say that depending on where that moment fell in relation to what's happening in the action of the scene that the action might be a little bit different.

We did some table work in New York of all of the plays. We worked with a number of actors who have been in Suzan-Lori's work in New York over the years. And even they, in the way that they would engage with each other, some of them–you actually saw them—would loom toward each other. It was quite striking the difference in the way that they took on their own inner feelings, their own inner selves. I feel like there's a lot of play inside those spells.

JR: The spell to me is so involved with the live presence of an actor. Do you think that way when writing a screenplay? In your novel? You've written different genres.

SLP: While I've only written one novel, *Getting Mother's Body*, I play with space in the novel. I can make a chapter very short and enjoy the space that it leaves at the bottom of the page and play around with silence 'cause there's nothing there. No, I wouldn't actually write in the spell. The reader would experience an explosion into silence. And it's great because it's a visual—a white—field. I play around with that too as much as I can, given that you have to hand the manuscript over to a typesetter or whatnot.

JR: The spell really happens in the mind of the reader.

SLP: That's what's cool about a novel. In a novel, the reader is the actor, the director, the designer, the costume designer, the lighting designer. They do it all in their head and it's great.

JR: I hope this doesn't push too hard on the creative process but I was wondering about this work in relation to your previous work, to the development of your theater from *Immutabilities* and *The America Play*...

SLP: I naturally look in the audience for Ellie Fuchs. I want to acknowledge her, who's here [today]. Elinor Fuchs is a professor at Yale. When you ask me how it relates, I say Ellie Fuchs is an incredible theater scholar and maybe Ellie will tell me [*laughter*]. Just tell me what it means.

Elinor Fuchs: I'm going to take this occasion to explode into silence.

JR: The way in which *Topdog/Underdog* takes earlier themes and develops them in different ways—it concentrates them, it seems as if it was getting into a smaller space. The ideas were just as big. The scope, even the stage itself, was reduced. Now, in *365*, a whole horizon opens up.

SLP: It's like *I Ching*—I know that I'm going to get this wrong—*The Book of Change*. The last one is like number 64 or something. You know when you hit the last one, you're going to have to start at the beginning again. *Topdog/Underdog* was like the end one. I've hit these places before in my writing. Or, if you do karate, when you get your black belt, you're starting all over again. You're beginning again. It's this coming down to the two-character play that's in one room and then you're a new person the next day. Which is about letting go. Instead of holding on to, "I'm going to write a whole bunch of two-character plays and put them on Broadway"—while my agent would be so happy if I did that, George Lange, he'd be so pleased—but instead of doing that I can't but listen to the voice speaking to me, the spirit, and the spirit says write a play every day of the year and call it *365 Days/365 Plays*. I said, okay, that sounds like fun.

It's also about, in a way, outreach. With *Topdog/Underdog*, we continued to reach so many people. I went over to India a couple of years ago and we went all around India. In every college where we visited, the kids, the Indian kids, would do a reading for me of *Topdog/Underdog*. Kids in India. The south of India too. Indian college students too, women, did a reading of *Topdog/Underdog*. "I am Lincoln." "I am Booth." This is our story. It's about getting out there and making a connection with people.

JR: And you've spread three-card monte across the world [*laughter*].

Audience Member: How do you know when the plays are done?

SLP: First, there's a great essay by Sam Shepard, the fantastic, fantastical playwright. Many years ago, he wrote an essay called "Time," I believe it is called, in which he talks about play length. He says, just to paraphrase briefly, a play should be no longer than it should be. Because people think, I have to write a play that I have to sit there to write a two hour, two act, or Shakespeare, a five act. A play should be no longer than it should be. I read that many years ago and it has stayed with me. I think that it is a brilliant essay.

Tennessee Williams. *Cat on a Hot Tin Roof.* The character Brick. Brick drinks until he hears the click. I write until I hear the click. There is an audible click. If you're listening in, I can hear when a play is done. And that's when I know it is finished. The thing is these plays, some take up this much room [a small amount] on the page, some seven pages long. Some have an average [run of] three minutes. Some run for ten minutes. Some plays run forever. There are several forever plays. For example, March 29th's performance. That play runs forever. There are some long ones in there. Just be warned.

JR: The influence of [Eugene] O'Neill is so strong.

BM: If I can just say one other thing about that question. It leads into some things that we're trying to get at through the festival structure. I hear that [question] and I ask, why is it that our assumption is that a play is two hours long?

One of the reasons that we believe that is that the theaters, the buildings that house theater and the audiences that they sell tickets to, expect theater to be two hours long. Many writers write things in forms that are [shorter], like a thirty-five minute event. What does a writer do with something where the click happens and it's thirty-five minutes long?

I created this venue in New York called Joe's Pub. One of the things that we did at Joe's Pub was we asked all the artists out there who were doing these things that were weirdly shaped, "Come and do it at our place." We wanted [Joe's Pub] to be a place where you're always surprised about how long something is, what it is, what the nature of it is.

One of the things about *365* that is so amazing is that suddenly we are all asked, how do I create a relationship with something [like] that? It's a really, really long play that takes a year. How do I go to it as an audience member? How do I approach it as a designer? If I'm only doing seven plays, do I look at all of it? It gets us to ask questions about what is theater and what can theater be. How do theater buildings and institutions need to expand their minds to be able to imagine different kinds of theater, shapes of theater so that we can make room for different kinds of things than just the two-hour, two-act play?

AM: What advice would you give to an aspiring playwright?

SLP: I am a morning person so I choose to get up in the morning and write. But I would suggest for those folks who are night owls or afternoon types, choose your favorite time to write. Don't try to get up at 5am, if that's not your thing. We were out very late [last] night at the launch in New York and, today, I was up very early, at four, walking around in NYC. It was a beautiful morning but I was up because—like Rebecca Rugg said—I was catching… the plays as they flew by because they're out at 4am and you just walk around with a net and scoop them up.

I am a very disciplined writer. In this country, we tend to think of it as beating yourself up. Discipline is just a lattice on which a beautiful vine can grow. It's a beautiful and loving thing that assists you in your efforts. It helps you show up at your desk every day. There were plenty of days that were difficult. Those are the days when you find out what kind of artist you are, when it's difficult [and] you show up anyway and get the work done. Those are the good days.

AM: What do you do on difficult days?

SLP: There were several, many days like that. There were many days. One of those days, when I woke up, I decided that I didn't have any ideas but that I would have to go through the motions. So, I sat at my desk and wrote, "Going through the motions." And then I thought wow, the motions could be a mountain range and the play could be about people going through the mountain range, a mountain range called the Motions. And this became the play for the day. It sounds silly. When we did the table work in New York, David Patrick Kelly, who is an A-list fantastic, fantastic actor—he does stage and screen—said he loved that play because, as he said to us, this is a play written on a day when all you had was the commitment, all you had was the commitment, and you wrote anyway and he loves it for that.

Some days all you have is your commitment, especially as an artist. Or, as a spouse. Sometimes all you have is the fact that you said, "Through thick and through thin," and that's all you have. It's a beautiful moment when you can show up and be present even on a difficult day. Sure, there were days like that.

AM: Prior to the publication of the book, what was it like to work with artists who could only see one piece, seven days or fourteen?

SLP: You look at the years that bracket your life and you think, "This is your time." That's what's exciting. To root yourself in the moment. To root yourself in the present moment that is the challenge. To allow yourself the resonance. Each one is about exactly what it is. If you have seven, work with seven. You know what I'm saying? My grandmother used to say, "Work with what you got."

EF: I'm trying to imagine the year that you spent doing this. One is that you got up every morning and it was a kind of meditation exercise. Or, maybe this was like one of those extended performances from the late '70s or '80s—I'm going to sit in this window for six months. What was your life like during this time?

SLP: It was kind of like endurance art but it was really, really trippy because it was endurance art done in private, without an audience. Very few people even knew that I was doing it. My very dear friend Bonnie Metzgar knew. I told her. My husband Paul. Other than them, nobody. It was endurance art done in private.

No, it was not a play a day for 24 hours. I would write the play in the morning. We were opening *Topdog/Underdog* in London. I was on my book tour for my novel. I was premiering *Fucking A* at the Public Theater in New York, and I was writing other things. I was writing a movie for Brad Pitt. I was teaching full-time at CalArts. Busy, busy, busy. This was my little treat that I had in the morning. Actually, it was not an offering to me. It was an offering that I made every day.

16

IT'S AN OBERAMMERGAU THING

An Interview with Suzan-Lori Parks

Kevin J. Wetmore, Jr.

July 12, 2006

From *Suzan-Lori Parks: A Casebook*
Eds. Kevin J. Wetmore, Jr. and Alycia Smith-Howard

This interview took place in Venice, California. Parks was preparing for the world premiere of *365 Days/365 Plays* as well as working on a new screenplay and the book for a Ray Charles musical.

Kevin J. Wetmore, Jr: Well, let's start with your writing; specifically, the process. How do you start writing a play?
Suzan-Lori Parks: I think it varies [*pause while she thinks*].
KJW: I find it interesting that when I asked you about writing, you picked up a pen.
SLP: [*Laughs*] I picked up the pen because I wanted to try it out, and then I could give you an accurate answer. Because it's different with every play – with *365*, and those are the plays that are most on my mind because we are going to perform them, God willing, starting on the 13th November and continuing for a whole year. When I wrote them, I would just wake up in the morning every day, wiggle my fingers around in the air and say, 'God, what is the play?' and some notion of some play would descend, and I would write it down. That's how I wrote those. With *Fucking A*, I was in a canoe with a friend. We were paddling along a river or lake – this was years ago. I was in the back of the canoe and I said to her, 'I'm going to write a play called *Fucking A*, and its going to be a riff on *The Scarlet Letter*. Ha, Ha, Ha', and I started laughing really hard. I hadn't actually read *The Scarlet Letter*, of course. It was one of those books that was assigned in high school but I hadn't read it. I hadn't wanted to. So we paddled around in the canoe, laughing, and we got back to land and dragged the canoe up onto the shore and the idea was still with me – I had been hooked. That was the

beginning of that play. So then I had to read *The Scarlet Letter*. Then figure out what about *The Scarlet Letter* had so sneakily hooked me.

KJW: So what started out as a joke became a serious play.

SLP: Exactly. It started as a stupid joke in a canoe...

KJW: Wonderful!

SLP: Or maddening. It's maddening.

KJW: Is writing a kind of madness?

SLP: I think so. We think writing cures the madness but it actually further exacerbates the cause. So you're never done – you're always chasing your tail. Or digging the hole. Or scratching. The itch that's never fully scratched, and the scratching just makes you want to continue – scratching, right? And, as you know, *Fucking A* started off as *Fucking A* and then split into two plays: *Fucking A* and *In the Blood*....

KJW: Has that happened in your other writing? Where a play leads to another, different play? Did it happen with *365*?

SLP: *The America Play* led to *Topdog* but there was more than a 5-year gap between those two. *FA* and *Blood* came out as almost-twins. And with *365*? My intention to write a play a day led me from one play to the next. The plays are strung tighter like beads with grace as the string – but they're not plot – or story-connected.

KJW: So there was no writing the play, and while you were writing, thinking, 'Oh, there's tomorrow's idea'?

SLP: Not really. It was such a crazy and wacky thing that I was doing all on my own. A newspaper interviewer a few weeks ago said, 'We should do this every year; commission a writer and get them to write a play a day and then produce it all over the country'. And I said, 'Yeah, but this project is *writer* initiated'. This was done all alone. I wish I could thoroughly describe the feeling of writing the *365*. It's like running a marathon without the crowd cheering you on. You know? Like the first guy who ran the marathon [in Greece]. There was no crowd cheering, 'Go! Go!' He was just running on his own, with a mission. But to return to your original question, every play starts differently.

Topdog/Underdog was kind of the same thing, in that it was a joke: 'I got an idea for a play: two brothers named Lincoln and Booth. Ha ha ha!' Same maniacal laughter and my friend, Emily Morse, who is now working at New Dramatists (and has just had a baby that she and her hubby have named Lincoln) – Emily said, 'You better go home and write that play'. And I was like, 'Yeah, I know'. So I went home and wrote it and 3 days later I was done. It was wild. But the writing of other plays sometimes feels like working the rockpile. Hard labour, baby. You know it. But yeah – so my plays start in different ways – but often with laughter. That's the thing. Laughter is interesting. I was reading the *Bible* the other day. I know that sounds like a joke, but I really was. I was reading the *Bible* and Sarah, you know, the wife of Abraham, is there, and God says, 'You're going to have a baby'. And she's like 'Ha! You've got to be kidding!' And God says, 'You laughed!' And she's like, 'No, I didn't'. And he says, 'Yes, you did'. And she says 'OK, I laughed'. And the laughter is a kind of handmaid to her conception. The birth comes from the laugh. OK, maybe biblical scholars would differ, but it seemed like that to me.

KJW: Moving from beginnings, once you start writing, how do you settle on a form for the play?

SLP: There's a quote from Charles Olson, the poet – at least I think it's him, or it may be Robert Creeley – they used to write letters back and forth. And in one of their letters, one of them said, 'Form is nothing more than an extension of content'. So form and content are arm in arm. Sometimes my students would ask me, 'How do I write more poetically?' And I would ask them, 'What does that mean – to write "poetically"?' And then I would encourage them to listen more and think less about writing poetically. I don't really decide on a form. Form is the shape the thing takes in order to live, you know? It's not a decision, like, 'I'm going to buy the green car'.

KJW: So it's organic?

SLP: Yeah – the play takes the shape that fits it.

KJW: Do you revise or re-write a lot?

SLP: Oh sure, I'm a good re-writer. I think that's my talent – re-writing.

KJW: How do you know you're done?

SLP: I can hear it. You know Brick in *Cat on a Hot Tin Roof*? He's a drunk. He says he drinks until he hears the click. That's the same thing – I listen for the click. Not in drinking [*laughs*] but in writing – I listen for the click. And I can hear the click. And then the play's done.

KJW: So there was a click after three days for *Topdog*?

SLP: Uh-huh. I didn't even have to think about that play. It came to me like – *zoom*! Playwriting like that can totally ruin you because it's like being struck by lightning. And you have to be strong to be able to take the next step and after you write a play in that way you can't go tripping on yourself if you ever want to write again. Not when you write a play like that, but when you write a play in that way – when it just comes to you like lightning. There's no struggle, no effort. I've never been struck by lightning, but writing *Topdog* – was *like* being struck by lightning. I mean it was very much like – I tell people that it was like silver liquid was being poured from a silver gravy boat, poured down through the air and into the back of my head. I swear if I turned around I would have seen silver liquid being poured in to the back of my head. In fact, it wasn't *like* that – that's what it *was*.

KJW: Is the process any different when you're writing for film?

SLP: Yes and no. There's the writing, the re-writing, the listening to the voices, the organic thing – all that – it's the same even with film, because I find that I can write the story only if it really comes from my guts. Lots of people think screenwriting is like paint-by-numbers writing, and some might write that way. But I think most screenwriters would agree that, even with a set structure, there should be a passionate from-the-guts writing brought into the structure. And I have to write from the guts.

KJW: Given the way Hollywood devalues writers, does that make a difference for you? I mean there is a respect for the writer in the theatre – the playwright is sacrosanct and, in theory, we aim to put what the writer intended on the stage. There are numerous discussions in rehearsal about what the playwright meant. In Hollywood, it's, 'Here's your cheque, now get the hell out and we'll do what we want with it'.

SLP: It's a shame. It's a shame. It's like devaluing a person. It's like having a factory and not valuing the folks on the assembly line. What it is, is short-sighted and stupid. And it's not true for everybody in the business. There are producers who value writers. There are directors, especially if they write themselves, who value the writer they're working with [*laughs*]. Actors – I went to the set of *Their Eyes Were Watching God* and it was incredible. The actors were so appreciative. The costume designers, the lighting designers, everybody who was part of that project was valued. Even though all I did was an *adaptation* of Zora Neale Hurston's book, and I felt so privileged to have a chance to work on the project and adapt the novel, they all said, 'If you hadn't come on board, we wouldn't be here today'. So there are Hollywood folks who value writers. But too often, there are the industry people who don't see the connection between what the writer does and the final product. Just like there are people who don't respect their parents, or don't respect the earth. We all come from the earth, and, in a movie, the writer is the person who first creates the thing we all play with. There are people who disrespect the writer's creative process – but, like *whatever* to them, right?

KJW: You're a couple of decades into your writing career, but you've said there is no such thing as a Suzan-Lori Parks play.

SLP: Yep.

KJW: It makes me think again of Hollywood, where an actor friend of mine says he knew he had made it when he saw his name as a 'type' – 'We're looking for a so-and-so type actor for this role'. One can become a type out here, regardless of what you do.

SLP: In the late 80s, when we were doing *Imperceptible Mutabilities in the Third Kingdom*, a lot of people loved it. And some people didn't know what the hell we were doing. They said, 'What?' And then we won the Obie for it. That was really great. Then I write *Last Black Man* and so many people said, 'Why didn't you just write a sequel to *Third Kingdom*?' Because they'd caught up to what I was doing by then and so they expected me to repeat myself. But I had written *Last Black Man*. I was already doing something else. And not because I *wanted* to do something else, but because I had to be true to the Spirit. The Spirit says 'Write the next thing'. And I write it. If it means I've got to go into uncharted waters to write it, well, there I go. But people were like, 'Do the Suzan-Lori Parks thing', which in 1988 to them was *Imperceptible Mutabilities in the Third Kingdom*. That was what they *thought* was my thing. But, actually, my thing is to listen. And there are plenty of people who get to tripping on one swell and just ride the same wave forever. Maybe that one swell is their thing. Not me.

I listen to the Spirit. The Spirit speaks through a channel and the channel has to be kept relatively clean. I say relatively because we all have our gunky habits. Like, I like cake – I eat too much cake, and I am sure cake gunks the channel. So if you stop doing your thing, and start doing only what the world dictates – then the channel becomes gunked up and it becomes more and more difficult to hear what you *should* be doing.

KJW: So it's not just a refusal to conform to expectation…

SLP: It's not a refusal; it's an awareness. An awareness that there is a greater knowledge and a higher power. That there is a higher source that is much smarter than me. The me that was born in 1963 and grew up in Germany – you know what I'm saying – there is a source that is much more knowledgeable than I am. There is a Self that is a lot bigger than my self. I'm very aware of the source that makes my plays and I want to stay in tune with that source and so I keep listening. It's an active, not a passive listening. So I keep listening and I write *Last Black Man*. I keep listening and I write *The America Play*. And just like *Black Man* isn't *Their Kingdom*, *America Play* is not *Black Man*. *America Play* isn't 12 figures with strange names all telling this jazz poetic story about a man who died and doesn't know where he's going to go now that he's dead. *American Play* is not *Black Man*. It's something else. It's this Lincoln thing. Why Lincoln? I don't know why exactly. But I am staying true to voices.

KJW: Do you listen to music while you write?

SLP: I used to.

KJW: Not so much anymore?

SLP: I find it distracting. Because, these days I actually listen to the music. My husband, Paul Oscher, is a musician and music is a big thing in our lives. It's hard to write and actively listen because I get distracted. These days music totally pulls my head.

KJW: So is writing actually an act of listening for you?

SLP: Oh yeah. It is for me. It's not thinking. It's not imparting a message. It's not having something to say to the people. For me, it's just listening. I tell people I don't have things to *tell*, but I have things to *show*. People say, 'What does your play mean? What should I think about? What are you trying to tell me?' Watch the play. Tell me what *you* think.

KJW: One of my teachers used to say, 'Plays don't mean – they generate meaning'.

SLP: That's a great line. That's true. That's it. That's exactly it. That's the role of the audience. When you go to see a play you shouldn't just sit there like you're being fed tapioca pudding with your mouth open. You're actively divining meaning. You're there in the theatre with a divining rod, going, 'Where's the water at? Where's the meaning? What is the meaning?' That's your job as the audience member. But to get back to your question what is a Suzan-Lori Parks play. Fast-forward to after *The America Play*. These days, there are so many people who don't know my early work when they meet me they say, 'Oh, you're just a Broadway playwright'. And I just crack up laughing. And then there are people in the downtown art scene, you know, New York City below 14ᵗʰ Street, folks I love and adore, because that's where I came up artistically, but so many down-towners hated that *Topdog* was on Broadway. So many of them were like, 'You betrayed us and your roots because you did a play on Broadway. You're not "Suzan-Lori Parks" anymore'. It's big-time funny to me. Who is Suzan-Lori Parks? Look at this [*points to tattoo*]. It's Sanskrit. Written on my arm forever. A gentle translation would be 'Follow God, the inner guide'. It's from the Yoga Sutras. It's Sutra 1:2.3, which is very important to me. It says 'Follow God'. Not 'Follow the fans'. Not 'Follow the audience'. Not 'Follow the market – make sure you make money'. It says: 'Follow God, the inner guide'.

KJW: The Sutra number makes me think of the importance of numbers in your plays. *365* being the most obvious example, but you play a lot with the meanings of numbers.

SLP: [*Laughs*] I don't know about numerology. I don't know anything about it. I read my horoscope in the newspaper, but my knowledge of numerology is limited. My choice of numbers has something to do with rhythm. But, yeah, the numbers themselves – in *The America Play*, Brazil keeps saying, 'I was only five. I was only five'. And in *Last Black Man* there's '6 by 6 by 6'. And there are the five fingers of fate in *In the Blood*. Although that's also just because there are five fingers on my hand – meaning: The meanings here go way deep but they're not 'intellectual' and they're not pre-thought out. With *365* – it just rhymed: *365 Days/365 Plays*. That was why I thought a play a day would be so fun: the title rhymed. That kind of stuff is like the heartbeat. It's there and it's strong but most of us don't have to think about it much.

KJW: There's such a sense of the interconnectedness of things in your plays…

SLP: Wow. That's a play in *365*. *The Interconnectedness of All Things*.

KJW: Synchronicity, eh? [*laughs*] That's one of the things that strikes me about your work. You talk about 'rev & rep', but I would add a third: 'ref'. It's not just revision and repetition, but also reference.

SLP: Oohh, that's good! 'Rev and rep and ref'.

KJW: Reference to outside elements runs through all your plays, whether it's Booth and Lincoln, whether it's the *Scarlet Letter*, or even your own work, there is this constant stream of outside reference that always gets drawn back in. Rev, rep, and ref.

SLP: Yeah. It's weird. I mean, what's smart about *Topdog*, for me, is that it does keep pointing to *The America Play*.

KJW: But *The America Play* already points toward so many other things, and in some ways points forward toward *Topdog*.

SLP: Sure, but the first Lincoln character doesn't know that he was pointing forward toward this other play in the future. Although, the Foundling Father is following in someone's footsteps – so we could assume that he's thinking of someone who is *ahead* of him. Hmmm… But, hey, that's a LONG conversation. We would have to re-invent the wheel of time to figure that one out [*laughs*].

KJW: Well, speaking as someone who has been in the audience for both, I was retrospectively sitting in the audience of *Topdog* thinking I was in a funhouse, wondering which is the real thing and which is the mirror.

SLP: [*Laughs*] Right. Don't ask me, I don't know.

KJW: But what is the experience for you then, when you see these things on their feet? What do you feel when you're looking at your own creation? Are there moments of discovery? Does someone else take your work and show you things about it, and it's a sort of accidental genius?

SLP: Moments of 'genius' are all blessings, but I wouldn't say my moments of genius are accidental, in the sense of the one who stumbles on a nugget of gold and doesn't know it. Mostly I write something that's good, I know it. It's like on a train or a subway. I always stand at the place in the car where you can see all the other cars. And I love that moment when you round a corner and all the cars line up and you can see all up and down the whole train. I love that. I could just stand there and do that for hours. And that's how you know when it's good – it all lines up and you can see it straight down the middle. And the parts of my plays that people think are really good, I usually know beforehand. It's not a surprise. That doesn't make it any less cool when people dig it, it's just not a surprise. Cause I felt it while I was writing – that lining up with the Bigger Thing. It's not, 'Me me me – I did this'. It's more like, 'I got in line with the Bigger Thing'. It's like an eclipse or a sunset. Like that moment at sunset where there's that flash of green light or a full moon when you go, 'Whoa – look at that!'

KJW: So you're writing, looking for a particular conjunction or alignment.

SLP: Right, right. Like the hole in Lincoln's head and the (w)hole of history, and they line up and all of a sudden, through that (w)hole hole comes the play.

KJW: There's something very Zen about that, very satori. That lightning flash that briefly illuminates the landscape and makes everything clear.

SLP: Right. And you can capture it and write it down so that it can offer illumination to the people who do the play, or see the play, or read the play. That's what I've found with a play like *Topdog* that has been read by so many people. The lighting comes, the writer writes it down, and then the people are able to re-experience that illumination. I just met two people – I was in Denver for meetings on *365* – and two different people at two different theatres doing *Topdog* in Colorado. One at Shadow Theatre in Denver and the other was at Steel City Theatre in Pueblo, Colorado. Or the groups of college students I met in India did staged readings of *Topdog*. Far out. It's cool knowing you made something that years later is still giving off light. It's wild how theatre works, because it's a living thing. Unlike a film, which is up on the screen and, while it provides pleasure and entertainment for those who watch it – it's not a living thing. A film is pretty much a done deal by the time a mass audience sees it. With a play, you're hanging a script out there, saying, 'Enter into this, step into these shoes, feel the fire', and, through their living-witness energy, lots of people get to participate in a very direct and immediate way and they get to create something new and specific to their own experience. You're hanging a naked live electric cord out there and saying, 'Hey, hang on to this'.

KJW: What is America? You wrote *The America Play*. Many people see you as one of this generation's great American playwrights. So what is 'America'?

SLP: America is different now from what it was when I wrote *The America Play* (around 1994). Does the definition of America change depending on the political dynamics – who's in the White House? Who is in the big (White) House? [*laughs*] It changes.

KJW: Can you give a snapshot of right now, before the premiere of *365*, what is the America that that play is being born into?

SLP: I get to go to all these communities where people know my work from long before *Topdog/Underdog*. And I get to say to them, 'You're invited to the party'. These are theatre people – and granted, it's tricky – some are conservative, but most of them aren't. We're not in it for the money. So our politics may be more progressive than someone who owns a chicken slaughterhouse in Arkansas. I'm not down on America. America is a place where so many things can happen. I think often we get steered in the wrong direction. There are an overwhelming number of people in this country committed to doing the right thing, even though we're going in the wrong direction. And it is a country of diversity, and that is our strength. And it is a country where, thank God, because of the sacrifices a lot of people have made, there has been some positive change. I'm still amazed at that. I grew up in the 1960s. We've still got a long way to go, but we have, as a country, come a long way. We are more accepting of our diversity than some other countries. Remember that World Cup of Football shit, where some Europeans shouted monkey chants at guys of African descent? Sometimes we are more accepting of others. We're not the most accepting, but we are working at it. I think we're making progress. We do a lot of shitty and stupid things also, but I am not one of those America-haters. Hate is the easy road. Too many of my people shed real, live blood so that I can be sitting here talking with you. And I will never forget that. I think a lot of people take for granted the progress this country has made. But I will never forget that. I know my parents worked hard so that I could live in a house a block from the beach in California. The meter maid, a black woman whose name is Sharon, we hang out and chat. She says, 'Girl, there ain't none of us but you on that street'. She wants me to know that there aren't a lot of 'us' living on my street. So what is America? America is working toward progress. And we can do so much more good. And the dream is so beautiful – that's why the heartache is so great. Most of my characters are consumed by heartache. But that's because the dream is beautiful, not because America sucks.

KJW: Because there is a promise and a hope. And there is a recognition that it doesn't have to be this way, but we're not there yet and that causes the heart to break.

SLP: Right. Right. Or we're so far from it. My characters often feel that no matter what they do, they can't seem to make any progress. Lincoln in *The America Play* is following in the footsteps of a man who lived in the past. He's walking forward in the footsteps of someone who is behind him. What does that mean to him? He gets terribly confused and angry and lost.

KJW: Isn't that a wonderful metaphor for life in America anyway – we're all confused and angry about the past. And the idea is, can you transcend it?

SLP: Sure. Yeah. We try. We all try.

KJW: You said you don't write for audiences and you don't write for yourself. I believe the word you used was 'figures' – you write for the characters themselves.

SLP: Now I write for God. Let's just cut to the chase. Now I write for God. That's all. Not God in the, 'Oh you go to church and it's the God that your priest with his limited ability to talk about God is allowed to talk about God because he is hampered by the Vatican and stuff'.

KJW: You grew up Catholic.

SLP: Yeah, I grew up Catholic.

KJW: I feel your pain.

SLP: [*Laughs*] So you understand what I'm talking about. Not in that kind of God, but the God without limitations. The Source. The 'That That is All That'.

KJW: 'I am that I am'.

SLP: Yeah – that one. I write for That One. It's being a lightning rod – you're struck and then you pass the voltage along to the people.

KJW: Let me switch gears. Your plays are full of violence: emotional, physical, verbal, deadly. People get shot. Marlin Perkins has a gun.

SLP: Horrible. Horrible [*laughs*].

KJW: Why all the violence?

SLP: I don't know. I always liked Greek tragedy. So that's part of it.

KJW: Does it relate to what you were saying earlier about having hopes and dreams, but the everyday reality gets in the way? Like Lincoln, for example, he's following…

SLP: Do you mean the Foundling Father as Lincoln or Abraham Lincoln? We have to distinguish.

KJW: I actually meant Booth's brother [in *Topdog*].

SLP: Oh – that I don't know. I was talking about the Foundling Father.

KJW: Even with the Foundling Father, if you take a job as Abraham Lincoln, there is a bullet at the end of your career. Or at least there is a bullet at the end of the job. And in his case, there is a bullet every 5 minutes. Although, now I'm going to move away from my own question. One of the things I found most beautiful about the play in an intellectual sense, is that it's all about the inaccuracy of history. We're not even sure about Booth's words – *Sic semper tyrannus*, or 'The South is Avenged'.

SLP: Right, right.

KJW: That history itself is rev, rep, and ref.

SLP: Well, it's just like sitting here going over the details of my chronology. Apparently I've been born in five different years and places and I went to Yale and a lot of this isn't true. What you read about me is not always true and sometimes different every time.

KJW: You've become one of your own characters.

SLP: But I think I was all along.

KJW: That's deep. That's deep.

SLP: [*Laughs*] But, you know, right? I must have been.

KJW: Bonnie Metzgar calls *In the Blood* a 'now play'. But you're known for history plays. So 'now' means 'history'?

SLP: Well, I'm known for history plays, but actually, the plays were never 'history plays'. Like Faulkner says 'History is IS'. So my plays often feature historical figures. But they're all 'now' plays. Especially the ones after *Venus* – *Venus* was like passing a test. I always felt that *Venus* was my black belt. These days I practice yoga, but before that I practiced karate for 7 years. Word is, after the black belt, everything changes. It's like you start all over again. I always felt when I was writing *Venus* that I was getting my black belt in playwriting, and after the black belt you start all over again. I knew the characters would be different after *Venus* and after *Venus* came *In the Blood*, and *Fucking A* and *Topdog* and *365*. But, to me, the plays have never been history plays. They're all about the intersection of the historical and the now. Even *In the Blood* is about that intersection because it is not based on *The Scarlet Letter* but *The Scarlet Letter* is one of its parents, let's say.

KJW: Is writing plays a joy, or is it a form of suffering?

SLP: It is a joy, I mean, it's difficult. Hard work is mandatory, suffering is optional. I'm more like the Buddhist kind of writer – suffering is an option. Hard work is not an option, but I think you choose to suffer. There's a lot of joy in writing. And when you get to meet the people who do the plays – everyone from the movie star people like Don Cheadle and Mos Def and Jeffrey Wright to the people at the Steel City Theatre in Pueblo, who are like the Mod Squad, they are so cool, Dorothy, Corey and Kennedy are their names – and there are hundreds, thousands like them all across the country and when I get to meet them, I feel very lucky.

KJW: Your first novel came out a couple of years ago.

SLP: Loved writing it.

KJW: Is there another one coming?

SLP: Yeah. Yeah. Yeah. I'm writing one right now. I started out as a short story writer.

KJW: Mr. Baldwin's class and influence.

SLP: Yeah, that's where I began.

KJW: How is it different than writing plays?

SLP: It's not, really.

KJW: It's the same thing?

SLP: Not the same – because when you write a play, your writing constructs a doorway, and through that door will enter the audience, the actors, the director, the people who create your play onstage. Writing a novel, you still write a doorway. But it's a different kind of doorway – because they don't need to bring a novel to life and walk in it and inhabit as they would a play. But the writing process is similar whether a novel, a play, a song, a screenplay, because it's all still writing. It's all still this [*picks up pen and mimes writing*]. Same thing. I write more on a computer now.

KJW: Do you ever write long hand?

SLP: I wrote *365* long hand.

KJW: Really?

SLP: Yep. It was while I was teaching at CalArts. I quit CalArts a few years ago.

KJW: You've taught at several places now. How does your writing shape your teaching and teaching shape your writing?

SLP: My writing doesn't change. I keep the two activities pretty separate. I didn't go to grad school myself, so my teaching methods are totally informed by my own writing process: 'Here, hold this live wire. Here, hold this live wire. Here, hold this live wire. Go straight to the nerve. Go straight to the guts'. Not much theory and lots of practice. I love writing. I enjoy my students quite a bit. But it's also something I can only do in short bursts – teaching. After a while I gotta get back to full-time writing. My students are all great, though – I love you all.

KJW: You've talked before about voyeurism and certainly a lot of your writings have people watching other people. In *Devotees in the Garden of Love* the women watch the battle. People watch the Hottentot Venus. *Girl 6* certainly concerns voyeurism. I actually want to flip the question and ask you the opposite – about performing. It seems to me that your characters are very self-aware of their own performances in their circumstances. And they perform for each other. Is there an interest in human performance? As a species, can we not stop performing?

SLP: That's an interesting question. As you were asking it, I was looking around and watching these other people. As my husband Paul says, 'We're more of ourselves when we're being watched because, as a species, we don't live alone'. An essential part of human *being* is performance. So there's a play about a brother who pretends he's someone else in the daytime and he has the same name of the person he is pretending to be, and when he gets home he has to pretend to be someone else to hide his underhanded motives from his brother. All that makes for a hall of mirrors, or a wave pattern. The characters perform and they're aware that they are being watched. They are each other's audience and their awareness of audience somehow makes them aware of us. The hall of mirrors is also a wave pattern. And in every wave pattern there is a spot where it goes quiet – where the mirrors go blind. But I don't intentionally write it in. It just happens because I'm writing a play in which the characters are trying to be – or, at least, figure out who they are. Gee, the weird way I write plays.

KJW: Weird but successful. It seems to be working for you. What was the impetus behind *365 Days/365 Plays*?

SLP: It started as a far out joke. I was hanging out with Paul, my husband, and I said, 'I'm going to write a play a day for a year and call it *365 Days/365 Plays*. Ha ha ha'. And I started laughing, right? And he says, 'That'd be cool'. And he's a blues musician, so he doesn't think theatre is cool. Because he really *is* cool, right? So he got me to thinking maybe it would be cool. Maybe it would be fun. And I started. Now, looking back, I realize that I was making a sort of daily offering, a daily devotional gift to the art form that has given me so much. And now it's huge. It's a love train. Shortly after I finished writing the plays I showed them around and a couple of theatres wanted to produce them, but in a very conventional way. But *365* is so different, I wanted them produced differently. At the core of the plays is something I've started calling 'radical inclusion'. To write a play a day for a whole year, you have to dismiss the bouncer who works the door of your creative mind. All ideas are welcome. All ideas are worthy for play-making. Somehow I wanted the production of the play cycle to dovetail with this 'radical inclusion'. But I didn't know how. So one day I'm hanging out with Bonnie Metzgar, who I've known since 1989, and we're sitting around thinking about how a production of *365* can be different and fun. And we're like, 'Maybe lots of theatres could do it – like 365 theatres!' And that was crazy. It was like saying, 'And then we're going to go to the moon!' It was just that nutty – 365 theatres doing the plays. And we were driving around Denver in her car. She's the Associate Artistic Director of Curious Theatre Company and she also teaches at Brown University. And we're just riffing, driving around and talking wild and the more we talked the more we thought it would be cool to get 52 theatres in seven cities to do the plays *simultaneously*. Now we've got over 14 cities. And its growing every day. With 'The 365 National Festival', all interested theatres and parties are welcome to join in and share in the world premiere. Big theatres, midsize theatres, small theatres, children's theatres, university theatres, high-schools, senior centres, dinner theatres, seasonal theatres. It's a love train. It's definitely a love train. We go out and we meet people. At first they can't believe that a Pulitzer Prize-winning playwright is sitting down at the table saying, 'Hey, want to do some of my plays?' and I'm only charging a licensing fee of a dollar a day. It's experimental theatre. So many groups around the country are participating. TCG [the Theatre Communications Group] is doing the book and they will list every theatre involved in the premiere.

KJW: Speaking of the Pulitzer. You're in that rare club – only 11 women have won the Pulitzer for drama.

SLP: Really? Only 11?

KJW: Only 11 since the award was established.

SLP: When was the award established?

KJW: 1918. It's mind blowing when you think about it, especially in 2006.

SLP: But they don't give it every year.

KJW: Well theoretically, they do give it every year, it's just some years the committee decides there is no play worthy of the award.

SLP: Do they ever *not* award the prize in other categories? It's kind of funny, don't you think?

KJW: True. But hasn't theatre always been the bastard at the family reunion? We have to get invited to the party but not everyone's happy about it.

SLP: True [*laughs*].

KJW: And there is this notion in our culture that writing for performance is 'cute'. Books and print and text are literature, but writing for performance isn't really writing.

SLP: People say plays aren't really complete until they are performed. But plays are complete – they just exist in another realm, and we, because we are human beings in a material world, must perform them to make them real for us. Plays written on paper are alive, they're just not alive for humans because we are in our bodies. *Topdog* felt alive before anyone else read it, before anyone performed it. *Venus* felt the same way. Switching gears for a minute to talk about *Venus* – I lecture and I tour and sometimes people have questions about *Venus*. They've seen a production and they have concerns. They always ask me to clarify my take on her situation. One: saying Venus had a hand in her fate is not the same thing as saying it's all her fault. It's very important that people understand that. If you want to see what hand she had in her fate, according to my play, look at the play. Don't listen to your friend talk about the play – they may have seen a production, but if you want to get a clearer sense of what I said, you could also read the play. At the beginning of the play the Brothers ask Venus if she wants to go away. She's not aware of the subtleties of what they are asking, or of the trap that exists for her. But she is, like most poor people, willing to exchange her labour in order to get out of a poverty-stricken situation. It is important that people understand that. It's a difficult play, because I don't say, 'Blame it all on the white guy'. We each have a hand in our fate – even if it is just a small hand. And admitting that is part of the process of liberation. Neither is *Venus* about dumping all the blame on the black girl – and if that's how you read it, you may have missed some of the deeper points. But hey, I also get lots of fan mail from folks who have read/performed/seen *Venus* and say it's their favourite play ever. The play is about love, so I guess it hits people hard.

KJW: As you yourself have said, its so difficult to talk about race in America because we want to make it so black and white, pardon the pun.

SLP: The main thing folks misunderstand in *Venus* is not so much the 'race' issue, but the 'blame' or the 'responsibility' issue. But, yeah, talking about race requires, if you will, a discriminating mind (not racial but time and spatial) and we aren't encouraged to think clearly and deeply in this country.

KJW: *Venus* is your most written about play.

SLP: It's a love play, and it's difficult. Later in the play, after Venus has spent time in England, the Doctor asks her, 'Do you want to go to France' and she says 'yes'. Why? Because the Doctor's hands are clean. He has clean hands. She wants to go with the man who has clean hands and who is nice, instead of staying with the Mother Showman who beats her and steals from her and invites men to rape her. Showing that she has this much agency is not blaming the victim. Neither does it let the victimizer off the hook. But if you're hip to this you can be transfixed by her story, wounded, and then healed. Her dream of a better life is so beautiful and she just misses realizing it. She misses realizing her dream to be someone of means who could send money home and maybe go home and live as a wealthy woman. And there are so many people who love that play. So many people who've performed in the play and have told me that it's made such a positive change in their lives.

KJW: In the past, you've disavowed the label, 'African-American Playwright'.

SLP: Not exactly. But that label is like saying, I write 'Suzan-Lori Parks plays'. I am an African-American woman and I am a playwright. But our culture too often uses labels as limiting – to denote what is expected of you and what rooms you are allowed to enter. If you're an African-American and a woman and a playwright, with those labels, too often the thinking stops because the assumptions leap in and folks think they can go on autopilot about you or your work. You SHOULD do this sort of thing; the subjects and topics your work addresses are confined to a particular list. When the label goes on, the thinking mind turns off – so I suggest we turn off or explode the label. When people feel they need to use a label, I've sought to hip them to a more accurate, wider-ranging definition.

KJW: Your plays really do show ethnic identity in flux. Hester and her multiethnic children. Lincoln played by an African-American man in whiteface. There's this whole deconstruction of the notion of ethnicity in your work which is wonderful.

SLP: Black characters, like all characters, ask the fundamental questions of 'who am I and what am I doing here?' Those are the questions that the characters in any good play ask. Hamlet is asking them. Lear is asking them. Oedipus is REALLY asking them.

KJW: Well, to bring us full circle, that's what happens in 'the theatre industry'. My friend Javon Johnson jokes he's going to legally change his name to 'African-American Playwright Javon Johnson', because he never sees his name without that in front of it when a theatre does one of his plays.

SLP: [*Laughs*] Right, right.

KJW: You'll never see 'the play by Euro-American playwright Arthur Miller' or 'the new play by Jewish-American playwright David Mamet'.

SLP: Well exactly. Say it again – 'Jewish-American playwright David Mamet'. Doesn't it sound like we're asking him to crawl into a tiny box for us so we don't have to think about him as a great writer, and I think Mamet is fantabulous. To label him simply in terms of his race or ethnicity is to ask him to crawl into a little box. So I say, recognize the whole person and you don't depend on the label. If you're awake and you're hip to the work, you don't depend on the label. It's like me saying I had lunch with Kevin, 'my white friend'. Maybe there are some situations where you have to say that, but I don't know – sometimes we use labels so we don't have to think.

KJW: But in contemporary America, isn't race the elephant in the room? It's either the only thing we think about or it's this huge doing that we try to pretend isn't there.

SLP: For some people. But not for everyone. It's the thing that a lot of people THINK black people should be thinking about. And, not only should we be thinking about it but we should be thinking about it along certain predefined lines. We are encouraged to talk/write about race in ways that may be successful in the marketplace, but not so helpful to the people. And how many interviews with David Mamet discuss the subject of race? Hey, we're not gonna figure this out today. What we can do is to continue to embrace the work. That's where the transformation happens. And we can explode the labels. For example: if I call *365 Days/365 Plays* a 'black' play, my labelling it that way explodes the limited notion of what a 'black play' can be. And from here on out, a 'black play' can be seen as one that invites everybody to the table. And with this definition, we can more clearly appreciate the works of, say, August Wilson. The work will make the Change. It's cool how plays can re-make history. But, my plays are not the History Channel. Like with *Venus*, and with *Topdog*. So many people say, 'Why'd you have the brothers kill each other?' *Topdog* is not the 11 o'clock news. It's a play. It's a play. And at the end of the play, the actors take their bows. At the end of the 11 o'clock news, the shot-dead brother does not get up take a bow. He's dead. But woven into the play is an opportunity for two actors to come together, to work together and create a pageant. I did some of my growing up in Germany. There is this town, Oberammergau. Once every 10 years the whole town gets together and puts on a religious pageant. My plays are very much like that – the community gets together and creates this pageant. It's not just a vomiting up of history or a regurgitation of the 11 o'clock news. So the idea of pageant-making is intrinsic to it. For example, *In the Blood*. My favourite part of *In the Blood* is where I get to listen to the actors run around backstage because they have to make quick costume changes. I was thinking while I was writing the play, 'This is going to be good – Chilli is going to have to change into Jabber! Ha ha! Watch this!' The pageant is going on. The playing of the play, the inner workings of the pageant, is often very much in my mind as I write. Not so much, 'How will a director stage this?' but more – 'This is a text with a doorway in it, and through that door will come actors, directors, designers, scholars, audience members'.

KJW: So is that the closest we are going to come to the definition of 'a Suzan-Lori Parks play'? A new pageant?

SLP: For now. And I may change up. But for now, sure, you can say my work is a new kind of community pageant. It's that Oberammergau thing. Yeah, that works. And the violence sometimes in my work, sure, like in every good religious pageant there's blood. And passion. And a miracle, maybe. But mostly there is an invitation for the community to come together and put on a show. Sure, it's very much an Oberammergau thing.

17

AN INTERVIEW WITH SUZAN-LORI PARKS

Shawn-Marie Garrett

Suzan-Lori Parks: Essays on the Plays and Other Works
Ed. Philip C. Kolin

Shawn-Marie Garrett: When you were first starting out, people used to talk a lot about the canon. And in your early essay "Possession," you refer to the "History of History" and "the History of Literature." Now that you've presumably secured a place in theater history, have your feelings about "History," about "Literature," changed?

Suzan-Lori Parks: They're not talking about the canon anymore? I feel strongly that it's okay to carve people like Plato, Aristotle, Shakespeare, in stone because their ideas are still alive. Funny how, at the moment we feel that someone will live forever, we carve them in stone. Stone = eternity, although we should remember they're not fixed. History and the historical are mutable, right?

    I love Shakespeare. And Shakespeare (still living, immortal) loves me back. In 1998 and 1999, when I was writing *Topdog/Underdog*, *In the Blood*, and *Fucking* A, I re-read all of Shakespeare's plays. A few years later at CalArts I taught a class called Shakespeare Read-through. I wrote down all of the titles of his plays and put them in a hat. Then we passed around the hat and each student picked one. We read all the plays that were chosen in the order in which the students wanted to read them, with the exception of the historical plays. We read those in chronological order— that made it easier to follow the lineages. I didn't assign any papers. I only asked everybody to read the plays, show up, be ready to talk about them, and read aloud. There were no right or wrong answers, no dumb or smart comments. The students got really excited because they felt they'd been freed from having to regurgitate conventional thought and they felt that Shakespeare was allowed to live again. And I had fun too! *Henry VI*, *Parts 1, 2*, and *3*—those are my favorites.

SMG: What do you take from Shakespeare for your own work?

SLP: Everything that's there.

His characters have heart and brains in a very balanced combination. Which means they have soul, and that's what shines forth.

A lot of playwrights write with brain power, there are a lot of ideas out there, and you feel like you're being lectured to, at least I do, because I'm not of the camp, not of the tribe, that likes a lecture. When I go to see a play: it's playtime! (Which can sometimes be some deep serious shit). Then there are other plays that have a lot of heart, a lot of *oooooooh*, a lot of feeling. The very academic play with a lot of great ideas, or the Hallmark-Movie-of-the-Week play. Those are the extremes. Shakespeare's plays have soul, with the mind and heart in perfect balance. That's what I love about his work, and that's what I seek to emulate. Those are the footsteps that I'm working to follow in.

SMG: I'm glad you brought up the question of soul because your plays are, among other things… "spiritual" is perhaps not the right word…

SLP: I don't mind. I'm not offended. Look at my arm (*gesturing to three identical Sanskrit tattoos on left arm*), possible translations: "Follow God," "Submit yourself to your Essential Goodness," or "Go with the Flow." There was a man at the farmers' market the other day, a gentleman who was selling—I don't know if he was a *gentleman*, he was a lovely man—who was selling green vegetables. And I purchased my snap peas and he looked at me and I thought "Oooo"—you know that moment where, someone is looking at you with great curiosity and all you're thinking is "woops, I must have made a mistake." In this case I'm thinking "I didn't give him the right amount of money." I have difficulty counting. So I'm looking at him, what does he need? Another dollar? And he's staring at me with this expression, and he's darting glances down at my arm, and I'm thinking, I need to give him more money, and he's looking at me, looking at me, and he says, "Your arm. Îśvara." He was reading my arm. Awesome! That's my favorite phrase, îśvara-praṅidhânâd vâ, which is from the yoga sutras, chapter 1, sutra 23, or sutra 1-2-3, easy as A-B-C, god bless Michael Jackson.

SMG: Speaking of which… any thoughts?

SLP: Yeah, MJ passed away about a week ago. I do feel like we let him down. And by letting him down, we let ourselves down. And every time people would laugh at him… they were laughing at that part of themselves—maybe not all of us have it, but that part of us that felt like we were never "in," and wanted so much to belong, never were accepted. He was brilliant and admired and could never feel the love. And I so wanted him to have a comeback because I believe in… the Resurrection. God bless MJ. So sutra number 1-2-3, easy as A-B-C, îśvara, which means "Go with the Flow," and I have it on my arm three times, each time larger and larger.

SMG: Do you still practice yoga two hours a day?

SLP: I practice as much as I can. I've been to India twice, I studied Ashtanga yoga with Sri K. Patabi Jois, who we call *Guruji*; he passed away about a month and a half ago. Recently I've switched gears and I'm enjoying Bikram yoga. It's an experience.

SMG: You were raised Catholic…

SLP: My religion these days… it's like a buffet. There are so many good things to choose from. I admire the spirits and the gods and the healers and the saints. Ganesh I wear around my neck, and I think Jesus is great, and often misunderstood, just like Michael Jackson, and Mohammed laid down some great things too. And then the modern-day folks like Mother Teresa and Gandhi and Martin Luther King. I think they're all manifestations of our possibility. And that's what theater does too. Beautiful imitations of God. We all are. The saints are great imitators of God. Shakespeare is a great imitator of God. Not God the guy with the beard who sits in the clouds, or who's painted on the Sistine Chapel… I mean God must look at that and say, "Nice! Very nice!" Like you would say to a child who presents you with a drawing and says, "Look Mommy, this is you!" And you say, "Beautiful! Good job! We're gonna put it on the fridge!" That's what I think God says when he looks at the Sistine Chapel: "Beautiful! Good job! We're gonna put it on the fridge!" I think it's the same kind of adoring, "How sweet! Doesn't look a thing like me. But glad that you did good in school."

I do… the more I do, the more the God-stuff comes out. It's creepy. It's unsettling in a way. It's not hard to talk about, but it's hard to live it. The more I work, the more it goes in that direction. Almost as if—hmm, as if I'm doing the art so that I can be given an opportunity to talk with people about the Spirit—instead of the other way around… With each work it's more and more. My new play, we go into rehearsal in January 2010—it's called *The Book of Grace*.

I try… there's part of me that's trying very hard to fit in. You know, just trying to write a normal play. But the more I listen, the more I hear, and then I go and get this "Follow God" this "Go with the Flow" tattooed on my arm three times, and I can't help but hear it more. The more I write, the more it's going in that direction. Writing *365 Days/365 Plays* was a devotional act. Or like with *The Union of My Confederate Parts: Father Comes Home From the Wars, Part 1*—I saw every performance of that play. There was such a "wyrdness"—w-y-r-d—the wyrdness of that play. I would sit onstage and watch it and I'd sometimes be thinking, "Who wrote this?"

What I love about Ganesh is, he's the transcriber of the Vedas. He's a writer! And he rides around on a mouse—that's my kind of god, right there. I've always felt this, but as time goes on I feel more and more that I'm transcribing. It's a powerful feeling, and yet, as Emerson writes, "I am a god in Nature / I am a weed by the wall."

SMG: Do you still write every day?

SLP: Sometimes "Follow God" isn't about writing every day. That's the thing about God, you have to listen. You can't make up your mind. God doesn't work so great if you set your idea of God in stone. God is mutable, change, right? And completely constant too—at the same time. So I work to roll with that. Several years ago, I could say, "'Follow God,' that means writing every day," but now I know that Follow God means Follow God. Sometimes I can't write every day. Over the years, it's become more difficult. It's getting wyrder and wyrder and wyrder and wyrder. People who climb Mount Everest get up there and need oxygen tanks and get dizzy—people who dive deep get the bends—it's like that. I'm walking a path where, sometimes you have to slow your steps, measure your breathing. "Writing every day" for me sometimes means "embracing the scary unknown and having compassion." I played guitar so much in this show [*The Union of My Confederate Parts: Father Comes Home From the Wars, Part 1*]; so some days writing would just be about that, or just reading a little. Or sleeping late, or reading about Michael Jackson—maybe that's what I'm supposed to do today. Maybe that's what the day was about: doing a good show; remembering the words to the songs and the chords too. Writing used to mean just "writing" but now maybe writing can include RIGHTING. Get right. Be right. Right. Write. Write on. Right on. These days I'm a little more flexible. That's the thing about yoga, it makes you flexible.

SMG: You've expanded the range of your activities: you've appeared in an independent film, you're slated to direct *Fences* on Broadway, you have a new play, *The Book of Grace*, opening at the Public in March of 2010, you wrote a poem for President Obama, "U Being U."

SLP: It made me very happy to write that. To give him a gift of love when he was just starting out. NPR put it on the radio. We need to remember that "yes we can" is a daily promise. We all have to live that mantra if it's going to work.

SMG: The image of the Foundling Father from *The America Play* almost seems to anticipate…

SLP: That's what a lot of people are saying.

SMG: The Lincoln connection.

SLP: The Lincoln link. And Obama is a foundling. He knows his parents, but he is orphaned now as our leader. The Foundling Father in *The America Play* was parentless. And nameless. When I wrote *The America Play* it was like the guy walked in the room and started talking to me, so I knew he existed. He is present in the universe. And so he manifests himself on stage, and he manifests himself in the White House.

SMG: Do you see your work differently, or do you think it will be interpreted differently, in the wake of Obama's election?

SLP: I don't really think about that. That's the thing about doing the kind of work I do, writing the way I do, it doesn't leave room for looking back.

Krishna and Arjuna are riding in the chariot in the Bhagavad Gita, and Arjuna is talking to Krishna like he's just some guy, and Krishna turns to him and opens his mouth and shows him the entire universe. And Arjuna's like, "Dude! So that's who you are!" I'm just staring into the mouth of God. It doesn't leave any room for thinking about the significance of a play I wrote in 1994... and not that it's not important but... I'm thinking more about guitar chords.

SMG: Are you going to cut an album?

SLP: If I get my courage up. I've written six new songs for *Father Comes Home from the Wars*.

There was a long time when I couldn't play one of the songs, "Bronze Star," without crying. That was the trouble I was having at the beginning of rehearsing this show. I really had to play the song a lot to be able to play it in public.

SMG: The title *Father Comes Home from the Wars* also appears in *365 Days/365 Plays*. Any relation?

SLP: "Oh I know this girl, her name is Jill, and she lives in Mexico..." "Oh I know a Jill! But she lives in New York." "Oh I know Jack! He's married to a Jill." "But that's another Jill..." "Oh her." It's like that. They're related in title. They're related in (*operatic tone*) "Theme." Or is it "Subject?"

SMG: Might the fourth part of *Impercetible Mutabilites* be a third cousin? There's another father who comes home from the wars.

SLP: Those are some of the biggest memories I have, of my father coming home from the war.

SMG: There are some plans in the works for you to direct August Wilson's *Fences* on Broadway.

SLP: Yes. The production was delayed because of the economy and because we want to make sure we can do it with the actors we really want to do it with. The producers want to keep the play in the 1950s, in the time it is set, but also really make it resonate with younger audiences today. I shared my ideas with them, and they liked them, and so we started working on it. Then the producers wanted to do it this spring, but I'd already committed to doing my play *The Book of Grace*. So they reassembled the team.

I enjoy directing. I enjoy being in the rehearsal room from day one. I enjoy being in tech. I enjoy talking to actors. I love creating pictures on stage. I've also enjoyed being in *Father Comes Home...*, although I don't think I was acting. I was just being. I was just up there being me. And playing the guitar along with the action, working with the actors. That was good scary fun.

SMG: *Father Comes Home from the Wars, Part 1* was underscored, almost like a melodrama.

SLP: Lucas Papaelias wrote the underscoring. I threw in some Robert Johnson licks. And it was really fun to play. We might do a cabaret together.

SMG: Is there anything about your success, about being a Pulitzer Prize winner for example, which has surprised you?

SLP: I have to say, it's very isolating. Wonderful Lynn Nottage has won the Pulitzer now, which is awesome. For me, for a long time, to be The Only One, I mean, the Only Black Woman winner in drama. To be The First One, the First Black Woman—and to have won it for a play that is so… it's a right-down-the-middle play. It's very lean and it does not apologize and it's just… right between the eyes. The play came down like that (*claps*) and it really does burn… it's like lightning, it burns the ground, the Earth, my own… psychological Earth, if you will. It was such a powerful experience. And that's what I mean about writing like I do now, it happens over and over and over. I have developed the muscles to deal with it, but at the same time, I keep waiting for it to be an easier process, a more gentle birth, but… they always seem to come like that, like "Whoooooaaah! Heeeere's anooother one!" (*squeals in mock-horror*). So the writing and the winning for me were isolating, in a way. But that's just what happens when you walk a path, that's just what happens.

SMG: Then with *365*, you opened yourself up in the most generous possible way.

SLP: Again, that was the right thing to do. Why did I choose the most intense gesture, why did the most intense gesture choose me… well thank you is all I can say because I guess that's what I'm supposed to be doing. Choose the most intense gesture and do it. That was the next thing. People said, "Why not do another Broadway play?" We did *365 Days/365 Plays* everywhere *but* Broadway! We did it everywhere! We did it in Beijing! We did it in Kenya! We did it in South Africa and Berlin and Moscow! We did it in places like Seattle and LA, and Atlanta and Texas and New England and Colorado and Old England. We were spreading the love and we were world-wide with it.

What good can this award, the Pulitzer Prize, do? What is it for? It affords the winner (and by extension, the community) some possibilities. So I wrote a play a day and then gave them away. We had a core production team of 4 people: Bonnie Metzgar, Rebecca Rugg, David Myers and me. We joined hands with awesome theatre artists from all over and we made it together. It wasn't even a thought, it was just the right thing to do: fling yourself open and say, "Let us play." To offer people a part. And how is that different from doing a play on Broadway, a play with $70 tickets, a play with Equity contracts? We had a big free for all. Which was the only right thing to do after the Pulitzer, after you climb the tower and hoist the flag and "Yaaaay!" and then you fling yourself into the mosh pit of people and say, "Let us play," and somehow that was the only right thing to do. And what was the next right thing to do? I come to New York, and I wanna be in Public Lab, which is 2½ weeks rehearsal time, no budget to speak of, a $10 ticket, run for a very limited time, no reviews cause it's a workshop production, plus I'm in the show playing guitar and singing… And what's the next right thing to do? I'm not even thinking about that… it's just "Ahhhh!" It's a little intense. And it does make it hard to… it makes it wonderful to be around people but it's also difficult.

SMG: Might there eventually be *Father Comes Home from the Wars, Parts 1, 2, 3…* through *9*?

SLP: God willing, yeah, that's the plan, that's the plan. There might be more. Who knows now cause now that I've seen Part 1 over and over and over, the whole cycle might change. I'm allowing myself to be flexible, which is very important. If my plan for a "9 part cycle" is too limiting, I'll change it up. If it's not what it's supposed to be then I'll go on and let it go.

Originally it was nine parts. I had it all blocked out; I had drafts of each one, a big draft of Part 9, which was like a 2½-hour play. But now watching it every night it's changing; it's actually changing. So who can know?

SMG: You had originally planned to stage Parts 1, 8, and 9 but ended up staging only Part 1, is that right?

SLP: Yeah. Yeah. We put on Part 9 one night, and I sat there and then I talked to Jo Bonney and Oskar (Eustis) afterwards, and I said we have not had enough time to rehearse Part 9, we have eight hours of rehearsal left, we have to stop, we have to stop. We have to say thank you to the wonderful actors who put in time on Part 9 but… it was too much to try to do in Public Lab. We only had three days of tech. Three days of tech to tech… Part 1 was an hour, Part 8 really is 45 minutes if we were to do it fully because it's a lot of structured improvs, and I'm performing during the intermission, and it's a live intermission, and I'm doing a lecture during the intermission, and then there are six songs, and then this big play at the end… But Part 9 isn't ready so let's just put it aside for now, let's just focus on Part 1, it's only an hour, let's only do two songs, and scale way back. So it was an hour of really well done theater. Eventually we'll do the rest. Cause the families come together in the end, the two families that you see in Part 1, there's a rupture, and we track them through the whole thing, and then they come together in the end.

SMG: In the present?

SLP: In the present-day.

SMG: One family tree is…

SLP: Penny and Homer. And then the other family tree is Hero and Alberta. And both family trees produce 2 different men, both named Smith. A Lincoln–Lincoln, Jill–Jill kinda thing. Or the Hester–Hester kinda thing. So both family trees produced a man named Smith. And one is a poet. And one is a critic.

SMG: The George Bernard Shaw-type of critic, or the consumer-reports-thumbs-up-thumbs-down-type?

SLP: I don't know. Right now he's more of a fan.

SMG: The Greeks seem to be circulating around this play, the *Odyssey* in particular…

SLP: I named the character Penny because I have a friend named Penny who died. Penny Lincoln. Really. Go figure. I named another one Homer because he stays home. You know me, there's not a lot of front-loaded thought. I don't think one has to have read any of those great Greek works to understand this story. And even when the characters refer to those old, old stories, they tell you the stories. It's not like *Finnegan's Wake* where you have to be in the know.

SMG: The weight of homecoming was a palpable presence in this performance.

SLP: Like I said, it's from my dad. My dad came home. From the Wars. That's what it's about. For me. It starts with that. I'm just talking about something I know, something which I can really only emotionally understand by looking at it through a play, through the framework of the big picture.

   Different writers have different methods—all of them valid and good. I don't get to my plays through thought. "Thought" in the conventional sense. I don't get to my plays through ideas. I think writing them would be easier if I did. Because ideas and thought, they're verbal, and I think my plays are preverbal. From my guts.

SMG: In a way, you've always been writing songs.

SLP: Thanks! All my writing is more like songs, cause in a song you're in the ocean, the ocean of emotion, and you're moving around, and you're trying to breathe, and that's what it feels like, trying to write. That's what I try to do. I try to sing to people.

SMG: And when you lay it down on the page…

SLP: A play is the road. You're giving an actor or a director the path. And the way a word is… if you put a word in the middle of the page, that's very different than if you put it on the side, and if you put a character's name in a line, that's very different than if you put it in the middle, with parentheses. Or italics, which can be very vigorous if used sparingly, like saffron. Italics are like surprises. Punctuation marks are jewels. With every letter I hold my breath and think, "Is it this or that? What best communicates the energy that's gonna course through the language, that's gonna tell an actor—whose instrument is finely tuned—how to shoot that energy through to the audience night after night, so they can ride that wave of language. It's very, very, very important to me how it is on the page, how it lies there. How it lies there in its grave. You lay them out right, and they can be continually and beautifully resurrected.

   Space. The rhythm of the words. Repetition. How the character is saying what she's saying. Each choice should indicate a specific emotional thing. Which can vary in color night after night after night as the actor continues making it anew. Is it y-o-u-r or y-r? With y-o-u-r there's more room. See what it feels like in your mouth, in your tongue, in your body. Allow the language to inform the choices. Read the words, and *feel*. My plays *beg* for feeling. They *beg* for the gut response. Let the stomach-brain, let the heart-brain, inform your head-brain, and not always the other way around. Because then we're getting to some deep stuff. And it's frightening. But it's also healing.

SMG: Do you read criticism or scholarship of your work?

SLP: I read what I feel will most help my process. Scholarship is important but for me—reading, it doesn't help me write. Reading scholarship about the works of "Suzan-Lori Parks" would take me outside the work. And I need to keep myself inside it, I need to be deep up in it, not outside intelligently observing, not at arm's length. Staying deep up in it: that's the best way for me to write my next thing.

18

CONVERSATION WITH
THE BOOK OF GRACE
PLAYWRIGHT/DIRECTOR
SUZAN-LORI PARKS

Dave Steakley

June 1, 2011

Dave Steakley: In *The Book of Grace* I'm struck that there are three characters who are each writing their own "book" and each of them is presenting their book to an imaginary audience.

Suzan-Lori Parks: Right. There's Grace who's writing a book called "The Book of Grace," and in her book she includes what she calls "the evidence of good things." Her husband Vet works for the Texas Border Patrol. He doesn't think much of books, but he's writing a speech in his head that he'll give when he accepts his award for a job well done. And there's Vet's son and Grace's step-son Buddy, whose book is going to be on Facebook and the Web. Each of these characters have their imaginary audiences they present their books to: Grace pretends she is reading her book aloud at a library—like writers do—to her imaginary audience; Vet imagines giving his speech as he practices it to himself; and Buddy imagines being seen by millions of people on the Internet as he gives his manifesto. What's cool is, through the magic of theatre, their imaginary audiences will become real, because the ZACH audience will be in those seats.

DS: The play riffs on the idea of how we create borders and fences and also deterrents, inside and outside of our homes.

SLP: Borders and fences—things that keep people out, things that keep people in. Vet works at the Texas border fence as a patrol guard, and his job is to keep people out and, at home, he's dug a hole in his yard as a deterrent— just to remind Grace that if she oversteps herself, she'll end up in that hole. The hole he's dug is a deterrent to questionable behavior, a scare tactic. And remember that great country song *Don't Fence Me In*? Holes and fences are related as deterrents because if you go to the actual border

FIGURE 6 *The Book of Grace,* written and directed by Suzan-Lori Parks, ZACH Theatre, 2011. Nadine Mozon as Grace. Photo by Kirk A. Tuck. Courtesy of ZACH Theatre.

fence, sometimes it looks like a big huge fence, and sometimes it looks like a regular garden fence on our side. But if you go and peek over into the Mexico side, right before the fence starts for them, there's this big hole, there is a "moat" on their side. So the "moat" on their side is a deterrent, like the hole.

DS: When you and I went to McAllen on a research trip to look at the border fence there were also big gaping holes within the fence itself.

SLP: Right. There are these big, huge "ginormous" gaps in the actual border fence. The border agents told us that they are waiting for more funding so that they can build some big swinging movable gates to fill in these holes. But in the meantime there is a gap, and to monitor that gap, they shine a big light into the hole, 24/7. Just so if anyone comes and runs through the gap, they can catch them, and exercise the law.

DS: Your play makes us think about the way families also create borders or fences inside and outside of the home.

SLP: Your neighbors have a fence around their yard and when the realtor showed me the house, the realtor said, "They have a fence because they have kids." Ah, to fence the children in, to keep the children safe so the children don't run out into the street. Sometimes it makes sense to have a fence. One could argue that civilization needs boundaries. We have codes of behavior. We have ways to behave around each other. We have appropriate ways to speak in meetings or in social settings; at work we have dress codes, things like that. Those are all boundaries, those are all fences. But then there are the fences that crop up, the borders that crop up between family members that are not always good. In our own families, sometimes we have people who are accepted and people who are not accepted. So civilization might need a kind of demarcation, but it also it can be a real negative thing too. Sometimes by keeping certain people out we're not allowing ourselves to include and expand and grow. That is why the American experiment is really amazing actually. Because you go around the world and you see similar people inhabiting countries, and then come back to America and you're like, "Wow, we've really done something great." All these different kinds of people with our different races, ethnicities, religions, and persuasions, are all, pretty much, co-existing. And that is really very, very cool.

DS: And now you're in Austin directing your play that is set in Texas.

SLP: My mom is from far west Texas, Odessa. We spent a lot of time there growing up. I feel like I am a Texan. The play is set near the border fence, which says something about the psychological state of the characters, much like Shakespeare's *King Lear*, in which there's a storm and the environment is reflecting what is going on in Lear's heart. The fence environment of *The Book of Grace* reflects what is going on in the hearts of these characters, as well as being an actual Fence that is dealt with. And the act of grace is the wisdom that passes all understanding, really. The act of grace is almost greater than the human mind can encompass. Our minds are rarely that expansive, that generous, that graceful. So we sort of have to believe in the possibility of grace and lean toward it and allow our minds to expand into it. And this allows for you to include people who are not like you, who do not believe what you believe in, who have done wrong. It allows you the ability to forgive and include them, which is a great act of bravery. The character Grace is a waitress and she's also a down-home, spiritual warrior. She's really committed to bringing together the estranged father and son. She's committed to creating this family because she wants a family and because they should be reconciled. She doesn't know how much this is going to cost her and it is going to cost her a lot.

DS: The play possesses a great juxtaposition in this family, between Vet who desires borders and Grace who actively entertains the idea of "grace"— something that's all expansive: containment versus something that is infinite and limitless.

SLP: Exactly. Vet is very, very human. And Grace is much more connected to the bigger way of living, which has its downsides because she, personally, has "boundary issues." These two people are married, just as we, each individually, are a married whole of two halves. One side of us is very human, the side made of clay, is married to the other side made of the spirit, and they are often in conflict. Your human side is often in opposition with your better nature and you're always, within yourself, trying to reconcile those opposites.

DS: They physically manifest in your characters differently based on the generation and age of the person.

SLP: They really do. Vet's the oldest guy and he is way, way back there before the written word. But he is very literate, very bright, very smart—

FIGURE 7 *The Book of Grace,* written and directed by Suzan-Lori Parks, ZACH Theatre, 2011. Nadine Mozon as Grace and Shaun Patrick Tubbs as Buddy/Snake. Photo by Kirk A. Tuck. Courtesy of ZACH Theatre.

doesn't write anything down but "writes" and "records" everything in his head. Grace, whose age is between Vet and Buddy, she writes things down using pen and paper. And then Buddy is the kid on Facebook and longs to be seen by the universe. These three world views, these three "books" collide in *The Book of Grace* and the play is an invitation to see your own family in this family, and to see your own story in this story, and to see your own limitations in the limitations of these characters, and to see the enormity of your own possibility in the possibility that you see expressed in the play. Like Grace says, "Camp David begins at home." I think that is really true. I am a firm believer that, if we could have more Camp David happening at home, if we could have more meaningful conflict resolution inside the home, we might have less need, we might have an easier time resolving problems that happen outside the home. If we could just work it out with the people we know then we'd have a much easier time working it out with folks we've never met.

PART II

Commentaries

19

REMARKS ON PARKS I

A Hunter College Symposium on the Work of Suzan-Lori Parks

Jonathan Kalb, moderator
April 30, 2004

Part One: Critics and Scholars

[The following, which was originally published in HotReview.org, Hunter online theater review, is an edited transcript of a symposium held at Hunter College on April 30, 2004, organized and moderated by Jonathan Kalb. This first of two panels (for critics and scholars) featured introductory remarks by Kalb, followed by twenty-minute presentations by Robert Brustein, Shawn-Marie Garrett, Marc Robinson, and Alisa Solomon, and discussion with the audience.]

Jonathan Kalb: This symposium has been organized in conjunction with the Hunter Theater Department's spring 2004 production, which is Suzan-Lori Parks's play *Venus*, directed by our faculty member Bill Walters, who is with us today and who will be speaking with us on the second panel. The show runs through May 9 and I encourage everybody to see it, not only because I want everybody to see all the work we do in the Theater Department here but also because I think that this playwright, even more than a lot of other playwrights, *really* has to be experienced in the theater if you want to understand what she is all about. The presence of her work in the theater, the challenges that her work poses to the theater, including her habit of casting spectators in the role of dubious historical witnesses whether they like it or not, are very much of the essence of her aesthetic. I feel sure that our panelists today will have a lot more to say on these issues. I have the honor of welcoming to Hunter today a remarkable array of theater scholars, critics and practitioners who have in part distinguished themselves through their work on Parks's drama. They have taken on the exciting and daunting task of focusing seriously on the sometimes difficult work of a startlingly new author in a period before others had provided any roadmaps for this, and everyone who turns their attention to Parks in the future, whether by writing about it or giving it life on the stage, owes a great deal to these writers and artists.

Just one point of clarification to begin with. For those of you familiar with her at all, Suzan-Lori Parks is probably known as the author of *Topdog/Underdog*, a play about two black brothers, one named Lincoln, the other named Booth, who live together in a seedy rooming house and whose names prefigure a tragicomic fate that both is and isn't obvious from the start. This play transferred from the Public Theater to Broadway in 2002 and was the first drama by an African-American woman to win the Pulitzer Prize. Parks won the Pulitzer one year after winning a MacArthur grant in 2001. It's important to establish here, though, at the outset, that *Topdog/Underdog*, a relatively naturalistic work, is not typical of Parks's other work before or after it. Parks has tried many, many different dramatic forms; in fact, she's something of a connoisseur of dramatic form. The works on which she built her early reputation were deliberate deconstructions of traditional linear structure.

Suzan-Lori Parks was born May 10, 1963, in Fort Knox, Kentucky, the daughter of an Army colonel who moved the family around quite a bit. By the time she was old enough to move out she had lived in six different states of the union and in Germany, where she attended a German school and learned the German language. She eventually graduated cum laude from Mount Holyoke College where she began writing plays at the encouragement of James Baldwin, one of her teachers. She came to the notice of the downtown theater community in 1989 for a play called *Imperceptible Mutabilities in the Third Kingdom*, done at BACA Downtown and later at many other theaters, which won three Obie awards. Following that, to mention only her full-length titles, came *Betting on the Dust Commander, The Death of the Last Black Man in the Whole Entire World, The America Play*, and *Venus*. *Venus*, as many of you know, is built around the historical figure of Saartjie Baartman, a black woman from South Africa who was brought to England in the early 19th century and displayed as a sideshow freak, The Hottentot Venus, because of her large behind. Then came *Topdog* and a pair of full-lengths that responded in different ways to Hawthorne's *The Scarlet Letter: In the Blood* and *Fucking A*. Although she has concentrated so far mainly on plays, Parks has also written a great deal in other genres. She wrote the screenplay for Spike Lee's film about phone sex workers, *Girl 6*, and is currently working on several other film scripts, as well as the book for a Disney musical about the Harlem Globetrotters, called *Hoops*. She has written many essays and she published a novel last year called *Getting Mother's Body*, which could be construed as a tribute to Faulkner's *As I Lay Dying*.

Now having listed all these titles and honors, I have still told you nothing about what the fuss is all about with this author. I've said nothing about her extremely provocative use of history, her fearless use of racist stereotypes to expropriate and diffuse what has been hurtful in other contexts, and I've said nothing about her fractured language, the way, as she puts it, she likes to bang

FIGURE 8 *Topdog/Underdog* by Suzan-Lori Parks, directed by Timothy Douglas. Bowman Wright (Lincoln) and Biko Eisen-Martin (Booth) at Marin Theatre Company (2012). Photo by David Allen (Marin Theatre Company).

words together and watch them do things. This is no cuddly composer of folklore. Her literary heroes are not easy writers but rather prickly and difficult ones like Faulkner, Joyce, Adrienne Kennedy, and Samuel Beckett, about whom she once said, "He just seems so black to me."

I want to turn things over to our panelists now and will end by reading a few lines from *Imperceptible Mutabilities in the Third Kingdom*. The figures here are in a flagrantly metaphorical boat located in a no-man's ocean called The Third Kingdom, somewhere between the United States and Africa.

Shark-Seer: How many kin kin I hold. Whole hull full.
Soul-Seer: Thuh hullholesfull of bleachin bones.
Us-Seer: Bleached Bones Man may come and take you far uhcross thuh sea from me.
Over-Seer: Who're you again?
Kin-Seer: I'm. Lucky.
Over-Seer: Who're you again?
Soul-Seer: Duhdduhnt-he-know-my-name?
Kin-Seer: Should I jump? Shouldijumporwhut?
Shark-Seer: But we are not in uh boat!
Us-Seer: But we iz. Iz iz iz uh huhn. Iz uh huhn. Uh huhn iz.
Shark-Seer: I wonder: Are we happy? Thuh looks we look look so.
Us-Seer: They like smiles and we will like what they will like.

Soul-Seer:	UUH!
Kin-Seer:	Me wavin at me me wavin at my I me wavin at my soul.
Shark-Seer:	Chomp chomp chomp chomp.
Kin-Seer:	Fffffffffff—
Us-Seer:	Thup.
Shark-Seer:	Baby, what will I do for love?
Soul-Seer:	Wave me uh wave and I'll wave one back blow me uh kiss n I'll blow you one back.
Over-Seer:	Quiet, you, or you'll be jettisoned!
Shark-Seer:	Chomp chomp chomp chomp.
Kin-Seer:	Wa-vin wavin.
Shark-Seer:	Chomp chomp chomp chomp.
Kin-Seer:	Howwe gonna find my Me?

Our mission today, one could say, is to try to help find Suzan-Lori Parks's "me." We'll give it the ol' college try.

Robert Brustein: I first came upon the rich, audacious, and singular talent of Suzan-Lori Parks in 1992 when I went up to Yale to see a production of a work with a marquee-swollen title, *The Death of the Last Black Man in the Whole Entire World*. This was actually her third in a series of plays with equally mind-boggling names like *Imperceptible Mutabilities in the Third Kingdom* (I think Alisa Solomon was the first critic to ever review that play) and *Betting on the Dust Commander*. These titles didn't quite match the length of Peter Weiss's *Persecution and Assassination of Jean-Paul Marat as Performed by the Inmates of the Asylum of Charenton Under the Direction of the Marquis de Sade*, or even Arthur Kopit's *Oh Dad, Poor Dad, Mama's Hung You in the Closet and I'm Feelin' So Sad*. But like all her plays, *The Death of the Last Black Man* suggested she had more in common with Kopit's avant-garde mischievousness and Weiss's supertheatricalism than with the formal and thematic conventions associated with contemporary American realism.

In those days Suzan-Lori herself was eager to distinguish her work in style from the more familiar domestic conventions of say, Lorraine Hansberry's *Raisin in the Sun* (which George C. Wolfe called "one of the last 'mama on the couch' plays") and in content from what she memorably identified as "the I'm-gonna-get-you plays of the '70s" (sequels to the "I'm-gonna-get-your-mama plays" of the '60s). Maybe that was because her teacher at Mount Holyoke was Jimmy Baldwin, the author of a famous essay called "Everybody's Protest Novel," in which he criticized the same sort of belligerent ideologizing in some black fiction writing. Whatever the case, Parks's writing has always been as much a product of Western postmodernism as of African-American consciousness and the black experience, an unusual amalgam of the two.

In this she had a literary prototype in Adrienne Kennedy, one of the earliest African-American women writers with more on her mind than race. "It's insulting," Suzan-Lori once said at a public symposium. "It's insulting when people say my plays are about what it's about to be black, as if that's all we think about, as if our life is about that. My life is not about race. It's about being alive." And she added, "Why does everyone think white artists make art and black artists make statements? Why doesn't anyone ask me ever about form?" Well if they did, people would have gotten an earful because Parks had been carefully schooled in the formalist breakthroughs of the postmodern school. Like other members of that movement, notably Gertrude Stein in *The Making of Americans*, and James Joyce in *Finnegans Wake*, for example, she is very preoccupied with deconstructing the English language. And like the author of a play called *The Blacks*, Jean Genet, who was one of the earliest writers to explore the way skin color influences consciousness, she is deeply concerned with identity and how the presence of the Other helps both to define and to obscure our sense of ourselves. At the same time, her work has been influenced a lot by music, both jazz and classical, from which she derives her concept of what she calls "repetition and revision"—that is to say, revisiting and revising the same phrases over and over again.

But despite her joyous encounter with music and language, it cannot be denied that Suzan-Lori is also writing plays about race. *The Last Black Man*, for example, is partly an effort to exalt black English into a kind of poetic code and to adapt English words to the black experience. As the play moves the audience through a kind of expressionist history of America, a character named Before Columbus reflects on a time when the Earth was flat, while another insists that the Earth was "roun" until Columbus made it round with a "d." In short, Parks deconstructs language as a means of establishing the forgotten place of African-Americans in recorded history. "You will write it down," she writes, "because if you don't write it down then we will come along and tell the future that we did not exist." "You will write it down and carve it out of rock." In the introduction to one of her collections, she adds quite beautifully, "One of my tasks is to locate the ancestral burial ground, dig for bones, find bones, hear the bones sing, write it down." This, I would suggest, is her way of endorsing the Czech writer Milan Kundera's definition of art as "a struggle of memory against forgetting." Her plays may sometimes be about oppression, but she never limits herself to writing about oppression. As she says, "To define black drama solely as the presentation of the Black as oppressed is bullshit."

After *The Death of the Last Black Man* came two transitional works, *The America Play* and *Venus*. *The America Play* was her first stab at the Cain and Abel relationship between Abe Lincoln, here called the Foundling Father, and his murderer, John Wilkes Booth. *Topdog/Underdog* was her second treatment of the subject, a sign that she is given to taking a story and revising it. In both works the central figure is a black man trained to reenact over and over again Lincoln's murder at the hands of Booth at Ford's Theater during a production of *Our American Cousin*, which was playing there when Lincoln was shot. *Venus*, on the other hand, is about the celebrated Venus Hottentot, as she was called.

By the way, that word Hottentot began as a derogatory term for the Khoikhoi tribe in South Africa. It was coined by an Afrikaner who said, "They only have two words, 'hot' and 'tot,'" and that's the way the word came into being. It was later applied to "Venus Hottentot" who was abducted from her South African home in the early nineteenth century to become a phenomenon of English freak shows because of her gargantuan buttocks and breasts. Despite obvious temptations, however, *Venus* is not a victim play and never pushes sympathy buttons. Parks's Venus is hugely exploited but always retains an aristocratic dignity and *sang-froid* laced with a gentle irony. She is exhibited, she's manhandled, sexually violated, infected with the clap, anatomized and, finally, autopsied by physicians who think they have found the missing link. Yet the play is not only an indictment of white racism but of European smugness and insularity as well. In short, it is less a victim play than a powerful dissent from European concepts of female beauty.

Like *The America Play, Venus* was a transitional work in the sense that Parks began then to subordinate her linguistic experimentation in order to concentrate more on theme and character. This had the result of making her work more accessible, until with *In the Blood*, a contemporary version of Hawthorne's *Scarlet Letter* about a homeless black woman and the black preacher who seduces and abandons her, she finally produced a popular work. Her next play, *Topdog/ Underdog*, even enjoyed a short run on Broadway, and as Jonathan told you, won the Pulitzer Prize. But just as that work covered the same material as *The America Play*, her most recent work, *Fucking A*, was a second look at the Hester Prynne story, the one she adapted in *In the Blood*, with the heroine wearing a scarlet "A" for being an abortionist.

Parks's style was undergoing changes as well. The dialogue of *Topdog/ Underdog* is composed in highly syncopated rhythms, the verbal equivalent of the modern jazz riffs that the director George C. Wolfe used as transitional motifs. In her previous plays, Parks's explorations were performed in a highly charged, imagistic language that kept the poetic content higher than the sociological substance. In her recent, more accessible if less reverberant plays, she uses increasingly naturalistic language and domestic themes. As in *Topdog/Underdog*, she is more concerned about what she calls family wounds and healing than with big historical flourishes. That may be why, instead of experimental artists like Marcus Stern, Liz Diamond, and Richard Foreman, who are the directors associated with her earlier work, her plays are now being staged by more mainstream artists like George C. Wolfe and Michael Greif. No one can predict where this unpredictable dramatist will go next, whether she will break out into fresh uncharted territory or remain content with a modest, if seedily furnished room in town. In any case, she is definitely an artist whose future work one awaits with the greatest anticipation.

Shawn-Marie Garrett: The title of my talk today is "The Venus Hottentot is Dead: The Historical Saartjie Baartman." Saartjie Baartman is the name of the woman who became known by the appellation "The Venus Hottentot." So I'm here to fill in a little historical background about the character, because while the play frequently refers to the little evidence that exists about her, it's certainly an imaginative version of the character.

The South African Baartman, under the stage name of The Hottentot Venus, was shown before paying crowds in London, in the English provinces and in Paris during the early 19th century. She died at the age of twenty-six in Paris in 1815. Her death is the starting point in *Venus*, and the play's most repeated refrain is "The Venus Hottentot is Dead." Parks perhaps anticipated that *Venus*'s audiences would need reminding on this point; for of all of Parks's figures, Venus is the least likely to stay dead anytime soon. Parks views her historical characters as having continuing life as "effigies," to use Joseph Roach's term, or "repetitions with revision," to use Parks's, that appear throughout history, as Robert Brustein mentioned. The same sorts of patterns repeat themselves, perhaps with revision. Saartjie Baartman isn't just what James Baldwin, Suzan-Lori Parks's teacher, called one of the many thousands gone. Nor is she one of the sixty million to whom Toni Morrison dedicates her novel *Beloved*. Like Morrison, Parks, in her plays before Venus, tended to concentrate on the unknown dead victims of the long international shame of the slave trade. Yet Saartjie Baartman is different. For many South Africans, she is a martyr, a secular saint.

In 1996 a South African Professor of Archaeology named Andrew Sillen called Baartman a metaphor for what has happened to his country. The few Americans today who have heard of her have probably heard about her from the buzz about Parks's play and its productions throughout the country. When the play premiered and told Baartman's story, Parks took on a new role in a way as a playwright, something more akin to Brecht's idea of a writer who gives the audience pleasure through teaching. Her previous plays were much more playful linguistically than *Venus* is. More literal and less poetical than in her earlier work, Parks's *Venus* is a conduit of the real past. Its Brechtian structure and language, its songs, mark a mutation of Parks's dramatic form, and Baartman's bones seem to require that. Parks does draw on the same inter-textual strategies; that is, she pulls from historical sources and mixes them with dramatic dialogue, as in her earlier plays. *Venus* is—mercifully, in my opinion—as far from documentary drama as those earlier plays. Yet Baartman's ordeal is described in *Venus*, in all its violent and perverse particularities, through a fragmented structure and multiple ironic distancing devices.

So who was Saartjie Baartman? Through uncertain means and for uncertain ends she left South Africa and ended up in London in 1812. It is thought—and this is reported on slim evidence in a book called *The Shows of London* by Richard Altick—that her father was a drover, or a driver of animals, who was killed by a Bushman, or Hottentot as the Dutch called them. Then she was taken to London, probably by force, to participate in a freak show. Those events are depicted in the play. In London she achieved a minor morbid celebrity as a sideshow freak called

The Hottentot Venus. She appeared nearly naked and crowds were particularly attracted by her butt. This appears again and again in historical documents.

Altick called her "steatopygic to a fault." Steatopygia is a medical condition that many doctors insist some South African women still suffer from, which involves having a large ass. In fact, it has to do with retention of water and other things that are completely to be expected in the environment in which those women have lived for centuries. In any case, spectators were also attracted by her genitals and private viewings could be arranged. Again through unknown forces, Baartman ended up in Paris in 1813, performing her show—which is to say, being shown off by somebody else. Parks questions this business of Baartman's agency. She sees Baartman as a diva. She gives her a kind of choice that the historical Saartjie Baartman probably would not have had, a set of rights and a will that she would not have been granted.

The French were even more fascinated by her than the English, for theoretical as well as erotic reasons. The preeminent French naturalist Georges Cuvier, who is for the French what Charles Darwin is for the English, was looking for a scientific basis for race at the time, as were many so-called naturalists, and Baartman seemed an ideal object of study. Naturalists regarded Baartman's race—which was not just African but the sub-race of Africans called the Hottentots—as "the true missing link." That's a quotation from Cuvier. After Baartman's death, Cuvier (who appears in Parks's play as the Baron Docteur) performed an autopsy on her corpse and published his results to great acclaim. He also made a plaster cast of her body and, most astonishingly, preserved her genitalia in a formaldehyde jar. These were put on public exhibition at Musée de l'Homme in Paris, where they remained until 1978. At that point I guess they decided they were a little embarrassing.

There were Peruvian genitalia and other genitalia then too. The Musée de l'Homme had a habit of preserving exotic women's genitalia, and also the brains of great male European scientists. Shelves of brains and genitalia. To paraphrase Shakespeare: a spectacle for mechanic slaves and quick comedians, a study for science and death.

The historian William B. Cohen writes that Baartman was so famous in French naturalist circles that she "dominated much of French scientific thought about Blacks for the remainder of the nineteenth century." Soon after her remains were removed from public display, Baartman's case was reopened by scholars and scientists contra-colonialism. In 1982, Steven J. Gould wrote an account of visiting the Musée de l'Homme. He writes in his evocative style about the labyrinthine innards and back wards, which is a pun Parks exploits but Gould misses. And his account reads like something out of Joseph Conrad, a white man's primal scene. Here's what he says, after recounting holding the skull of Descartes and looking at the French scientist Paul Broca's brain: "Yet I found the most interesting items on the shelf just above, a little exhibit that provided an immediate and chilling insight into 19th-century *mentalité* and the history of racism. In three smaller jars I saw the dissected genitalia of three

Third-World women. I found no brains of women, nor any male genitalia. The three jars are labeled 'une négresse,' 'une péruvienne,' 'la Vénus Hottentotte.'" Hot on Gould's heels, many scholars picked up the story of Baartman and she became once again exhibited, displayed, theorized, but this time in scholarly conferences and discussions such as this one.

A few words on the contemporary events that surrounded *Venus*'s premiere, purely coincidentally. Baartman descended from, as we've said, a group of Africans known derisively as Hottentots or Bushmen; even today many people call them the latter. The real name of their tribes are the Khoisan. Sadly, they've practically been eradicated through genocide. In January and February 1996, before *Venus*'s premiere in the U.S., the Griqua National Congress in post-apartheid South Africa, which represents the Khoisan tribes, intensified its pressure on South African policy makers to secure the return of Baartman's remains to South Africa from France. The Khoisan are generally light-skinned and identify themselves as neither Black nor Colored, according to apartheid's lingering categories, and at first the GNC's efforts were rebuffed because they lack the political muscle of, say, the ANC. Interestingly, not a single American newspaper picked up on this Baartman controversy in 1996, while it was all over European newspapers. In the year 2000, Baartman's remains were finally returned to South Africa, and she was really greeted there as kind of a secular saint. A great celebration was held and she was given a proper burial, which, according to the traditions of her people, is essential and necessary for her to pass on to the next phase of life.

A couple of other contemporary creative writers have also picked up on Baartman's story and it's interesting to compare their approaches to Parks's in *Venus*. In 1979 the white South African poet Stephen Gray conceived an immortal Baartman figure, an Earth mother Venus who reverses the putdown she endured in life. This is an excerpt from his poem, in which she effects a kind of Dionysian revenge:

> Saartjie Baartman is my name and I know
> my place I know my rights I put down my foot
> and the Tuileries Gardens shake I put down
> my foot and the Seine changes course I put
> down my foot and the globe turns upside down
> I rattle my handful of bones and the dead arise.

In another poem, by the American writer Elizabeth Alexander, who is also a playwright, Baartman resumes her mortal dimensions. It is a very naturalistic telling of Baartman's story. Like Parks's, Alexander's Baartman is the family entrepreneur and a kind of diva. For Parks, Venus's downfall comes when she merges her public and private personas; that is, when she succumbs to the love affair with the Baron Docteur. Alexander imagines Baartman's inner life and memories as her only sanctuary. Here's how she imagines Baartman thinking:

> … there are hours in every day
> to conjure my imaginary
> daughters in banana skirts
>
> and ostrich-feather fans.
> Since my own genitals are public
> I have made other parts private.

Interestingly, Alexander also reveals the secret of the Hottentot Venus's fabulous popularity. The Venus character explains,

> … I rub my hair
> with lanolin, and pose in profile
> like a painted Nubian
>
> archer, imagining gold leaf
> woven through my hair and diamonds.

In the end she fantasizes a kind of Jacobean revenge against Cuvier.

> If he were to let me rise up
> from this table, I'd spirit
> his knives and cut out his black heart…
> so the whole world would see
> it was shriveled and hard,
> geometric, deformed, unnatural.

Of course, "deformed" and "unnatural" were the qualities that Cuvier sought to ascribe to all Hottentots, and by extension all Africans, through his autopsy report on Venus. Unlike Gray and Alexander, then, Parks denies Baartman justice. Her play is not a melodrama or a tragedy. She grants Baartman and the audience only whatever comfort lies in performance because it repeats, because it revises. Parks moves Baartman out of the familiar form of revenge fantasy, where both Gray's and Alexander's Venuses, different as they are, seek a divinity to shape their ends. Parks's Venus, like the figures in her earlier plays, can only keep on "waving back," to borrow a phrase from *Imperceptible Mutabilities in the Third Kingdom*, where figures in Middle Passage keep waving goodbye to their African selves and the distant African shore. Baartman, in a sense, also keeps waving back. That's the justice that Suzan-Lori Parks can imagine for her in the present.

Marc Robinson: I want to begin by quoting one playwright's vision of an ideal theater, a theater he famously said would be located in a cemetery "where graves are being dug all the time."

Before burying the dead man, carry the corpse in his casket to the front of the stage, let his friends, enemies, and the curious sit in the section reserved for the audience, let the funeral mime who led the procession divide and multiply, let him turn into a theatrical company, and let him recreate the life and death of the dead man, right in front of the corpse and the audience, afterwards, let the casket be carried to the grave in the dead of night, let the audience finally leave— the feast is finished. Until another ceremony, occasioned by another corpse, is worthy of dramatic performance—not a tragic one. Tragedy must be lived, not played.

The writer, of course, is Genet, and this scenario (from his essay "The Strange Word *Urb*...") anticipates many of the procedures and themes of *Venus*, not least its own funeral mime in the person of the Negro Resurrectionist overseeing a reenacted life of Venus after presenting her body and announcing her death. The passage also names the deliberately unresolved tension between exhumation and burial—or, more generally, exposure and concealment—in many other Parks's plays.

It's an ambivalence for which Genet found a simple theatrical sign. In the stage directions to *Deathwatch*, he insists that the lighting be as bright as possible all the time in the otherwise tomblike prison cell. The condemned may be out of sight, buried alive in a hole, but they are not unseen. There is always a spectator monitoring their actions. The characters, denied privacy, are always on stage. The same harsh, unremitting light should fill both the stage and the house of *The Screens*, Genet wrote to Roger Blin, that play's first director, "because I should in some way like both actors and audience caught up in the same illumination, and for there to be no place for them to hide, or even half-hide."

There may be no place to hide or even half-hide in Parks, either, so habitual is her characters' theatricality and so pervasive is the accompanying surveillance. Yet she nonetheless recognizes the strength of an undertow pulling the action down and out of sight. The characters' response to this extraordinary force *is* the action. As many critics have observed (Una Chaudhuri, Greg Miller, Alice Rayner, and Harry Elam among them), Parks's theater occupies a perforated landscape. Her stages are pockmarked with ditches, pools, and graves; the text with lacuna; the bodies with wounds; the narratives with secrets and other recesses from which authoritative meaning won't emerge. This is a theater in perpetual retreat from visual, verbal, and physical presence, recoiling as readers and viewers reach toward it. We have each made our own list of its hiding places: under the porch or in the slave-ship hold in *The Death of the Last Black Man*; under the bridge in *In the Blood*; *The America Play*'s Great Hole and, less obviously, Lucy's pledge of confidentiality; in *Venus*, the cage, cell, and dark bedroom; and, in many plays, the privacy of footnotes and the anticipatory silence before speech or the helplessness after it. These aren't mere absences or omissions, as some have described them, but arenas of action. Here, in the spaces opened up whenever the action sinks below the surface of declarative language, social behavior, and expository action, Parks's characters engage with histories both individual and cultural, seize and sift the very matter supporting their presence, and confront aspects of themselves that can't be regularized into dramatically manageable form onstage or in spoken language.

Not that these recesses are wholly divorced from Parks's relentlessly spectatorial culture. As in Genet, the idea of privacy exists only as a simulation, teasing characters with promises of a security it can no longer fulfill. "Yr only yrself when no ones watching," Parks writes, hopefully, in *Topdog/Underdog*, welcoming the irony that the brothers are actually quoting one of Lincoln's voyeuristic customers. Is there ever true solitude in Parks's theater? A naturalist and, later, a photographer hover over the action in *Imperceptible Mutabilities*. Hester's bridge is regularly invaded by policemen, welfare officials, and vandals scrawling graffiti. The needy and the menacing burst in on the Hester of *Fucking A* just when she settles into the first private hour of the night. In *Topdog/Underdog*, the most intimate companion of one's seclusion becomes the most intrusive spectator. The action of that play exists in a state of permanent inhibition, as the brothers are always spying on one another or fearing discovery. One brother looks in, unnoticed, from the threshold, or eavesdrops behind a screen. The other hides his possessions—money, porn magazines, weapon—from prying eyes or tries, futilely, to smother the shame that follows his own moments of self-consciousness.

In her recognition of the pull exerted by subterranean spaces, literal or figurative, Parks extends a tradition of concealment in American theater, or more precisely, African-American theater. The oldest hole swallowing her own is in William Wells Brown's 1858 play *The Escape; or, A Leap for Freedom*, the first play published by a black American writer. Its most memorable image is a deep pit in which a slave is kept prisoner by a sadistic overseer. (That synonym for slave owner, as Parks recognized in *Imperceptible Mutabilities*, nicely captures the relationship of spectatorship to possession.) Jean Toomer's *Kabnis*, the play buried in his 1923 novel *Cane*, places the title character in a murky cellar where he must face a painful ancestry he thought he understood above ground. "I get my life down in this scum-hole," he says. Marita Bonner's 1928 play *The Purple Flower* envisions a dimly lit level below the thin "skin of civilization," as she calls it. The latter repeatedly cracks—"a thought can drop you through it," she says—and plunges Bonner's characters into an atavistic past.

More recent works make Parks's imagery seem all the more inevitable. Amiri Baraka's *Dutchman* is set in what he famously calls "the flying underbelly of the city," a hot, cramped subway car. Another subway car appears in Adrienne Kennedy's *The Owl Answers*. Kennedy's *Ohio State Murders*, nearly contemporaneous with Parks's major early plays, is set in the underground level of a university library, with a single window hung far above the stage. At night, the play's playwright-protagonist retreats here to consider why her theater is so preoccupied with violence. Of course, the best-known hole in American literature is in Ralph Ellison's *Invisible Man*, and its protagonist's monologue sets the standard for all subsequent self-interrogations. In all this theater, as in

Ellison's novel, characters who have had invisibility forced upon them use it to study their disguises, compromises, and inhibitions, if never wholly to shed them. They also surrender to elemental fear, anger, and longing, these emotions no longer cut to fit any landscape other than their own. (In *The America Play*, Parks writes that the Great Hole "gave a shape" to the Lesser Known.) Out of sight, all these characters hope to arrive at insights penetrating, candid, and self-surprising.

In Parks's theater, the pits, underbellies, and cellars of these earlier writers appear as replicas and echoes (to cite two forms from *The America Play*), or rather, throughout this theater history, each void can be seen as citing an earlier one, digging deeper into a shared absence. In fact, the digging, as the Lesser Known and the Negro Resurrectionist know, is as important as the hole. Parks makes the most of theater's temporality to confront the experience of losing, not just the subsequent recognition of loss—of retreat, not mere vacancy—and of the dynamic struggle either to resist it or, more often and more surprising, to welcome it and, by trying to control it, to turn it to one's advantage. As Elizabeth Bishop advises in "One Art," "practice losing farther, losing faster."

Images of falling or sinking recur obsessively in Parks's theater, as if each sequence advanced by a few segments one endless, metaphysical descent, the ground forever lowering just as the characters near it. (Is this a vision of the original Fall from grace as rendered by a playwright who acknowledges Catholicism's formative influence on her theater?) The Foundling Father slumps repeatedly in his chair after being "shot." Kin-Seer in *Imperceptible Mutabilities* sinks through the ocean after being jettisoned from a slave-ship. An Icarus-like pilot in the same play falls out of the sky onto Sergeant Smith. The sky itself seems to fall on Hester during the eclipse in *In the Blood*, an experience that makes her feel as if "the hand of fate with its five fingers [were] coming down on me." Miss Miss imagines (falsely, it turns out) her own drowning in the short play *Pickling*. "Down down down," says Black Woman With Fried Drumstick. "Down down down down down." Perhaps this is her account of Black Man With Watermelon, who tumbles through the experience of dying over and over but never reaches the bottom of death.

As characters fall, so too does the idea of character. The Foundling Father, already a fallen version of the real Lincoln, dwindles further over the course of the play, present only as a Lincoln bust early in Act II, then a Lincoln penny, then even further reduced to an intangible face on the TV that reruns the play's first act, now, in a final diminishment, played in silence. So runs down memory. As Lucy and Brazil try to retrieve the past, it dissolves in their hands and before their eyes. This erosion of character has its equivalent in just about every Parks play. Bodies turn to maimed bodies, turn to body parts, turn to facsimiles of body parts, turn, finally, to mere words for those parts. In this last instance, I'm thinking, of course, of the glossary at the end of the printed version of *Venus*, perhaps meant to be read and staged as part of the body of the text, on par with its footnotes. (Here too, the corporeal associations of the word "footnotes" are hard to ignore.)

The regression doesn't stop here. The glossary asserts an authority that Parks deliberately withholds in her other plays. This procedure involves more than interrupting speech with silence. As memorable in themselves as are Parks's famous "spells," equally important are the passages of falling toward the moment when silence reestablishes order. Here, to borrow an image from Bonner's *Purple Flower*, we can imagine the thin ice of the play's verbal civilization cracking and the speakers plunging through a languageless chasm, so horrifying that the silence at the bottom comes as a relief. At least *that* is stable. In sequences that parallel bodily dispersal and decay, writing itself slowly recoils from our attention, as characters burrow into private, coded modes of expression, or pull back even further to a time when they could not or would not express anything.

Enacting a kind of reverse evolution of language over the course of several plays, Parks seeks ever stronger ways of troubling, if not wholly burying expression. Each departure from established language initiates more extreme retreats. After the vernacular are the echoes of the vernacular, or, in *Fucking A*, the still more remote, exclusive vernacular of the made-up language "TALK." The buried language of the written footnotes is more accessible than the unwritten ones (in *Last Black Man*). The preverbal sounds of the glottal stops, quick intakes of breath, and tongue clicks subside to the shaped silence of the spells, which finally sink deeper still, toward the unshaped silences in which characters hear themselves trail off into an unvoiced question or a dash. (*The America Play* ends in one.) All are ways of marking the sudden failure of any dramatic structure, verbal or silent, to support its characters. A beautiful line from *Last Black Man* captures this dissolution of language and the desperation to retain it before it rushes away. "My text was writ on water," says Black Man With Watermelon. "I would like to drink it down."

Venus could be another text "writ on water." Parks labels its scenes in reverse order, starting at scene thirty-one and ending with scene one. The structure suggests the melting of a solid into fluid, or the shedding of skins; what once had bulk, presence, slowly disappears until nothing remains. Nothing, or everything. Perhaps the play's structure is the inverse of the dying that goes on throughout Parks—her theater, with this play, returning to its newborn state, or even to some earlier stage in which, on which, actors haven't yet turned into characters, haven't submitted themselves to our attention, a time when everything was still potential, a state of grace.

Does Parks preserve whole strata of experience and emotion by refusing to show them in her theater? Venus is famously said to have died of "exposure." Hers is only the most obvious instance in which performance is manipulative and distorting. The three-card monte spectacle in *Topdog*, the mountebank preacher in *In the Blood*, the phony Lincoln in *The America Play* (reminding us, further, that Lincoln was of course killed while watching a play): theater in Parks is always associated with fakery and always a dangerous and unprotected space. When her invisible men and women reject such duplicity and sink into their holes, they seek secure fact, not illusion, an image of experience that is real, not merely realistic. They compulsively measure their surroundings, weigh and take stock of its contents—actions that they believe are the first steps toward having a history and, as she puts it in *Last Black Man*, "hiding it under a rock." They honor pledges and keep secrets, save money, pickle things in mason jars. They take photographs, write and save letters, keep records and monitor those kept by others, balance the budget. In every case, Parks's characters are working to "hold it hold it hold it," as all the characters say seven times at the end of *Last Black Man*, thereby filling their voids with knowledge, however unexalted. As Lincoln insists in *Topdog*, "If you dont know what is, you dont know what aint." Sometimes the holding is simply a matter of usage. Black Man With Watermelon says, "You: is. It: be… You: still is. They: be… Remember me." At other times, the same need is satisfied less articulately. During the spells, the characters are claiming moments of silence, not merely observing them. They mark them with their particular styles of refusal. The silence literally has their names on it.

Such serious and busy activity returns us to Genet, and I want to end with another look at his passage about a cemetery theater. At the end of the passage I quoted, Genet makes a careful distinction: lives enacted on this gravesite stage are "worthy of dramatic performance—not a tragic one." He adds, "Tragedy must be lived, not played." In Parks, too, there is the same assertion of the difference between the playable and the unplayable, and the same cordoning off of territory for life uncorrupted by the theater. Every action, every aspect of character in her theater implies a world of incident and psychology not shown, impossible to show, saved from the fate of being shown. As Venus says, "Love's soul… hides in heaven… Love's corpse stands on show." Up in heaven—or down in a hole. Parks presents us with the drama lodged between the two sites, but the tragedy flanking it remains obscured—"lived," as Genet said, "not played." In her plays, we see the stereotypes, archetypes, variations on literary characters, facsimiles of historical figures—masks all—but the people they stand in for remain submerged, causing anxiety by staying just below the surface—landmines, to borrow an image from *Imperceptible Mutabilities*, that might explode if we're not careful. The true "tragedies" of the woman in *Venus*, of the two men in *Topdog*, of the family in *Imperceptible Mutabilities*, of the race in *Last Black Man*, and finally, of the nation in *The America Play*: Parks knows that there is no way to do them justice in the simplifying medium of theater, the medium that, as Brecht said, "theaters everything down." She rejects her art to save her subjects. That she does so within her art preserves her own self-protective ambiguity. We can't pin her down. "Miss me… Kiss me," says Venus, sounding like Parks herself as she rejects and summons us in an unbroken circle, simultaneously mourning loss and trying to compensate for it.

Alisa Solomon: I would like to begin by challenging a particular narrative that has become popular in mainstream journalism since Suzan-Lori Parks won the Pulitzer Prize. This narrative describes her starting out with promising but largely obscure early plays championed by a few white intellectuals until she was triumphantly rescued by those who knew better, George C. Wolfe and The Disney Corporation, who guided her toward the writing of characters you can sympathize with and plots you can follow and sometimes even predict. Of course, I'm exaggerating but only slightly. The embrace of Parks by the mainstream has seemed to require, among some critics—not any of my esteemed colleagues here, of course, but at least among some daily reviewers—a sort of denunciation of her earliest plays or a valuing of them primarily as immature sketches that prepared her for the more complex and controlled canvases that she's created in the last couple of years. The situation reminds me a little bit of how modern drama surveys typically treat Ibsen, tracing a clear progressive trajectory from overwrought verse dramas to realistic paragons. The prose plays themselves, evolving like an ever more fit species, shedding soliloquies, asides, and all the integuments of the well-made play as they creep, then crouch, then culminate in the upright masterpiece of *Hedda Gabler*. A grand narrative like this is, at best, misleading. Worse, it tends to turn us into forensic dramaturgs, pushing us to read the earlier plays primarily for clues of the full-fledged works that will follow. I want to stave off that tendency by focusing today on Parks's first play, *Imperceptible Mutabilities in the Third Kingdom*. I do not want to ask how it introduces themes and formal obsessions that emerge more fully later or that are left aside in *Topdog/Underdog* or *Fucking A* or *In the Blood* (plays that I admire very much). I want to look at *Imperceptible Mutabilities* for itself because it's a powerful work in its own right and really ought to be produced and studied more often.

I don't have time to give a full reading of *Imperceptible Mutabilities*, so I want to talk a bit about Parks's general project with language and the startling dramaturgical strategies that she invents in this play. Let's begin precariously balanced on a ledge, that is, with a character standing on a ledge, a window ledge contemplating jumping, specifically Mona in the opening scene of *Imperceptible Mutabilities*. Her roommate is fixing eggs while Mona is peering over the abyss. Part of the complication of these characters is that they call themselves Mona and Chona but they are officially called Charlene and Molly. So Mona, Molly, is standing on the ledge:

Charlene: How dja get through it?
Molly: Mm not through it.
Charlene: Yer leg. Thuh guard. Lose weight?
Molly: Hhh. What should I do Chona should I jump should I jump or what?
Charlene: You want some eggs?
Molly: Would I splat?
Charlene: Uhuhuhnnnn…
Molly: Twelve floors up. Whaduhya think?
Charlene: Uh-uh-uhn. Like scrambled?
Molly: Shit.
Charlene: With cheese? Say "with" cause ssgoin in.

Molly: I diduhnt quit that school. HHH. Thought: nope! Mm gonna go
            on-go on ssif nothin ssapin yuh know? "S-K" is /sk/ as in "ask."
            The little-lamb-follows-closely-behind-at-Marys-heels-as-Mary-
            boards-the-train. Shit. Failed every test he shoves in my face. He
            makes me recite my mind goes blank. HHH. The-little-lamb-
            follows-closely-behind-at-Marys-heels-as-Mary-boards-the-train.
            Aint never seen no woman on no train with no lamb. I tell him so.
            He throws me out. Stuff like this happens every day y know? This
            isnt uh special case mines iduhnt uh uhnnn.
Charlene: Salami? Yarnt veg anymore.

I begin here not simply because these are the opening lines of the play, but
because the impact of language on self-definition is so crucial here. It's
important throughout the play and quite powerfully in the last section,
"Greeks," which chronicles the tragic disintegration of the Smith family,
as the breadwinning father, a sergeant overseas, works for his mysterious
distinction. But in this first scene the effects of language on self-formulation
and social possibility are most explicit. Parks focuses here on black English and
its proclaimed inadequacy in mainstream America. Interestingly, she does not
strike a tone of complaint. Indeed, in interviews and post-play discussions of
this early work, Parks was often adamant about not being pegged as a political
writer of a particular kind or as a black writer of a particular kind, specifically
those who churned out what she called "those I'm-gonna-get-you-whitey
plays" of the 1970s. And as you heard, she said around this time, "It's insulting
when people say my plays are about what it's about to be black—as if that's all
we think about, as if our life is about that. My life is not about race. It's about
being alive." With startling imagery and a lyrical sense of wordplay, Parks
dramatizes this very predicament.

   The characters in *Imperceptible Mutabilities*, among them slaves in middle
passage, contemporary black women being spied on by a white naturalist
through the medium of a giant cockroach, a proud and proper family awaiting
their father's return from military service, certainly represent different aspects
of African-American experience. But it's through the everyday surreality of
what it means for them to be alive that Parks's allegorical absurdism achieves its
power. Grounded in history, yet given to fanciful flights of language, formalistic
in its conventions yet full of compassion, *Imperceptible Mutabilities* theatrically
incarnates and uses the double-seeing of theater itself to call attention to our
own experience as spectators of that incarnation, of what W.E.B. Dubois called
the "double-consciousness" of African-American life. That's not to say that
Parks gives us stories of conventional characters struggling with a familiar
assimilationist identity crisis, searching at once for their roots and for the road
out of the place where they're rooted. Instead, she stages that consciousness
itself, pulling apart language and image, pointing at their innards, and sometimes
reconstituting them anew.

Though Parks is an admirer of the avant garde's most staunch stager of the conundrums of consciousness, Richard Foremen, her minings of the mind are less cerebral than his. You might say that Foreman stages the left side of the brain and Parks the right. Where Foreman's non-narrative spectacles are driven by the sparkplug fire of connecting synapses, Parks's stage poems follow a dream logic in which sights and sounds melt into one another without losing their own shapes. So in one scene when loud Foremanesque buzzers punctuate *Imperceptible Mutabilities in the Third Kingdom*, for example, Parks's twining of the disparate elements of slavery in that scene, into a single excruciating image, occupies an emotional terrain that's far more moist than that of distanced Potatoland. Parks delineates her characters' anger, madness, and fear, and at the same time she steps a bit away from them to reveal the double-consciousness not only that her African-American characters experience, but also with which they are perceived from the outside. Thus, she is really doubly dealing with double-consciousness. While investigating the outer and inner worlds of African-American life from the inside, she is also showing how both are viewed from the outside, punched into relief by definitions and descriptions made by white folks.

With her stage imagery and her experiments with language, Parks pulls taut this tension between inner and outer life, between black and white worlds, between reality and appearance—a project that is inherently theatrical because it has at its core the question of representation. In the opening scene I read a moment ago, we hear the voices of women in the dark while slides flash overhead. In an interview, Parks explained, "You have these fixed pictures projected up there and down below there's a little person mutating like hell on stage. I'm obsessed with the gap between those two things." And she added, "This dynamic parallels the relationship between preconceived images of African-Americans and real people." At the same time, Parks explores a similar dynamic in the relationship between language and theater. In drama she says, "Language is taken from the world, refigured and set on the page and then taken from the page, refigured and set loose in the world again." But since language in this literary sense had historically excluded African-Americans, Parks's undertaking is doubly complex. She explains, "At one time in this country, the teaching of reading and writing to African-Americans was a criminal offense. So how do I adequately represent not merely the speech patterns of a people oppressed by language (which is the simple question) but the patterns of a people whose language use is so complex and varied and ephemeral that its daily use not only Signifies on the non-vernacular language forms, but on the construct of writing as well? If language is a construct and writing is a construct and Signifyin(g) on the double construct is the daily use, then I have chosen to Signify on the Signifyin(g)."

In doing so Parks uncovers the power of language to be performative, that is to call action into being, both in historical terms, as language can oppress as well as express, and in theatrical terms. The very typography of her scripts addresses this latter sense. Parks's early plays look like long dialogic poems. There are no stage directions and little in the way of moorings for the unsuspecting director. But Parks insists that movement is contained within the speech itself. Often leaving out punctuation that would delineate formal pauses, she lets words run together to find their own rhythms. And with a self-conscious nod to Zora Neale Hurston's seamless welding of the so-called folkloric and the so-called literary, Parks makes music of everyday usage. Even the way a word is spelled can imply stage action. "The," t-h-u-h in her scripts, signifies thuh, a slump, while t-h-e, "the," makes the body do something different. What's more, for African-Americans the distinction can mean the difference between work and unemployment, even between life and death, which brings us back to Mona on that ledge in near suicidal torment over the difference between "ask" and "aks."

Throughout the play, as in this scene, Parks plays with language, punning, changing a letter to shift the ground of the world within her words, tugging on the tension of what's known as standard American English and black vernacular. It's an issue Mona recognizes clearly. She says,

> You lie down you lie down but he and she and it and us well we lays down. Didnt quit. They booted me. He booted me. Couldnt see thuh sense uh words workin like he said couldnt see thuh sense uh workin where words workin like that was workin would drop my phone voice would let things slip they tell me get Basic Skills call me breaking protocol hhhhh! Think I'll splat?

Conversations between these two women alternate in this first section of *Imperceptible Mutabilities*, which is called "Snails," with monologues delivered by the white Naturalist, who is observing the interactions and behaviors of them, among them. His exaggerated language contrasts that of the women whom he's spying on. He says, "Having accumulated a wealth of naturally occurring observations knowing now how our subjects occur in their own world (*mundus primitivus*), the question now arises as to how we of our world (*mundus modernus*) best accommodate them." His diction is a comic yet sinister, white patriarchal discourse. Parks shows how egregiously he is missing what's going on in that apartment, in large measure because his language simply cannot describe or encompass it. Though I certainly don't equate Parks with her characters, I have, I confess, sometimes anxiously wondered whether she wasn't commenting with this menacing Naturalist on the white critical establishment that might also seek to accommodate her work in whatever "*mundus modernus*" happens to be the fashion of the moment. Gauging the work on its own terms, of course, is the best and only way to avoid that trap. It's also the best way to keep Suzan-Lori Parks out of the meta-narratives about playwrights' careers and keep ourselves open to the inexhaustible conventions of Suzan-Lori Parks's great theatrical imagination.

Questions and Discussion

JK: I want to use my privilege as moderator to ask a few of my own questions first. Shawn, I'm just curious, do we know how Baartman died? The play says she died of exposure but do we know that? And you mentioned that Suzan-Lori Parks invented the love affair with the doctor. Is there anything about a love affair in the historical record?

SMG: The question of how she died is really interesting because nobody knows what she died of. There is repetition with revision here, as I said: in the late twentieth century, we've revised Baartman for our own purposes through the theater, through poetry, through scholarly texts, anthropology, and so forth. Everybody's still seeking the explanation, you know. What's the bottom line?—to pun on the play's main image. There are currently five different published explanations of her death. Richard Altick supposes that she died of alcoholism. That's one possible explanation. Another possible explanation is, as Suzan-Lori writes, she died of gonorrhea, and Suzan-Lori calls it "the clap," an obvious, very funny pun. Another explanation argues that she died of exposure because she was kept in a cage and probably caught some sort of virus, cholera, chill, who knows? There's another historical account that holds that her racial inferiority alone—not only was she African but this inferior form of African—would have contributed to her death. That's a historical source. In my chapter on this play, I resolve not to get to the bottom of this issue. There's no record of why she died. All that's known is that she died at the age of twenty-six.

The love affair is a fiction, as far as the historical record is concerned. However, if you read the autopsy report, and a lot of it is actually verbatim in the play, there are these fascinatingly bizarre moments where Cuvier says, for example, "Her foot was very alluring." There are hints, in other words, of desire throughout the autopsy report, and you can think about the need to get under the skin of this character— "creature," as he calls her—as really a form of desire. I think Suzan-Lori picked up on this, which from a modern point of view might be seen as a perversion or a horrible violation—this posthumous violation of her body as a sort of desire, the desire to literally penetrate the body of this strange woman. Cuvier also, in one of the creepiest moments of the autopsy report, writes about her labia. One of the mysteries of the Hottentot women had to do with their genitalia. They were thought to have very elongated and extended labia. Nobody knows now whether this was because of the habit of decorating the labia, or because of a quote unquote racial characteristic. In any event, it did seem to Cuvier that Saartjie Baartman's labia were elongated. And in a certain moment in the autopsy report he describes taking her labia and pulling them to measure their length. He pulls them up and around and says, "They form the shape of a heart." Now we can assume the great scientist was not talking about the muscle that pumps blood here but rather about the two-dimensional valentine. So there are all these odd moments in the autopsy report where I would guess Parks thought, "Hmm." But no, they didn't really fall in love, as far as history knows.

JK: Thank you very much. Bob, you mentioned that the later plays, which might be described as more social realist or Brechtian, were less "reverberant" for you. And Alisa talked about not liking the narrative about Parks progressing to good, healthy commercial plays. Could we have just a few more words on this transition from earlier to later works from both of you?

AS: I don't have anything against these recent plays. I like them, but I don't think it's necessarily a progress narrative. That's what concerns me. And who knows what she's going to do next? If we stick with the Ibsen teleology, then nobody knows what to say about the late Ibsen plays which are so interesting and exciting. Some of us love *Peer Gynt*, as well. So it's not that I think she shouldn't be allowed to write more narrative plays, more accessible plays, or that I don't find them appealing in their way. What I'm talking about is the idea that this is the line of progress and now she's finally coming into her own and finally doing what playwrights are supposed to do. That's the trajectory that I want to intervene in. Though I do find the earlier plays more resonant.

RB: Well I agree with you. I find them more resonant too. Perhaps because they're more difficult to understand and therefore you keep coming back to them, whereas the later plays are more easily accessible and there doesn't seem to be much left after you've absorbed it and digested it. That's why I said they were not as reverberant. But this is a normal pattern of American artistic creative development—to start in the avant-garde and then eventually to be captured by the Disney Corporation. I mean the same thing happened to Julie Taymor. It happens to everyone but Richard Foreman, so it's a normal American development.

AS: I'd actually like to add a question to this. I wonder if we might think for a moment about the material conditions in which Suzan-Lori's work first came to our attention, at BACA Downtown. Certainly her tremendous talent and craft and skill had everything to do with it, but if she were to come on the scene now, where would her plays get done? Do we have the kind of space right now where an unknown playwright could get a spectacular production by a great director like Liz Diamond in a handsome, well-appointed production with fine actors, that would get reviewed by everyone? The conditions have really changed, and one likes to think that the great talents will rise and be found anyway but I wonder: are there writers around right now that might be breaking new ground that we don't know about?

Question from the audience about the purpose of inserting a reading of the Baron Docteur's autopsy during intermission of Venus.

SMG: I would say it has a lot to do with some of the ideas that Professor Robinson talked about, the abyss. The play is cleaved in two like the buttocks and in the middle is a gap or a hole. There are moments in Parks's plays that she calls the nadir—the terrible, bad, bad, bad stuff—and I think this is one of those really painful things. She puts it in the intermission because, I think, she sees it as a kind of gap imagistically. I think the effect she wants is sort of hearing something going on and people wandering back and forth, and the character of the Baron Docteur continually says, "Please gentlemen go. Take your rest. Take your rest." I think you're meant to hear terrifying snippets of this secret, now-buried document, this autopsy report, and it's put in a place where it's almost not meant to be heard or seen.

★★★

MR: In the intermission you are asked to choose whether you are going to listen to it or not. You can or you can't.

Question from the audience about the repatriation of Baartman's remains.

SMG: What was left after Cuvier's maceration, as the French call it, was a plaster cast of her body and the jar of her genitalia. I believe that was all that was left. So only those remains were repatriated and buried. I'm sure that's not typical. I'm sure the entire body is usually buried. But just the symbolic return of those remains was extremely important to the Khosian people. It took the French four years to agree to return them.

JK: I'd like to add that my colleague Claudia Orenstein told me earlier that there was a production of *Venus* done in South Africa on the occasion of the repatriation of Baartman's remains. I found that extremely interesting in light of the fact that some people find this play troubling because it's not a straightforward victim play which presents her as a pure and noble heroine.

SMG: It was actually a fundraising campaign, that production, and it was coupled with a kind of special offer where people could go on a tour of South Africa in conjunction with the play if they donated a certain amount of money. It was a whole sort of interdisciplinary program to raise funds to bring the remains of Saartjie Baartman back.

Question from the audience about whether anyone on the panel had read Parks's recently published novel and, if so, what their views of it were.

SMG: I've read it. I think the novel is really joyful. I think it's more joyful than anything she's written to date. It feels confident to me. It was written, or completed rather, after she received the Pulitzer Prize. Whatever one thinks of the Pulitzer Prize, it is a kind of validation of one's talent. She also had received a MacArthur grant by that time. She had gotten engaged, married, and moved to Los Angeles and became the head of the CalArts playwriting program. I think the book really exudes confidence and joy. I also think it's significant that it's set in west Texas where she spent many years as a young person. She never used to talk about living there and now she has really recast herself as a southern woman writer.

Question from the audience requesting clarification of the Brecht quote "theaters everything down."

MR: I'm not going to suppose I know exactly what Brecht meant by that, but I think the demands of theatrical production, the commercial pressures on theatrical production, the requirements of character construction and narrative development and basic intelligibility, all simplify or oversimplify the vast, sprawling, and messy experience that some writers try to capture. They reduce what is a multi-dimensional world to one of two or three dimensions that can be staged. And Brecht, who was always a practical man of the theater, I think recognized that when you stage something you also betray it in some way, you compromise.

A: So you're saying that that applies to Suzan-Lori Parks? Or that it doesn't?

MR: I think in some of her works she's staging that very problem. I don't think she's found an answer to it any more than Brecht did.

Question from the audience about Parks's so-called "compromise" with respect to the avant-gardism of her earlier plays.

JK: This is opening up maybe too big a can of worms at a point where this session needs to be wrapping up, but I wonder if this issue doesn't need to be talked about briefly in terms of race. At least since the Harlem Renaissance, going back to W.E.B. Dubois and Alain Locke and before, there's been a discussion about whether literary experimentation was permissible in the African-American community. Throughout the 20th century there were always many voices claiming that African-American writers had an obligation to write plays that were "uplifting." Now, this is a pressure that not all of us share. All of us on this panel are white. And so I wonder if this fact doesn't just need to be stated and brought into our discussion.

RB: I think that's a good point. There's a tradition of privileged white avant-garde writers and avant-garde thinkers, among which I count myself, to remain on the fringe and, you know, piss into the tent instead of pissing out of it (to use Lyndon Johnson's tasteful phrase). For at least two hundred years now, artists have been trying to invent a new vision through creative dissent against what has gone before. That means continual revision, continual advance, continual rethinking, as it were, on an aesthetic level, which is quite different from the natural desire to become part of American life, to become assimilated into American society, to enjoy American prosperity with all its advantages and opportunities. Those are two different things. To ask anybody, black or white, to assume the hair shirt that goes with being an avant-garde artist, I think is presumptuous. However, we have to maintain that presumption or else the arts will never move forward.

20

REMARKS ON PARKS II

A Hunter College Symposium on the Work of Suzan-Lori Parks

Jonathan Kalb, moderator

April 30, 2004

[The following, which was originally published in HotReview.org, Hunter online review, is an edited transcript of a symposium held at Hunter College on April 30, 2004, organized and moderated by Jonathan Kalb. This second of two panels featured presentations by Richard Foreman, Liz Diamond, Leah C. Gardiner, and Bill Walters, plus a discussion period with the audience. It was preceded by a critics-and-scholars panel.]

Jonathan Kalb: Thank you for coming back. This is our second panel on Suzan-Lori Parks and we have with us this time a distinguished group of directors who have wrestled with all problems, challenges, and joys of doing Suzan-Lori Parks's work. I'm going to introduce them in the order in which I've asked them to speak and then, as in the earlier panel, we'll open it up to a more general discussion.

Richard Foreman has received a MacArthur Fellowship and been awarded the PEN Master Dramatist Award, plus nine Obies and many other prizes. He has designed and directed over seventy-five productions at major theaters around the world, including over forty of his own plays. I assume most of you have visited his Ontological-Hysteric Theater down in St. Marks Church. Six collections of his plays have been published, as well as many articles and a number of books in different countries discussing his work. Richard directed and designed the world premiere of Suzan-Lori Parks's *Venus* at Yale Rep and the New York Shakespeare Festival/Public Theater in 1996.

Liz Diamond is resident director at Yale Repertory Theatre and Chair of the Directing Department at the Yale School of Drama. Her productions at Yale include *Fighting Words* and *Rice Boy*, both by the Canadian playwright Sunil Kuruvilla, Brecht's *St. Joan of the Stockyards*, and Seamus Heaney's *The Cure at Troy*. Other productions of hers include Racine's *Phaedra* at American

Repertory Theater, Euripides's *The Trojan Women* at Oregon Shakespeare Festival, and *Of Mice and Men* at Arena Stage. Next season she will direct Strindberg's *Miss Julie* at Yale Rep and the world premiere of Octavio Solis's *Gibraltar* at Oregon Shakespeare Festival. Liz began collaborating with Suzan-Lori Parks in 1988 when Parks invited her to direct *Imperceptible Mutabilities in the Third Kingdom* in a workshop production at BACA Downtown in Brooklyn. She directed the world premiere in BACA's 1989 Fringe Festival and the show won three 1990 Obie Awards, for playwrighting, direction, and for Pamela Tyson's performance. In 1991, Liz directed *Greeks*, which was Part Four of *Imperceptible Mutabilities*, at Manhattan Theater Club's Downtown/ Uptown Festival, and she directed the world premiere of Parks's *Betting on the Dust Commander* at the Working Theater in New York. In 1992 she directed the west-coast premiere of *Imperceptible Mutabilities* at New City Theater in Seattle and *The Death of the Last Black Man in the Whole Entire World* at Yale Rep. In 1993 she worked with Parks on *The America Play*, conducting readings at New Dramatists and a workshop production at the Dallas Theater Center. In 1994 she directed the world premiere of *The America Play* at Yale Rep and The Public Theater in New York. Gail Grate as Lucy and Michael Potts as Brazil received Obie Awards for their performances in that show. You can see that Liz has been very involved in Suzan-Lori Parks's work.

Leah C. Gardiner's New York directing credits include *Kent, CT* at the Zipper Theater, *The Mother of Modern Censorship*, and *Immigrating Interludes* at Tiny Mythic Theater for Lincoln Center's Director's Lab. Her regional directing includes *A Streetcar Named Desire* at The Pillsbury House in Minneapolis, which was honored by the *Minneapolis Star Tribune* as one of the top ten productions of the season. She directed *Spunk* at the Oddfellows Playhouse in Middletown, CT, and, most recently, the Philadelphia premiere of Suzan-Lori Parks's *Topdog/Underdog* at the Philadelphia Theater Company. This premiere is what she'll be talking about today. Leah assisted George C. Wolfe on the New York premiere of *Topdog/ Underdog* and the Broadway production of *On the Town*. She has served as Director in Residence at the Public Theater and was an individual artist participant in the 2001 TCG Conference. She served as Resident Director for New Dramatists in 2002–03 and was a participant in the artistic leadership for The Women's Project and Productions. She's a graduate of the University of Pennsylvania and the Yale School of Drama. And I might add that she was one of Liz Diamond's students.

Bill Walters teaches acting and directing in the Theatre Department at Hunter College. Bill previously taught at Yale, Tulane University, and the University of Wisconsin-Milwaukee. His work as a director and choreographer has been seen throughout the United States and abroad, most recently in China. Bill is the director of the Hunter Theater Department's current production of Parks's *Venus*, and he'll be talking to us about that.

Richard Foreman: It's been a long time since I worked on *Venus*. I was originally interested in Suzan's work, I don't how many years ago it was, but at a time when

I had stopped going to very much theater. Up to the time I was forty I went to see everything. But then I couldn't take it anymore. So I was familiar with Suzan-Lori's work by reputation, and they sent me the script of *Venus* and as usual, I looked through it very casually. I thought: "This looks interesting because it says 'Venus' and there's a line of dialogue and then, with nothing else in between, 'Venus,' and dialogue, 'Venus,' and dialogue, then just 'Venus' and nothing." I thought that the texture, which is basically what I respond to first in all writing, seemed provocative and difficult and interesting. So I said, "Yeah, I'll do the play." Then I thought, "God, how do you do something like this?" So I went to the library and saw Liz's production on tape of *The America Play*, which I liked. I thought it was very interesting. Then, like I always do, without paying too much careful attention to the play, I tried to get a global feeling of what is going on.

Now, the first thing that always happens with me is I make a set. The story of *Venus* seemed sort of antiquey. I looked through a lot of books. I found a line drawing, an etching, in a book I had of the history of magic shows in the West, and there was something there from the 18th century, sort of a cage thing. Apparently somebody was using secret microphones to make voices come into that cage, but the cage and the people leaning into the set seemed related to the way that I imagined this play when I read it very casually. So I designed a set and made a model, as I always do, and went to my first meeting with George C. Wolfe… well, my second meeting… and made my first mistake. I made a number of mistakes doing this show. George said to me, "There's a lot of green in that set. You can do what you want but my experience has been that green sets never work" [*laughter*]. I thought, "I sorta like it but I don't know—I get to do exactly what I want in my own theater but if George doesn't like green, okay." So it wasn't green. That was a minor change that I didn't think was too serious.

Now, it appeared self-evident that George had been working with Suzan-Lori for a number of years in crafting this play. It seems to me that this was perhaps the transitional play when, as people have said today, Suzan-Lori was changing from being this wild, experimental artist to being, for better or for worse, a more commercially acceptable artist. It's my understanding that *Venus* was the transitional play because George was having her rewrite it to make the play more palatable as a normal evening in the theater for normal Public Theater audiences. As a result—and I didn't object to this—George thought there should be a lot of cuts. And I didn't disagree. Now, George was not there. I mean, George came to like two rehearsals, but he asked for cuts. And I felt, "Well, I'm doing this play for them." It was one of those situations when whenever we were talking together, we were sort of in league against George, who was the "commercial" producer. And then, when he would come around, we would sort of accept many of his ideas. Suzan-Lori was of course friendly towards George, having worked with him for two years, but I noticed that he was cutting a lot of the more abstract material. Now whether that's a mistake or not a mistake, I'm not really prepared to say because yes, it was difficult to make that material work, especially in the way I had decided to do the production.

To me art is nerve, a question of having the courage to do what you want to do. And I must admit: that's why I don't particularly like working with living playwrights. (Or even smart producers, and George is certainly smart.) I've worked twice in my life with living playwrights who were there at rehearsal, with Arthur Kopit and Suzan-Lori Parks. And I liked them both and we got along swell, but I must admit there's a built-in inhibition. When I'm doing my own play and we're rehearsing, I can say, "Oh my God, is that a stupid line. How are we gonna deal with this stupid thing?" Now I would never say that to another writer. I mean, Suzan-Lori might actually enjoy me saying that. (I don't know if Arthur would?) Nevertheless, there's this built-in hesitation and I think it influenced my production somewhat in a bad way.

When I read the text originally with this stop-and-go kind of structure, I thought somehow it needed lights on, lights off, click, click, adjustment, lights on, lights off, to reflect the very abstract nature of the play. I think I softened my initial ideas dealing with that. So when George was cutting the more abstract parts in my production, he was probably right in terms of what he saw in the rehearsal studio. By the way, he wasn't a dictator. It wasn't insistence. He just said, "I really have problems with this, this, that, that." And I was basically a hired gun, out to please without sacrificing my vision too much. I mean, there was nothing but my stuff on stage. It was still my production. I certainly can't deny that.

The only thing about the production, well there are two things about the production that I was pissed off about. This play imagines a world of English Colonial culture—represented by the Doctor character, then re-reflected in scenes in which the "freaks" put on little commentary "playlets" in the theatrical style of the time. For me those scenes were a big challenge. You have two worlds—how do they mesh without seeming too obvious in their message? When we were still in New Haven—I thought we could suggest the garbage (I use the word "garbage" in quotes) out of which the English society believed it was "extracting" the "freaks" they were putting on display in the side show by putting a lot of crumpled up newspaper all over the stage floor. Because the English world of the time was also a world of "garbage." And when George and Rosemary Tischler (who was George's assistant at the time—I think it was really her idea that I do the play) saw the play remounted in New York, with all this crumpled up newspaper on the floor—they came to me and said, "Well, Richard, the string, I know all that string in front of the stage, I know that's your thing. But the dirty newspaper all over the stage, I mean—why, Richard? Why?" I explained, but they weren't satisfied. Maybe they thought it didn't go with the Public Theater's neat image. So we got rid of that crumpled up newspaper. I think it was an aesthetic mistake but not a major one. The more interesting issue involved the very good actor playing the doctor. Adina, who played the Venus Hottentot, was somebody who read for us and in five minutes we all thought, "That's her, that's it, she's great." And she was. Peter Francis James is another fine actor and he read for something else and we really liked him, and Suzan-Lori and I both thought—"You know, couldn't he play the English Doctor?"

Well, he was black, but he was pale black, so we thought, what does it mean if we cast a black man as the doctor? We talked to George about it and said, "He's the only actor we've seen who can really cut it in this part." So he played the doctor.

Now, I rehearsed the play for, I think, six weeks. And I had Peter Francis James playing the doctor as a sort of bumbling, shy guy, who was falling over things. There were a lot of ladders on the set. He would trip on ladders. He had these little glasses, and was crumpling paper nervously in his fists. After the New Haven opening, George and Rosemary came to me and said, "Richard, why are you doing that to Peter? He's such a good actor and you're making him into this wormy little schlep." So my big mistake was bowing to their wishes, and changing Peter's performance. In New York Peter Francis James played it—a very good performance—more as a distinguished English gentleman of that period who was a serious man of medicine, a little disturbed by his feelings for the Hottentot Venus but nevertheless a man of culture and determination. In my original version, I identified him with myself perhaps, this bumbling intellectual who does these strange things. I think my original version served the play and its strangeness much better. I thought there were many fine things about the production but, as often happens in the theater, you compromise and you negotiate. If I had to do it again today I would try to have the courage to make it stranger than it was. Maybe people thought it was strange, but I think it should have been even stranger. That's really all I can say.

Liz Diamond: It's an honor to be here among these wonderful colleagues and to talk about a writer who remains my favorite living writer. Working on Suzan-Lori Parks's plays, as I look back on it, was really the great theater training of my life. We came up together. I'm ten years older than Suzan-Lori, but I was a classic late bloomer who backed into admitting that I really wanted to make theater and that I might have something worth other people paying a few bucks to see. It took me a long time to own my voice as an artist, and I was only beginning to when I met Suzan-Lori in 1988.

I remember reading a wonderful conversation that was published in the *Village Voice* between Richard Foreman and Elizabeth LeCompte. They were arguing back and forth about theater and at one point he said, "You know, when I go to the theater, I like it when it's like going to the gym. I want to go to the gym, the gym of art." I love that phrase because I think that working with Suzan-Lori was for me an eight-year gym for art. I learned so much about what theatricality is, what theatrical poetry is, about what it means to embody poetry in three and four dimensions, in space and time, about texture, the texture of language and how that becomes visible and audible on stage in an actor's body. These were really joyous years of shared learning and discovery for both of us. So I thought I might talk about some of what I learned working with Suzan-Lori.

I think the first thing I learned with Suzan-Lori, was how to read a play, which I kinda thought I already knew how to do. Perhaps I did, but my first encounter with her work was in a sense my first encounter with everything I didn't know about how to read a play. In 1988, Mac Wellman had set up a workshop for new experimental writing at BACA Downtown at the urging of the amazing and wonderful Greta Gunderson, BACA's artistic director. BACA Downtown was this crazy art gallery/performance space near the Fulton Mall and I was working there as a director. Suzan-Lori joined Mac's new work project. She was twenty-five. Mac read her play *Imperceptible Mutabilities in the Third Kingdom*, gave it to Greta, and said, "You have to do this. This has to be done." And they talked about who should do it, and it was my good fortune that they thought I might be a good match.

I read the play and I remember not knowing how to read it, not really knowing what was going on. Lines like: "How dja get through it? Mm not through it. Yer leg. Thuh guard. Lose weight. Hhh. What should I do Chona should I jump should I jump or what?" What was up? Only when we got together and Suzan-Lori read it out loud in my kitchen did I see that I needed to just get very simple. Simply say, "Okay, who's talking? Get through what? Where's the leg? What kind of guard?" Now you've probably learned in the course of this afternoon that one of the great, pleasurable features of Suzan-Lori's writing is that it's richly layered and loaded, fraught with word plays and puns and jokes in which one word starts to ricochet and bounce around and mean much more than it does on what you might call the dog shit level of reality. But I found that by starting there I could begin to direct her work. By saying, okay, here's a kid who is maybe half way out the window, has her leg stuck in the window guard, has a problem, and her sister is talking her back down from the jump with eggs, food, some nourishment. By beginning there we began to create something concrete. Making the abstract concrete is so much the problem of putting on theater, then allowing it to become abstract again in the imagination of the audience as they listen and hear this resonant language.

Early on, Suzan-Lori talked about how to cast the play and, as Alisa described, you've got figures that move from one part of *Imperceptible Mutabilities* to another. We had five actors and we knew we wanted a white guy to play the Naturalist and decided to cast him as Duffy in *Greeks* later on. He plays several roles in the play which are conventionally white characters, and then in the last play he appears again, as the last son of the Smith family, this African-American military family. Interestingly, this didn't cause any consternation at BACA Downtown, but it caused a near riot at Manhattan Theater Club when we did it the next year. The audience was deeply troubled at Manhattan Theater Club that Suzan-Lori had depicted a black family's only son—and the last child in the line—as a white person. They felt fooled with, played with. They felt troubled. They also felt, I think, obstructed in their understanding: "What do you mean? What does this mean?" They were vaguely threatened by it and didn't know what to do with it. All of which were understandable reactions. I don't think Suzan-Lori and I made it any easier with our response to their consternation, which was to say, "We just felt like it." We could have been more helpful. At one point when I talked to her about it she said something very interesting, which I found moving at the time and still do. She said she felt that it made sense because he was the "dream child" of this family—a statement that she declined to make at Manhattan Theater Club because she had no confidence that they would understand this. When I asked her what she meant she said: a black family would dream of having a child that they wouldn't have to fear for, and you don't have to fear for a white boy. He'll be okay. The thought that you might have a child that you wouldn't have to protect was critical in her exploration of this play. In some ways the dream comes true, the assimilationist dream of that play comes true in the end, which she sees as a kind of tragicomic fact.

Suzan-Lori was clear from the start that she wanted to write against the grain of mainstream American theater. She talked with great enthusiasm about wanting to fight the "belch factor" in the theater. She wanted to write plays that would be chewy and a little bit hard to digest, that wouldn't go down easy. She was genuinely interested in that. And I loved partnering her in that project. At the same time, neither of us saw these plays as opaque, as perhaps some did at the time. And we worked hard together to make them clear on their own dramatic and poetic terms. For example, *Imperceptible Mutabilities in the Third Kingdom*, at first was a four-part play—with four equal parts. One of the parts plainly did not belong. I told her it felt like a one-act; its own play. She agreed and replaced it with a poem, called "Third Kingdom" which she split in two and put as a kind of thematic environment around the three larger plays. Once she did this, the whole play worked. This poem provided, if you will, a kind of watery bed, a poetic bed, on top of which the rest of the play floated. The phrase "Third Kingdom" refers to that watery limbo between Africa and America and the poem was an elegy in which slaves on a slave ship described their dreams and fretted about where they were going and where they had come from and how deep the water was and what was swimming there under the surface of the sea. So we put the show in a container that was sort of oceanic.

We didn't have a lot of money. With *Imperceptible Mutabilities*, SLP put in $2000, I put in $2000, and BACA Downtown provided the space. Everybody worked for free, and the actors donated their performances. The man who created the photographs, Phil Perkins, did it all for free. That's how it happened. We painted the floor together one night—this dark, dark, dark blue-black. We created a sort of memorial arch under which Sergeant Smith stood in the last piece. We brought kitchen chairs for the Smiths in *Greeks* and a friend of ours built a giant mechanical cockroach that rolled around and took pictures. When we worked on our next big project, which was *The Death of the Last Black Man in the Whole Entire World*, everything changed because we suddenly had a budget. We had a longer run. We were casting with a casting director and it was a whole new world. It was an extremely hospitable world that opened up to us then. Yale Repertory Theatre invited Suzan-Lori to do *The Death of the Last Black Man*, and she invited me to direct it. And there we got to work with the set designer Ricardo Hernandez.

The Death of the Last Black Man is this gorgeous requiem for the last black man in the whole entire world. And unlike *Imperceptible Mutabilities*, which underwent a pretty massive change during our work together, *Black Man* was virtually complete when I got it. It was this masterpiece of theatrical theater. You have a man named Black Man with Watermelon and his wife, Black Woman with Fried Drumstick, and all these other figures: Yes and Greens Black Eyed Peas Cornbread, And Bigger and Bigger and Bigger, Before Columbus. When we first talked about the play I said, "Gee, uh, what, who are these people?" And she said, "All I can say is, all of them but Black Woman with Fried Drumstick are dead, but some are deader than others." And that was my first clue as to what might be going on in the play—which tells an extraordinary tale in which Black Woman sits on her porch and her husband's body and spirit come flying back to her. He lands on the front porch with the electrocution cap still on his head, having just been fried in the town square, and is distressed because he'd like to die. His body is dead. He wants to be laid to rest but he can't be, and the problem in the play is when and how will Black Man will lie down? When will he be allowed to cross the river and be laid to rest? He won't, it seems, until Black Woman accepts his story, and writes it down—writes it down and hides it under a rock, which is a refrain that's repeated over and over again by the least enfranchised figure in the play, Yes and Greens Black Eyed Peas Cornbread, an illiterate slave girl. This injunction is repeated across the play: "You must write it down. You must write it down and hide it under a rock." It's repeated until Black Woman finally hears it, and she doesn't hear it for pages and pages, until she's witnessed enough versions of Black Man's death that she can no longer deny his story. Then she promises to write it down. And he can lie down and at the end of the play he's laid to rest.

We staged it as, in a sense, a high mass. Suzan-Lori is Roman Catholic. I remember she said to me, "Whatever it is, it isn't Baptist and I don't want it to be Baptist. Don't give me the eruptions of song and gestures." She said, "It's cooler than that." And she said, "I promise you, the cast is gonna wanna go there. Don't go there." And it was very interesting because the cast did want to go there. Many of them were young African-American actors from black Baptist backgrounds, and they were terribly resistant to this cool, cool tone that Suzan-Lori wanted in the play. They finally embraced it because I think they saw what she was after. The end of the play is solemn, not ecstatic.

The America Play was a huge project for both of us and it was the one that took us to the Public Theater from Yale Rep. It was a wild ride and it involved huge debates about how to make it possible for the audience to enter the world of this play. I remember vividly, late-night sessions of notes with George Wolfe in which he'd say, "Marge has got to understand this." The first time he said this, I remember looking at Suzan-Lori and she looking at me—saying, "Who's Marge?"—before we realized that Marge was a kind of quintessential subscriber that he wanted to have access to this world. I understood that, and I wanted Marge to go to this gym. But I didn't want it not to be a gym. I wanted her to embrace going to the gym. This was hard.

We had huge issues relating to the design of *The America Play*. At Yale Rep, Ricardo Hernandez designed a beautiful container for this show, which takes place in "The Great Hole of History": what a suggestive and beautiful phrase from which to imagine a set! But the play also seems to take place in a hall of wonders. And so Ricardo created a conflation of those two images, a sort of mausoleum type space with white Formica walls reaching up to the ceiling, very rectilinear, very sterile, shiny black coal on the floor. At the Public it just became the black hole. We started chucking the black coal at the wall, obscuring what we had created at Yale and going for the one metaphor rather than the two or three or four. I continue to debate with myself as to which world I prefer. I loved the strangeness of the former, but I found the latter space really haunting and dark and more psychologically disturbing.

Regarding some things that were said earlier about *Venus* and Suzan-Lori: when we were talking about *Venus* as she was working on it, one of the things I remember exciting me about the play was its relationship to her own journey as an artist. In *Venus* Suzan-Lori explored that scary moment when an artist achieves, if you will, the apogee of her fame and celebrity, the moment when she suddenly moves from being a subject to an object. In a grotesque way, the objectification of the Venus occurs at the very moment she is at the height of her fame in London. This moment, when everybody knows her name, begins the tragedy of her disintegration. I want to say that, despite Disney and other would-be destroyers and dissectors of Suzan-Lori's body of work and soul, I'm not too worried about her. I don't think she's going to suffer the same fate as Saartjie Baartman. I think she's tougher than that. I also think she's more conscious than Saartjie had the fortune to be. She's used her privilege, her fabulous education, and her amazing poetic gift to undertake an ongoing exploration of who she is. And it's continuing in the novel, obviously. I don't think she apologizes for the more commercial work she's done, and I don't know what she's going to do next. I want to think that something completely astonishing is going to come out of this genuine happiness in her life, a sense of place, a sense of recognition that she's won from the world. I hope it does.

Leah Gardiner: Today, I am interested in providing you a visual representation of how I chose to direct *Topdog/Underdog*. I have with me slides of various aspects of the show in hopes of showing you how I, as a director, took Suzan-Lori's language to inform my approach to the play. I was interested in the theatrics of the piece. This defined a clear sensibility for the piece. As you can see from the first slide, Hunter's own Louisa Thompson, our set designer, created a proscenium within the proscenium. It was a clever way of enhancing the performance within a performance—very much present in Suzan-Lori's language.

In this next slide, Seth Gilliam, who played Lincoln, performed sitting in a chair, and there was an exaggeration of his character projected on the back wall. For me, this represented the idea that, here we are with a black man who is attempting in many ways to make himself larger than life and the only way in which, in our society, he can do so is by making a whole lot of money or by pretending. In this scene here, he's pretending.

Moving on to clothes: the costume designer, Andre Harrington, decided to use the layering effect by creating different odd costume pieces. If you look at the Lincoln character by the street playing three-card monte, he has cuffs around his wrists which have been cut off from a shirt, and he wore a dicky over that in place of a jacket. The cuffs for us represented shackles, historical shackles that slaves wore. For me they represent not just that but also the huge number of incarcerated black men in the United States today, whom Lincoln and Booth could very well join at any given point in their lives. So once again, this was taking a naturalistic thought and blowing it up in an attempt to react to Suzan-Lori's sensibility.

Then there was the sound. The final thing that, for me, set each section of the play very much had to do with history, and with different forms of the black community. I have a song that we played at the very beginning of the show, that our composer made and our sound designer overlaid with historical voices— from slave narratives of women all the way through to the voices of Shirley Chisolm and Angela Davis. We chose women particularly in honor of Suzan-Lori. There were a few men, but we kept them in the background. We wanted that effect: seeing these two black men on the stage while hearing the voices of these black women. So here's the song [*plays tape*], and just imagine hearing this over the sound of slave ships, old historical voices of women, just a very rich mixture that turned into a much thicker, more contemporary sound and set the tone for the production.

Finally, I want to read my director's statement, which will give you an idea of what Suzan-Lori means to me and what this production meant to me: "Everything old is made new again. Fashions return but with a different twist. Musical phraseologies which seem new emerge from the history bank of sound. Slang words from last week live in our culture for years. How often are we reminded that the old really isn't old, and that the new is not always new? As in anything rooted in the past, Suzan-Lori Parks takes her interpretation of what was and assigns a new voice to it. In *Topdog/Underdog*, Lincoln and Booth are not the historical characters as we know them. They are instead two modern-day brothers who after several years of separation come back together to revisit their past and redefine their present. Their history dictates their future, making that which appears old appear new. Like a jazz riff, *Topdog/Underdog* flows like a con game both inside and outside our consciousness. We swim in the river of the blues with a lot of stops and starts along the way. Soul music allows us to go deeper into their humorous sensibilities. Hip-hop guides our understanding of what these men endure, living in a confined space placed against the backdrop of urban America. We are presented with the culture of black life, musical traditions influencing the presence, the language, the sound and the rhythms of truth. We are participants, not merely spectators, in a historical-theatrical storybook, one which unfolds delicately but powerfully before our eyes. As with any epic drama, *Topdog* asks us to face the successes and the failures of our society. In its specifics, it presents boldly drawn characters who represent the beauty and poetry of our country. We are asked to celebrate life in its purest form through the eyes of these two brothers, peeling away at a historical backdrop made anew."

I'll stop for the sake of time, but I did have some ideas about the actors and the language. One person said during one of our talk-backs in Philadelphia: "There's no hip-hop in this play!" And I had to stop and think, but there's a beautiful exchange between the brothers when they are shooting the dozens—a term in the black community which plays on language: Lincoln says, "Sure, sure yer sure?" And the exchange is: "Sure yer sure. Ya sure?" Booth says, "I'm sure." "Ya sure? Sure yer sure?" And there's the hip-hop, that rhythm—da duh, da duh da duh, da duh, da duh da duh da duh—which has its origins in bebop. That musical combination alone, in my opinion, takes this play out of naturalism and moves it into much more of what Suzan-Lori really represents, that is a non-linear, a more theatrical approach to making plays.

Bill Walters: Well, I'm going to be very brief because, when Jonathan and I were first talking about this conference being organized around the production, I was very excited but I actually asked if I could be excused from appearing on the panel and just let the work downstairs speak for itself. As the time for the conference approached, though, I felt like I didn't want to seem like I was hiding and should at least make myself available for some questions. I'll say a couple of things about the experience I've had in working on *Venus* and then after that, let the work speak for itself.

I found very interesting what Professor Brustein was saying earlier this afternoon, that there has been a shift in the type of directors who have undertaken Suzan-Lori Parks's plays. This is a theme we've heard all day, but he made the point that so-called avant-garde directors were interested in her earlier works and more mainstream directors have been more interested in her later works. I would enjoy situating myself in the former group. I enjoy working with original texts, my own texts, adaptations, but in the university setting where you usually pick a preexisting play, I like picking plays that I can really push against and pull at and tug and stretch really to their breaking point and sometimes beyond—big plays, Shakespeare and other texts that can stand up to that kind of pressure, or else plays that are open-ended enough to leave you enough room to play. The last play I did with a group of students was *Dr. Faustus Lights the Lights* by Gertrude Stein which I think has more in common with Suzan-Lori Parks's earlier plays than with her later ones, since we're following that theme.

Venus has been said to be a kind of middle-ground, transitional play. The experience I found in working on it—and I knew this was going to happen, going into it—was that I actually had a lot less to do than I usually do as a director. In many ways she had already done the work that I usually try to do, which is push and pull at something until it's all twisted up and bent around. That's one of the reasons I enjoy reading her works, and going to watch her works. I definitely feel a sort of kinship with her artistically. So in looking at *Venus* and starting to work on it I really felt more than ever that my job as a director was to simply get out of the way and help the thing stand on its own legs, which are very strong I think. I don't find it as open-ended as a lot of her earlier works, and I would actually enjoy working on some of her earlier works for that reason. I felt like I was there mostly to help it stand on its own.

With that said, I'm already thinking—and we opened only three days ago—of all the things I wish that I had done and what I would do next time. Maybe I didn't let it be as crazy as it could have been either. Saying that I tried to simplify it is not to say there wasn't a lot of work to be done. I think it's actually a pretty difficult text to approach. Luckily, I felt a connection to it, and the main job was working with the design team to come up with a physical space in which this could live and its themes could resonate and its structure could take shape physically. Also, there was the work with the actors. Actors, especially younger actors, generally tend to try to make any kind of text feel natural, feel realistic. So one of my jobs as a director was to keep them away from that—let them flirt with it so it could seem like that if they needed it to but then move away. So there was quite a lot of work to be done. But I think, largely, it was kind of my job to stay out of the way.

One of the things that really draws me to all of Parks's work is the connection she insists on between form and content, which a number of people have mentioned today. She talks about how in her work the container, the vessel, shapes what is being put in it and vice versa, what she's writing about dictates the form that it takes. That's part of what I'm speaking about as a director. I usually like to mess with the structure a little bit, and in her work she has already done that, and I find that quite lovely and artistically exciting. One of the difficult things in *Venus* in particular is the way she has twisted it around and looped it back on itself. I think that can frustrate or infuriate some viewers because, as has already been said, it doesn't come out as a victim play. And it doesn't necessarily come out as a straightforward issue play. We had some really lovely discussions with the cast right from the beginning. Especially since I was working with students, I really felt like I had to address the topics and the themes of the play with them, and of course, as you can imagine, we never reached any kind of consensus whatsoever. And that's exactly the point of the work, as Suzan-Lori Parks says. She intends to raise questions and questions and more questions, but she refuses to provide pat answers. I have found it very rewarding to be walking down the halls at Hunter over the last couple of months and hear the various discussions coming out of the doors from various different classes discussing this. Several people have asked me over the course of this semester why I chose this play. And did I really feel like I had a right to choose this play? I think I'll leave that to the judgment of others, but I've had a wonderful time working on it and I think that in an educational setting particularly, it's been wonderful and rewarding. I definitely thank Jonathan for letting us follow through with the decision to do a difficult piece like this.

Questions and Discussion

JK: I would like to use Parks herself as my way into the discussion phase of this panel and quote one of her essays, called "Tradition and the Individual Talent." She writes in this essay: "Someone once told me, '*Venus* isn't really a Suzan-Lori Parks play.' To which I responded: 'There isn't any such thing as a Suzan-Lori Parks play.' What I mean is this. I don't discount the plays I've written but I do realize I am growing and changing as I grow. Once Miss X starts thinking that she can/should/must only write Xian literature and anything that is not clearly Xian is a betrayal of the great Xian tradition… once Miss X buys into the existence of an Xian style of writing and once that purchase keeps her simply and stupidly repeating her last best hit, then Miss X gets really stinky." Parks is talking here about getting out of the way. She's describing herself as a moving target, a river of spirit that we and part of her have to get out of the way of. So in light of that, I'd like to put this as a question to the director's panel. Is there any such thing as a Suzan-Lori Parks play? Can we take this quote at face value? We've been talking a lot today about early plays versus late plays, but Leah challenged Robert Brustein's statement about that and said that there really are things that thread through all the works that are very important, characteristic explorations of Suzan-Lori Parks. Leah sees them in *Topdog*. So is there a Suzan-Lori Parks play?

RF: I only know one Suzan-Lori Parks play well, so I'm not the person to ask. But I'm interested in this issue of "getting out of the way," because even though some people say my theater is totally solipsistic and I'm writing from a very personal base (I don't think so), I think the task of all writers, all artists, is to get out of the way. This is an issue that is interestingly revealed by Suzan-Lori. An awful lot of stuff can come through when you get out of the way. To me, art is interesting when you get out of the way and conflicting contradictory forces are what come through. They're not necessarily you, but they're contradictory forces. It is not, however, interesting to me to get out of the way as a writer or a designer, in such a way that you "go with the flow" of the surrounding cultural milieu. People have spoken today about development of a play in terms of the conflicting commercial or experimental worlds. To me, in the commercial world one hooks into the flow of the engine of the culture that is going along, chugging along in a certain direction; certain things are happening in the culture. But letting the work come to life by letting all the contradictions come through—this is not "going with the flow." It's allowing yourself to be upended by all kinds of things, like the strange way that Venus's dialogue appears on the pages of the text, things like that. And it's my own continual battle for art and against normal theater. I would make a comparison between Suzan-Lori, the experimental Suzan-Lori, and the way I did *Dr. Faustus* too. The other person who's more like Suzan-Lori than people realize is Kathy Acker, who mostly wrote novels and did a few plays. I did an adaptation of one of her novels. Acker is a writer very close to Suzan-Lori in generating this energy and getting out of the way so that contradictory things can collide.

LG: Suzan-Lori told me the most interesting thing with *Topdog*. She said that the play was channeled through her. She moves around a lot when she writes, she's constantly moving, and I'm curious about whether each of her previous works was channeled the same way she described. With *Topdog*, she said, she was moving around, moving around, moving around, and all of a sudden something said, "Sit!" And she sat, and the play came out, and she was just a vessel. She said it's as if a hole in her head opened up and the play just came through and within a few days the play was done. So if, in fact, that is the process in which she wrote the other plays, I would wonder if, in fact, that helps define what a Suzan-Lori Parks play is.

RF: I've gotta try that *[laughter]*.

LD: I've done, what, five of her plays, and a couple of them in different configurations, and there are ways in which tremendous images and poetic strategies go through them all. There's a musicality that happens in some of her more elegiac writing that you can hear from play to play to play. I can give an example. In *Imperceptible Mutabilities*, Mrs. Smith, in one of the most gorgeous speeches in the play, which is said more than once, says: "On thuh horizon any day now soon. Huh. You girls know what he told me last furlough? Last furlough I got off that bus and thuh sky was just as blue—wooo it was uh blue sky. I'd taken thuh bus to thuh coast. Rode in thuh front seat cause thuh ride was smoother up in thuh front. Kept my pocketbook on my lap. Was nervous. Asked thuh driver tuh name out names of towns we didn't stop at. Was uh express. Uh express bus. 'Mawhaven!' That was one place—where we passed by. Not by but through. 'Mawhaven!' Had me uh front seat. Got to thuh coast. Wearin my brown and white. 'You ain't traveled a mile nor sweated a drop!' That's exactly how he said it too. Voice tooked up thuh whole outside couldn't hear nothin else." Etcetera.

   Then in *Black Man*, you get this amazing speech where Black Woman with Fried Drumstick says, "Yesterday today next summer tomorrow just uh moment uhgoh in 1317 dieded thuh last black man in thuh whole entire world. Uh! Oh. Dont be uhlarmed. Do not be afeared. It was painless. Uh painless passin. He falls twenty-three floors to his death. 23 floors from uh passin ship from space tuh splat on thuh pavement. He have uh head he been keepin under thuh Tee V. On his bottom pantry shelf. He have uh head that hurts. Don't fit right." Etcetera, etcetera. For me there's a voice there that's unmistakable. I don't know how to articulate it outside the words themselves. Now in her writing, lots of different figures speak in lots of different ways. This happens to be an extremely fluid melodic, vowel-filled, open-sounding song, right? Then she's also got speeches that are extremely clipped and staccato. Like the speech in *Black Man*, "Do in diddley dip die-die thuh drop. Do drop be dripted? Why, of course." Staccato, rhythmic, high-speed riffing is replicated across the plays. You get it in *Imperceptible Mutabilities in the Third Kingdom*, in Aretha Saxon in the second play. So I do think that there are these gorgeous, poetic and musical sounds and a strategy of wedding sound to sense and insisting on the plasticity of language and on the way the actual sound of a word creates, if you will, character (as in Shakespeare), that informs all of her writing.

RF: Well, like all writers, she doesn't always know what she's talking about when she's talking about herself. Of course there's a Suzan-Lori Parks play—and what you describe is these two different versions. But I heard everything you were talking about in the second staccato version already present in the first version.

LD: Yes indeed. Fair enough.

LG: Here I would argue that *Topdog* is very much within the same genre. "Watch me close, watch me close now, watch me close." It's the exact same duh-du-duh, duh-du-duh. It has the same kind of rhythm. There are lines that have the same musicality, staccato, the jazz. It's consistent throughout her plays.

RF: And I would propose that when she says, "There is no such thing as a Suzan-Lori Parks play," she's saying it for polemical and justifiable reasons, and all of us experience this. Every play has to be approached and dealt with—as an audience member or as an artist working on a play— inch by inch. It's the inch-by-inch work that distinguishes goodness from badness, not, "Oh, I have a great theme in this play, I have a great overall structure." Nonsense. It's the inch by inch—Is it true? Is it really happening? Does it really reverberate with other things in the play? Any artist wants to say, "No, you can't make a simplified global pattern out of me or my work"—a global Suzan-Lori Parks play. She doesn't want anyone to say, "I'm going to see a Suzan-Lori Parks play tonight and I can relax because I know what I'm going to get," because that stops you from doing your inch-by-inch work.

Question from the audience regarding the difference between the experience of directing Suzan-Lori Parks plays and directing other authors' plays.

LG: Well, I had a great first day of rehearsal. One of my actors, who is a television actor, an intelligent actor, sat down as we were about to read through and said, "I would just like to let you know something. I have no idea what this play is about. I have no idea." And I could've done one of two things then. I could've shot myself, or I could've just said, "Right, well, let's just dive in." Luckily I just decided to dive in. But that was the first time I've cast actors who I've not auditioned, and it was also the first time I ever had an actor say, "I have no idea what she's saying, what this play is. I don't understand it." The one thing he did understand, though, was the rhythm and the music.

LD: I imagine it's changing a lot over time, directors' experiences with actors on this work. Back in the early nineties—which was, you may remember, some of you who are old enough, a period of very passionate exploration of ethnic and political identity: feminist plays, African-American plays, Asian-American plays—there was kind of an explosion of work in this way. When I started working with Suzan-Lori there was some question on the actors' parts about a white director working on Suzan-Lori's plays. I remember the first rehearsal for *The Death of the Last Black Man* up at Yale Rep, we had a lot of student actors in the show, along with some wonderful professional actors. There was a very interesting tension in the room. The kids who were in this very traditionally white institution had been doing Shakespeare and Molière and all this stuff, and they were finally getting to work on a contemporary play with a contemporary voice, telling stories which in many ways they considered theirs. And there I was. The professionals, the older actors, had really no issues with this whatsoever but watched and waited. But there was a lot of tension around the table about this. A student raised her hand at one point and said, "I've just got to express a certain concern here that, Liz, I mean, Suzan-Lori, why'd you pick her? Why'd you pick her?" Suzan-Lori talked about that for a minute and said, "What are you asking?" And the student said, "Well, she's not black." And Suzan-Lori turned and said, "You're not?" And it was a great diffuser—at that time a kind of necessary moment.

    I found it very exciting. There was a lot of cultural border-crossing I got to do, a lot of learning while working on these plays. The actors would pour out their stories and their relationships in connection with this text. Sometimes Suzan-Lori embraced that and sometimes she wanted to stop it because she felt that it was getting in the way of the work. In particular, there were actors who would look at the writing on the page, as Alisa described, you know you look at a word like "t-h-u-h" and extrapolate from that that a kind of black vernacular was being asked of them. And Suzan-Lori would get very angry and say, "They've gotta read it. They've gotta read it word for word." Inch by inch. Inch by inch. Absolutely hew to what's on the page. She said, those spellings are not a license to speak, carte blanche, in a kind of youthful black vernacular across the play. It's somewhat abstracted. So it was interesting that that would raise great hackles, particularly among young actors, who would get very concerned about what she was saying about that speech. So quite ahead of anything that would happen in the transaction between audience and stage, there was in the rehearsal hall all this material about art and race raised in those early days, and perhaps now as well, these great emotional issues surrounding the politics embedded in the aesthetics in the writing.

JK: Liz, you mentioned before that Suzan-Lori did not want the extroverted emotional expressions of the black Baptist tradition in *Black Man* when you directed it. And yet that play is very ceremonial. Suzan-Lori is clearly interested in ceremony and ritual. Everyone in the play is, in a sense, looking for the ceremony that *Black Man* needs to be finally buried, and with that the women can find rest too. So when you talk about abstracting black vernacular, I wonder if maybe what she wants is not actual ceremonial expression from life but rather something that's intentionally artificial, that she has invented, and that you therefore have to find and define in the theater. Is there a parallel here?

LD: One of the first things we did when we worked on *Black Man* together was to go up to St. John the Divine and St. Patrick's and attend some masses together. She was raised Roman Catholic. So was I. We were both recovering Catholics maybe. Both of us had certain kinds of deep attachments, I must say, visceral attachments to certain aspects of what you might call Catholic ritual—the drag, the fancy clothes, the gold, the incense, the Latin in my case. I was old enough for that. And a certain terribly stately, slow process. I think in her case it was very much connected to rhythm. She was resistant to bringing Baptist rhythms into the piece, particularly at the end. She wanted more the call-and-response of the Catholic Church, which is very slow and cadenced. I don't know how to describe it musically, but it's kind of a formal, strict, metric rhythm, as opposed to the more propulsive bending rhythms you might hear in a Baptist church. And that's what we went for.

Question from the audience requesting clarification of Leah Gardiner's remark, "We are participants, not merely spectators," in her director's statement for Topdog/Underdog.

LG: Well it's interesting—if I can piggyback on what Liz was saying about religion and the Catholic Church. If you think about how the Catholic Church works, you participate by going up each week for communion. You go to confession. There's a kind of participation in the ritual that exists within the Catholic Church. I think that with Suzan-Lori's work, in particular in *Topdog*, it's important for the audience to participate in what's happening up there. These are familiar characters, familiar people to us who cross racial boundaries. Their economic plight relates to any country, any place in the world where poverty exists and people are struggling. We all understand what that is, and if we are conscious beings, we can be participants in that and not necessarily spectators. It could be the artist in me who's hoping that everyone in the world does that. I could be idealistic in that sense, I suppose, but I do feel like in this particular play, in order to get the more visceral response to what's happening on stage it's important to see yourself as someone who's up there and in there. I think that the music is the thing that draws you in and makes you a participant and not necessarily a spectator. In our production, people were tapping their toes and swaying just because the kind of music that we chose allowed them to participate like that.

Question from the audience requesting clarification about a director "getting out of the way."

BW: For my part, I certainly didn't intend to say that you just show up at rehearsal and sit back and watch it all unfold. There are still a lot of choices to be made and there's still a lot of listening to be done to the text. And in a text like *Venus*, all the things that we talked about, the way that it's set on the page, the spellings, the rests and spells that she includes, everything goes into the structure of how she's built this thing. It has something to do with, I think, listening to exactly that, the tensions that she had built into the script in creating an atmosphere in which these things can start to come to life on their own. Essentially, she has given you all the chemical ingredients and it's a matter of setting up the appropriate environment for them to do their thing. But that requires very meticulously creating that appropriate environment.

RF: If I could just add to that: this is very important for all artists. It's one of the hardest lessons I had to learn as a director. I'd be sitting there in rehearsal all the time looking with a focused attention, saying, "Why is she doing it that way? No, no. What can I do to make it better?" Then at a certain point you realize that's wrong, and you sit back, and instead of focusing on that and figuring out why it's not working, you open your field of vision, use peripheral vision, use a wide field of vision. You go into a semi-daze. You glaze over. And you say, "Oh, she's doing it that way and she's bad, that's bad, but in that badness there is a necessity and a goodness that we have to learn how to exploit." So you, the director, have to go back and forth between making decisions and letting it be what it wants to be, the material, the performer. You often forget that—you have to let it be.

JK: I think that's a great closing comment. Thank you very much to all of our panelists.

21

THE BIRTH OF *THE DEATH OF THE LAST BLACK MAN*

Recollections of the First Staging

Beth Schachter

This essay tells the story of directing the first production of Suzan-Lori Parks's *The Death of the Last Black Man in the Whole Entire World*. I will describe how I came to work on the project as well discuss the play's characters and figures. The essay shares the thinking process to key decisions that Parks and I made and, in addition, offers some historical contextualization of the 1990 BACA Downtown production.

How We Got Together

The first full production that I saw at BACA Downtown was Parks's collaboration with Liz Diamond on their terrific production of *Imperceptible Mutabilities in the Third Kingdom*. I was fascinated by Parks's work. What I could not have articulated then about Parks's themes, unique style, and the power of her work has since been said eloquently by scholars like Harry Elam, Alice Rayner, Philip Kolin, and Harvey Young, and critics like Margo Jefferson and Alisa Solomon. Without identifying it as such, I connected to the Bakhtinian dialogical tension that lies at the heart of *Last Black Man* – the carnivalesque that bursts out through the language turning classical forms of literary tropes and realism's norms inside out. The energy of the repressed other, the unruly poetry of the hippest of cool, plays itself out center stage.

With a nudge from that downtown genius writer, Mac Wellman, NWP Literary Manager, I became a member of Brooklyn's BACA Downtown's New Works Project Group (NWP) in 1989. This meant that I could use the fantastic space that was the upstairs studio theatre, formerly a church, to create short pieces of work to present before my fellow group members. Parks saw my first auteur directorial effort working with a text drawn from, and I say this with all the humility of hindsight, *Moby Dick*. She was attracted to the dance-theatre-like qualities of the movement and the song-like evocations of language taken from the novel. The ten-minute selection of performance focused on images of Pip, the drowned African American cabin boy. So it was Pip who brought Parks and me together. Parks asked me to direct a section from her next play for one of our New Works showings. The script was not complete at that point. Parks was still writing it, but already the play challenged the usual parameters of dramatic literature. Parks and I presented a short cutting from one of the Chorus panels, drawing heavily for inspiration from the Supremes and New Orleans jazz funerals.

NEA Grant and Production

We were then encouraged to apply for a National Endowment for the Arts grant – this was back when there were such things. Our ideas about the project were articulated in the grant application. *Last Black Man* is, as Parks wrote in our proposal, "a requiem mass in the Jazz aesthetic." We further wrote:

> Like a musical score, the phonetic spellings capture the musical sequence of sounds to create this mythological landscape. Repeated beats, lines and words create dramatic tension as the characters struggle to empower themselves through their language.

Greta Gundersen was the Director of BACA Downtown when we did the first showing, and she helped us considerably with the NEA application. We won the NEA grant for $10,000, which seemed like a generous budget for my first New York City full-length show. Bonnie Metzgar, who had become the Director of BACA Downtown by the time we did the full production, also found additional funds. Ultimately, we had approximately $17,000 to spend on the show. Parks was hit with an extra financial burden because she personally had to pay the tax on the grant, which seemed particularly unfair as we all had such limited personal finances at that time. When push came to shove, in terms of payroll during the production, we had an iconic downtown moment in which I had to ask the actors if we could pay them three days late as funds had not yet come in… they generously agreed to the delay.

Characters and Figures

The journey of the play moves through multiple deaths of the Black Man; he will ultimately be electrocuted, drowned, lynched, and will fall to his death. With each death, the Figures call for an increasingly permanent record of what has happened. From writing in the dirt in the Overture, the Chorus progresses, in the play's last scene, to call for writing that is carved out of a rock so that their history will endure. The scarification of the rocks will attest to the deaths that have come and gone before: to the history of a "great nation fallen on hard times" as Parks says in her piece, "new black math" (*Theatre Journal*, December 2005, 579).

The structure of the script suggests that there is a familiar world with the Black Man and Black Woman on their front porch, a purgatory of his deaths and returns and her rituals of welcoming back by killing all of the neighbors' hens. It was of prime importance to us to generate the stereotype-size characterizations of the Black Man and Black Woman, but at the same time, to cultivate smaller relationship exchanges and moments of comedy. Their journey was the focal point of this production. The Chorus, made up of the nine Figures, was instrumental, as Parks shared with me, in being helpful to the couple as they tried to unravel the mystery of their positions in limbo.

The Figures, on the other hand, were not so concerned with life or death for themselves. They were concerned with history untold. Parks was insistent that they were "Figures" rather than characters. In other words, they were like fetishes. One way to understand a fetish, as Robert Stoller has written, is to recognize it as "a story masquerading as an object," in this case as a Figure (*Observing the Erotic Imagination*, 155). They seem to move through several evocative but not logical landscapes. They create asynchronous shifting worlds of icons drawn from the culture, language and unvoiced histories of African Americans. They serve as cultural memory for the Black Man and Black Woman.

Some of the Figures in the Chorus mirror the Black Man, some the Black Woman, and others refract black cultural images. And Bigger and Bigger speaks the rage of being stereotyped and trapped, in Bigger Thomas' case, in jail and circumstances that bring him only death. Old Man River Jordan and Ham rise up from the past to push the Black Man into knowledge of his own inheritance, learning that appears to be both powerful and painful. Prunes and Prisms carries the self-hatred and anger generated in the Black Woman by a world that tells her she cannot be beautiful with her large lips. Prunes and Prisms references Joyce's writing. Parks told me that Joyce had written that saying "prunes and prisms" multiple times in the day will reduce one's overly large lips. Yes and Greens Black-Eyed Peas Cornbread and Lots of Grease and Lots of Pork bring stereotypical African American culinary culture to the stage. Voice on thuh Tee V is a different sort of cultural force, and Before Columbus represents the indigenous peoples who generously helped Columbus when he came calling and "asking to borrow a cup of sugar" (*Last Black Man*, 104).

Queen-Then-Pharaoh Hatshepsut was, I think, one of the final Figures to take her place in the script, but she is a crucial member of the Chorus. Queen-Then-Pharaoh Hatshepsut took shape through a combination of Parks's interest in making a connection between ancient Egypt and African culture and my own limited knowledge of Egypt from a trip there. I shared my interest in Hatshepsut, one of the few female pharaohs. This amazing "King," who ruled Egypt from 1479 to 1458 B.C., had a stepson, Thutmose III, whom she kept from the throne. She built great monuments, but after her death, Thutmose tried to erase her cartouche (the visual sign of her identity) from all of her buildings, apparently, to "methodically wipe his stepmother, the king, out of history" (Chip Brown, "The King Herself," *National Geographic*, April 2009). The *National Geographic* article describes how Thutmose III did a spectacularly good job of "smiting the iconography of King Hatshepsut… At Karnak her image and cartouche, or name symbol, were chiseled off shrine walls; the texts on her obelisks were covered with stone (which had the unintended effect of keeping them in pristine condition)." Parks was struck with the historical turnings of, the vicissitudes of, Egyptian rulers and the erasure of what had seemed like permanently written fame. I believe that Parks was also wrestling herself with issues of laying claim to "writing it down." She may have had qualms about speaking on behalf of these powerful figures at this point in her own development. So it was also to herself that she spoke when Queen-Then-Pharaoh Hatshepsut delayed the action in the Overture by saying, "Not yet. Let Queen-Then-Pharaoh Hatshepsut tell you when" (*Last Black Man,* 101). The Black Man cannot move his hands and, perhaps, Parks was keenly aware of the risks of moving hers across the keyboard.

The Chorus want the Black Man, Black Woman, and the audience, to recognize and reject the stereotypes placed upon them. Then the Black Man and Black Woman, in addition, must connect with their anger before he can be given permission by his "kin" to pass on. By the end of the play, the Black Man does indeed move his hands. He and his wife have both accepted that he is dead and will be "go gone now now" (116). The Chorus, at times, appears to torment The Black Man, denying him the capacity to move his hands, yet, the Figures also clearly claim his death. They struggle to make sure that the audience takes responsibility for the forces behind his murders. Ultimately, the Figures in the Chorus have come to move along with the Black Man, once they agree that they will have left their marks in rock so that they cannot be ignored.

Directing and Dramaturgy

In many ways, the events of the play were mysterious to me initially, but I had an intuitive sense of the ways in which the "rep and rev" that Parks has described ever since this early point in her work created conversation, sermonized with call and response, joked with the audience, sang out jazz riffs ("do in diddly dip die-die thuh drop") and generated other kinds of interactions (130).

Differentiating each iteration of lines and motifs was much of the work of my directing, exploring, and articulating the subtle reasons for the repetitions of lines and sections. I was interested in giving the audience a strong experience of the Africanist contradictions and mythic sense of history in the script. For instance, what changes allowed the Black Man to relocate his likes, his own identity, in fact, so that he could triumphantly call out with renewed romantic feeling to his wife, "SPRING-TIME!" (127). He does so even as she is, in contradiction, stuffing him with feathers in a kind of taxidermy. These kinds of questions made up the bulk of the conversations between Parks and myself. Although we certainly talked about specific sounds and what the impulse was behind language like Old Man River Jordan's "ya-oh-may/chuh-naw," a version of "Yes, oh me? Shit, no," as he described what the Black Man said when confronted with his own death by lynching (112). We, however, focused primarily on the rise and fall and rise again of the increasingly urgent crises of the play.

The play enacts a ritual in which unquiet spirits come to find peace, but ultimately claim only history. Just as Parks is taking the stage time and space for these haunts, so to do the Figures claim control over the Black Man's final crossing over to freedom. With Parks's liberation having written it down and the Figures calling for the Black Woman to write down the fabricated absence of African Americans, the play ends with a brief breath of freedom. It is a moment so delicate that they all call out "Hold it" to try and hang onto that transient experience (131). Previously placed on Ham, the blame is lifted and put where it belongs, on Columbus and the colonial powers for endlessly murdering the black man from past to present to future.

Some of our other dramaturgical conversations were about the end of the play. I recall talking to Parks at various cafes in New York and Brooklyn about things that "turned." As she wrote in the Overture, "without that /d/ we coulda gone on spinnin forever. The /d/ thing ended things ended" (102). For the ending of the play, she was searching for what had turned in the play's ritual. What had progressed through the repetitions and revisions of the Overture, three Black Man and Woman panels, and three chorus scenes? Which elements had transformed into something else? We discussed how the earth turned (spun), dirt was turned for planting, and time itself turned with the revolving seasons and years. The kin sometimes seem to be turning on the Black Man. The begats speech turns into an auctioneer's slave-selling speech. Feeding him drumstick turns to feeding him feathers. Ultimately, Parks crafted an elegant climax for the Black Woman in which she comes to realize that "Thuh dirt itself turns itself. … Winter pro-cessin back tuh back with spring-time" (128). At the end of the fifth panel, "Thuh Garden of HooDoo It," the Black Woman has moved through the years and is "getting down," as she said in the Overture: "uh whole line gone roun… You comed back. Yep. Nope. Well. Build uh well" (128).

Production Choices

Along with continuing work by Parks to finalize the script, she collaborated with me on all major production decisions. Our first significant set of decisions came with casting and design. I hired a wonderful team of designers: set by Sharon Sprague, lights by Brian McDevitt, costumes by Toni-Leslie James, and vocal work with Mark Bennett. We also found a terrific casting director who did the whole project gratis: Suzanne Ringrose.

Parks and I spent time on the costume and design conceptual process. When and where *did* this play take place? How were we to create the simultaneity conjured up by the script of past, present, and future? I recall that Parks and I decided to get out of the city to get some clarity on the sets and costumes. We stayed out in East Hampton at an inn where I had been a chambermaid, and we talked and walked and sat in the graveyard out there. Amongst the old New

England gravestones, we decided that the Civil Rights Era was to be the basis of the costumes. Parks was particularly interested in the ways in which blacks were careful to appear particularly well-dressed when taking part in sit-ins and protests for the movement. She explained to me that they were protecting their middle-class status and making clear that they belonged; they had the dignity of citizenship no matter what assaults and dangers were heaped upon them. I was excited about the idea of highlighting the 50s with the black and white scheme that was ultimately conceptualized (with the exception of the Black Woman's pink print dress). I thought it would bring the Chorus together in a cohesive way. Fanni Green, for instance, as Yes and Greens, was a vision of a proper African American lady dressed to be seen in public in the 1950s. Her tight yet conservative sleeveless black dress gave her a stylish look and a small headdress endowed her with a sense of maturity and authority. These period costumes lifted the style of the production by offering realistic outlines but with minimal detail. There was also a whiff of a jazz hipster's world in the costumes for Ole Man River Jordan and Queen-Then-Pharaoh-Hatshepsut.

In determining how to cast the production, Parks and I discussed the nature of the cast's ethnicity. As she has described in her introduction to the play as it appeared in *Theater*, "When *Last Black Man* premiered at BACA Downtown in Brooklyn, it was a multiracial cast because I didn't have any feeling at that time that it needed to be an all-black cast. I didn't want people to jump to some easy political point about the play and sum it up in some quick statement" (Summer/Fall 1990, 244). Liz Diamond subsequently suggested to Parks that the play be cast entirely with African American actors and Parks agreed. I suspect that mine may have been the only cast of the play with ethnic diversity that included a Japanese American actress, a Filipino actress, and a blue-eyed white man.

It seems quite strange to look back and imagine why we would have thought that this play, with its poetry drawing upon the lyrical qualities of a certain black vernacular, should be cast this way, but there were several factors. Parks, I think, may have been concerned about the play being seen too simply, too literally. She may have wished, as she has often written and spoken about, to have audiences and reviewers give priority to her forms and structures and not just "diagnose a message." It may have been that she was also working out her own identity as an African American experimental playwright and did not wish to be pigeonholed solely as a black writer of black experience. In addition, multicultural casting was at the front of some theatre artists' minds in this 1989–1990 moment. Harry Newman, creator of the Non-Traditional Casting Project, was a member of the New Works Project, and he had written several persuasive essays and had also arranged for panels on the topic. We had a sense of responsibility to the larger community of minority actors.

The multicultural casting may have made the show harder to grasp even while it may have gone some way to creating a wider view of postcolonial subjects. Parks and I decided that James Himelsbach, our white actor, was the best actor for Before Columbus, and we felt that we could use his whiteness to ironize the speeches and interactions with that character. This strategy had moments of success, and equally, generated moments of confusion. But, Parks and I were committed to as widely mythic a world as possible, and we saw that happening by being able to bring together multiethnic bodies that could speak back to stereotypes of marginalized people of color.

The strength of the casting was, I believe, in the vocal performances. Leon Addison Brown's charming Black Man's Holy Fool's innocent questioning and anxious pleas drove much of the forward motion of the show. Pamela Tyson, Black Woman, used her edgy intensity to offer access to the frustration and dark irony the character wielded like a sword in her own defense. Ching Valdez-Aran seduced with a nightclub siren's Queen-Then-Pharaoh Hatshepsut's crooning "my mans uh all men" (113). Jasper McGruder's rich bass as Ham spoke back to decades of shuck'n jive performances of blackness largely by white performers in blackface minstrelsy. Patrice Johnson's Prunes and Prisms and Michael Jayce's And Bigger's commanding tones of audacious anger grounded the piece in the face of the constraints upon the Black Man as well as on the Black Woman.

Margo Jefferson summarized the set nicely saying it functioned "as a home, a church, a graveyard, a town square. Each has a moment of truth and trauma" (*Village Voice*, October 2, 1990). The walls of the theatre space were painted a nighttime purple with Basquiat-like figures scattered graffiti-like on several actual walls of the space. Sharon Sprague's set also featured a country church façade with an altar with a glowing bowl of eggs, a tv, and a large watermelon perched on top of the television. All of the altar's objects came to life during the show by being activated through use or lighting moments. In the upper right center of the space was a raised porch platform with two chairs upon it. In his *New York Times* review, Mel Gussow noted that the watermelon on top of the television was "the primal symbol of the play and, without embarrassment, a kind of life sign" (September 25, 1990). Watermelons functioned in numerous ways in the show, and a sign of nature and growth was certainly one of them. They also represented the loaves and fishes Christ creates and multiplies as well as, in contradiction, the deaths of individual black men under constraint, like the watermelon that first prevents the Black Man from moving his hands. In addition, in the show, Ham sat polishing a large watermelon on his lap: a symbol for the shoe-shine service "Uncle" performed. Lastly, it served as an eternally regenerating aspect of black resilience, growing as it did from one to three to many. We thought carefully about the image on our cards for the show. We finally decided upon an old-fashioned drawing of a watermelon sitting on the seat of an electric chair.

The Era and The Artists

Looking back I see a production very much of its moment in the beginning of the early 1990s in NYC and at a particular point of the rising action of Suzan-Lori Parks's career. The NWP and BACA Downtown were uniquely invested in artists like Parks and had already successfully produced her first major show.

The group consisted of artists working in juxtaposition to mainstream theatrical paradigms; the particular spirit of the NWP was to function as outsider-art-maker challenging various structures of authority. The mission statement for the group reads as follows: "The New Works Project at BACA DOWNTOWN sets as its primary function the creation of a residence theater group committed to the support of sharp, aggressive, intelligent and unconventional theater works." The New Works Project promised to make theatre that would raise, as Mac Wellman put it, "a joyful hell in a small space."

This was an era of David Greenspan, Reza Abdoh, Ping Chong, Karen Finley, and the Wooster Group. They created transgressive characters whose identities critiqued normative constructions of gender, sexual identification, race, and ethnicity in the crossover period of Reagan-economics and the Bush administration – a period in which government funding for the arts became a favorite conservative scapegoat.

There were other playwrights like Suzan-Lori Parks in the late 1980s and early 1990s who addressed the question of how identity was constructed through social forces. They eschewed realism's fixed verisimilar boundaries of subjectivity in favor of an x-ray post-structuralist vision of ideology rendered visible. Then marginalized writers like Parks, Wallace Shawn, Mac Wellman (the Literary Manager of NWP), and Erik Ehn (fellow NWP member), for instance, all interrogated the nature of subjectivity by marking the presence, absence, and fragmentation of both characters' and performers' bodies. As with her fellow language-focused writers, the body was an even more than usually important matrix of signification for Parks. Uniquely, I think, Parks used novel physical scenarios and images depicting her figures' ritual and emotional processes.

Last Black Man, as Parks herself has noted, explodes realism, undoing a genre that can be recognized partly by its desire to keep its own constructed-ness invisible, to hold onto the status quo. With *Last Black Man*, however, Parks creates a poem that spirals outward insistently asking formal questions and troubling the usual tightly knit affirmation between illusionistic stage world and an individual spectator's stable sense of reality.

Works Cited

Brown, Chip. "The King Herself." *National Geographic* online, April 2009. (Available from: http://ngm.nationalgeographic.com/2009/04/hatshepsut/brown-text). Web.

Gussow, Mel. *The New York Times*. 25 September 1990. Print.

Jefferson, Margo. "Limbo Tale." *Village Voice*. 2 October 1990. Print.

Parks, Suzan-Lori. "Introduction to *Death of the Last Black Man in the Whole Entire World*." *Theatre* (Summer/Fall 1990): 244. Print.

Parks, Suzan-Lori. "new black math." *Theatre Journal* 57.4 (December 2005): 576–583. Print.

Parks, Suzan-Lori. *The America Play and Other Works*. New York: Theatre Communication Group, 1995. Print.

Stoller, Robert. *Observing the Erotic Imagination*. New Haven: Yale University Press, 1985. Print.

22

AN INTERVIEW WITH DIRECTOR LIZ DIAMOND

Philip C. Kolin

January 2013

Liz Diamond is the Resident Director at Yale Rep and the Chair of Directing at the Yale School of Drama where she has taught and directed for 20 years. She has enjoyed a longstanding friendship and artistic collaboration with Suzan-Lori Parks begun in 1988 with her award-winning production of *Imperceptible Mutabilities in the Third Kingdom*. Diamond has also collaborated with Parks on four other of her works, including *The Death of the Last Black Man in the Whole Entire World*, *Betting on the Dust Commander*, *The America Play*, and substantial portions of *365* at Yale and in New York. I interviewed Diamond on 29 January 2013 by telephone with several subsequent conversations in February and March.

Philip C. Kolin: When did you first meet Suzan-Lori?

Liz Diamond: I met her in the spring of 1988. I was four years out of graduate school, running around downtown New York trying to make my way as a theater director. A good friend, the writer, Mac Wellman, had encouraged me to do some work at BACA Downtown, an exciting new art gallery and performance space in downtown Brooklyn.

PCK: Since BACA is so crucial to understanding Suzan-Lori Parks, could you describe it?

LD: It was an old 2-storey parochial school, with high ceilings, a steep staircase, and wainscoting. Very plain and practical architecture. The performance space was on the second floor, and was about sixteen feet to the ceiling and maybe 40 feet square. Over to one side there was a kitchen area that served as a backstage.

PCK: Would you sketch the history of BACA Downtown?

LD: BACA Downtown was created by the Brooklyn Arts and Culture Association, a citizens' arts association founded in 1966 to promote the arts in Brooklyn. In the late '80s, wanting to draw to Brooklyn's downtown area younger, experimental theatre and visual artists, musicians and multi-disciplinary artists, BACA found an abandoned school there to convert to a performance and gallery space. They picked the perfect person, Greta Gunderson, a visual artist living nearby, to launch the place. She brought in a brilliant young man, Kyle Chepulis, to help her and together they cleaned the place out, made two beautiful galleries on the ground floor, put in a light grid and sound gear upstairs, and opened the doors. Artists started submitting work and projects and very quickly word got out that Greta had the taste and the drive to create an arts scene. She would pretty much let you do anything as long as you cleaned up after yourself. For my first show with Suzan-Lori, our designer, an installation artist named Alan Glovsky, replaced the stairway railing with a hot water pipe that was entirely too hot to hold. I can't remember why! There was nothing that Greta would say no to if she thought it was imaginative, original, provocative, and fun. Greta helped launch many young artists, including Anne Bogart, Jeff Jones, Ruth Margraff, and Mac Wellman, as well as Suzan-Lori and me.

So I was working at BACA Downtown, when Mac Wellman, who had been leading a writers' group there, asked me to read *Imperceptible Mutabilities in the Third Kingdom*, which he and Greta wanted to premiere in BACA's first annual Fringe Festival. Suzan-Lori was a member of the writers' group and Mac thought she was simply brilliant. Mac and Greta thought we would work well together. I don't think they had any idea—well maybe they did—just how much Suzan-Lori and I would enjoy working with each other.

PCK: What were your first impressions of Suzan-Lori Parks?

LD: We met for the first time on a rainy day at the Opera Café on Broadway, across from the Lincoln Center. I went in, looked around, and saw an athletic looking young woman with short little dreadlocks and a huge grin. She was laughing. We started talking and that was it. It was a *playwright/director coup de foudre*. Suzan-Lori amazed me. And moved me. Because she was crystal clear about her talent, about her work, and, pretty quickly, about wanting to work with me. I had read *Imperceptible Mutabilities in the Third Kingdom* prior to our meeting. I was dazzled by the language—its rhythm, its poetry. I didn't feel I knew what I was reading yet, or quite how to read it yet, but having read it out loud to myself before meeting its author, I knew I held in my hands something completely new, and powerful. And then I met her and the feeling was confirmed. Here was a poet: a gifted, fiercely ambitious, theatrical poet.

PCK: When you read it did you have any idea that Suzan-Lori was embarking on a spectacular career?

LD: "Spectacular career" is not the phrase that came to me when I met Suzan-Lori. "Major artist" is what I thought. I thought she was brilliant.

And I thought she would succeed in doing what she wanted to do, which was to create a body of powerful, lasting, important work. Reading *Imperceptible Mutabilities in the Third Kingdom* for the first time, I thought, "OK—I can't quite crack the code yet but it's full of powerful images, it's incredibly funny, and it's gorgeous to say out loud. It has astonishingly varied rhythms and textures, alliterative and onomatopoetic patterns, and virtuosic, politically-charged word play." There were puns within puns. The stories in the play were funny, and heartbreaking, all at once.

PCK: Yes. Commenting on *Imperceptible Mutabilities in the Third Kingdom* in a BACA-sponsored publication *New Writers Journal*, Suzan-Lori claimed that the play came to her through voices that she had heard. Elsewhere she said that no one spoke like her characters did. Certainly in a language-driven play like *Imperceptible Mutabilities* we hear voices.

LD: She wasn't kidding when she talked about hearing voices. In her early life as a writer she would say that she didn't see her plays, she heard them. She still describes "transcribing" speeches, which she hears very clearly in her head. To this day she can recall the uncanny sensation of writing down Ham's Begotten speech—in *The Death of the Last Black Man in the Whole Entire World*—on a paper napkin as it came to her whole, while she sat in a café in New Haven. Of course, for me, as a director, the fact that Suzan-Lori didn't so much see, as hear her plays, was an irresistible invitation. Because I felt I *could* see them. The characters' voices conjured immediate and powerful visual images to me. I saw the figures in her plays, what they wore, how they moved, and the environments they might move through: a nightmare hospital bed; an apartment infested with roaches that were actually surveillance cameras; the Great Hole of History; The Garden of HooDoo It—these were gifts for a director and designer. It was a gift to have the artistic freedom to figure out how to embody this visually rich, multi-dimensional poetry.

PCK: Would you argue that what Suzan-Lori did for the late 1980s and early 1990s was comparable to what Adrienne Kennedy did in the 1960s, that is, to transform the landscape of American theatre through language?

LD: Suzan-Lori's plays, like Adrienne Kennedy's, are on every serious syllabus of modern and contemporary American drama. But in addition to her plays, Suzan-Lori has written screenplays, novels, essays on the writer's craft and on the theatre. She has had serious artistic and commercial success, winning the Pulitzer for *Topdog/Underdog*, and helping make *The Gershwins' Porgy and Bess* a Tony-winning Broadway hit. (She revised the libretto.) She continues to write important new plays, like *The Book of Grace*. Suzan-Lori is a very private person, but she gets out there and engages with the public. For *365 Plays/365 Days* she travelled all over the country, meeting participants and audiences. She is right now doing another of her "Watch Me Work" series at New York's Joseph Papp Public Theater, where she invites the public to join her for a couple of hours weekly to write and talk about their work together. All this artistic output and activity has had a major impact on the next generation. Greater than Kennedy's? More direct, to be sure. I hear Suzan-Lori's subversive wordplay, jazzy rhythms, stylization, long riffs, and dramatic confrontations in the plays of such exciting younger American writers as Marcus Gardley and Tarell McCraney, just to cite two. I also see Suzan-Lori's way of being a playwright—her hands-on engagement with the hurly burly of theatre making—as having a strong influence on these and other younger writers. Young playwrights feel they need to be savvy about the marketplace, and break new artistic ground, all at once. Parks has done that, is doing that. And they admire this.

PCK: What was it like collaborating with Suzan-Lori on reading a script for production?

LD: Before we got down to work on *Imperceptible Mutabilities in the Third Kingdom*, we just hung out, drinking cups of coffee and sharing our biographies with each other. We joked about our families, and being raised Catholic. She told me all kinds of hair-raising stories about growing up in an African American military family and living in Germany. I told her my crazy stories about growing up in a small house with 4 kids in a very white suburb of Boston. We shared stories about our years at the women's colleges we went to. We shared a lot of very personal stuff.

PCK: What happened next?

LD: Then we just sat across the table from each other and read the play out loud. I had Suzan-Lori start and then I joined in. A director can learn a great deal, hearing a writer read his or her own work. It was instructive to hear and watch Suzan-Lori read the text. She read simply, carefully attending to her punctuation, and pronouncing her idiosyncratic spelling in a way that was not a dialect—but a poeticization, a heightening of everyday American dialects, black/white, urban/rural, educated/unlettered. This was a stylization that invited the listener to really listen to the way a word was bent and shaped by the speaker, and to appreciate the political significance, and the singular beauty—or ugliness—of these linguistic inventions and deformations. Gradually I would join in, and we would read the play out loud together going through it page by page. I would ask questions to glean everything I possibly could about given and present circumstances, intention and objective… seeking answers to questions about dramatic action inside the text of the play. I began to see that the information I needed was there, embedded in the language: Mona squeezing through the window guard to sit on the ledge and consider suicide; Aretha lying in a hospital bed, newly toothless, dreaming of her past lives; Sergeant Smith standing atop his dreamed-of desk, dreaming of earning his military "distinction." The way this information seemed to shimmer in the text, "hidden in plain sight," suggested that the staging needed to be similarly graceful, non-literal but also non-abstract. The task was to put these "concrete metaphors" onstage, so that the real-life truthfulness of the characters' struggles would resonate, universalized through stage poetry.

PCK: Suzan-Lori's language deconstructs the idea of stereotypical African American speech, doesn't it?

LD: Yes. With that first read-through, I understood what Suzan-Lori meant when she insisted, with real vehemence, that it wasn't dialect. She had seen African American colloquial language and gesture represented in American theatre, film, and TV, and she felt its use there was a form of abuse that shut the listener's ears to the specific human life of the character. The spectator could say—"I know that character"—when in fact they did not. Stereotype is a central aspect of racist thinking and a big part of Suzan-Lori's artistic project could be said to expose the racism—conscious and unconscious—by deconstructing the use of stereotype in representation. Suzan-Lori knew that if actors weren't disabused of the notion that her text's idiosyncratic spellings signified a "realistic" regional, cultural, ethnic dialect, her entire poetic/political point would be lost. Obviously, Parks' language partakes of colloquialisms, speech rhythms, and moving imagery, the rich landscape of everyday speech heard in African American and other American dialects, present and past. It celebrates their rich, densely meaningful variety and beauty. But her language also reveals the suffering, the betrayals, the hypocrisies, the dishonesties, the bombast, and the yearning *inside* these dialects and locutions. The slight distancing effect of her poeticized language allows the listener to hear the speaker's unconscious assumptions, lies, needs, fears. Her language is a psychological x-ray that exposes the soul of the character, and a sociological x-ray that reveals the soul of the community. Understanding this was the first step toward my understanding Suzan-Lori's work.

PCK: How did the two of you convey that important point to actors?

LD: We just told them, and reminded them, and reminded them, and reminded them. I gave them lots and lots of notes. Actors generally would initially see Suzan-Lori's text as invitations to play stereotype. We'd see heads snap, hips cock, and faces set in ways that we'd seen black people represented for years onstage. Suzan-Lori would shake her head and say, "Oh God, here comes the stereotype." The actors, understandably, did not realize at first that they were being invited to do something else, something richer and infinitely more artful and truthful.

PCK: How did you get the actors to understand what was required?

LD: By letting them in on the joke. By inviting them to do what Brecht was asking his actors to do (which is what great comic actors do automatically)—which is to be *conscious as actors* of that which the character may be unconscious of—which is the gap between what they think they are saying and what they are actually saying, between what they want to project and what they are actually projecting. Between what they are doing and what they think they are doing. When an actor becomes aware of this gap, or contradiction, they can subtly and artfully select when to expose that contradiction—by a shift in emphasis, a betraying gesture, and when to let the text do the work and sail on. Once the actors understood what the language was revealing about their character's self image and understanding of their place in the world, they could play the roles with much greater objectivity. They could let the mask slip, "protest too much," exposing, ever so delicately, the chasm yawning under their character's most fervent assertions. This of course could have led to hideous "commenting," when the text in fact required a fervent commitment to the stakes. But it didn't. Suzan-Lori's work requires delicacy, high intelligence, inventive physicality, compassion, and a subversive sense of humor. We were very, very lucky to work with actors who brought all of these gifts to the work.

PCK: Did Suzan-Lori participate in rehearsals?

LD: Not so much. But she would watch and respond and share her notes with me. They were good, specific, practical notes.

PCK: How did the script evolve for *Imperceptible Mutabilities*? Did it change much from the first draft that you had seen?

LD: Early on in working on *Imperceptible Mutabilities of the Third Kingdom,* I had a gut feeling that the second part, *Flounder,* didn't belong in the play. That whole section seemed to come from an entirely different set of concerns. It seemed to want to be a stand-alone play. Suzan-Lori agreed, but felt very strongly that *Imperceptible Mutabilities* needed to be a four-part play. Realizing that for Suzan-Lori, the play was an episodic composition, comprised of a set of discrete panels, as in a medieval altarpiece, helped me think about what it was that made this "panel" wrong." This one panel just didn't contribute to the whole telling of this tragicomic tale of "non-evolution." Suzan-Lori was never shy about protesting an idea that did not feel right, but this one did, so she pulled that section out. Now she felt we had a new problem: a panel was missing. I felt, meanwhile, that we didn't so much need a new panel as a way to get from one panel to the next. What "moved" these figures, who changed character name and situation but remained somehow the same (Chona/Charlene to Anglor Saxon to Buffy Smith...)? And so I asked if Suzan-Lori could create a kind of passage between panels. What could she write that would help the audience link the stories within each panel to one another, thematically, poetically, if not literally? I felt the underlying theme of these panels—of the crushing weight of racism on our history, the human disappointments, betrayals, and abuses it causes, and its power to mutate victim and perpetrator in ways we may not perceive, but nevertheless betray in our speech—needed to be thrust up, so to speak, for the audience to grasp. The progress of the figures in *Imperceptible Mutabilities in the Third Kingdom* is actually *backwards.* From snails to slugs...

PCK: So regarding the removal of the second part of *Imperceptible Mutabilities*, what happened next?

LD: We dove into the question: what made the whole greater than the sum of its parts? One day we were talking and I just asked: "What's the Third Kingdom? We are in the Third Kingdom, and the mutabilities, the imperceptible mutabilities are taking place in the Third Kingdom. Where is that?" It seemed to be the medium, the space within which this whole event takes place, but I couldn't see it or hear it yet.

PCK: What was Suzan-Lori's response?

LD: She said, "It's the ocean. It's the Atlantic, it's between. It's the space between." My eyes just popped and I said, "You've got to write that." She was on her way to the MacDowell Colony. I urged her to try and write, even at risk of seeming too obvious, something called Third Kingdom, some kind of poem to get us from one part to another. She wasn't sure if it would qualify as the fourth panel, which she wanted for the play. But she said she would try. I will never forget the day she called me and said, "I've got it, I've got it. Just a minute. Wait, I am going to fax some pages." And out from the fax machine poured this unbelievably beautiful choral poem, *Third Kingdom*. And that was it—the 4th panel, the container of the whole play, and, since she wrote *Third Kingdom* in two sections, the passages that I needed to move us from panel to panel.

PCK: It's beautiful writing and has an evocative effect.

LD: Within the rest of the play, I can't recall any significant rewrites, save some small cuts or line re-assignments. She did some cutting and clarifying in *Snails*. We struggled with that part, to glean who is doing what to whom and who is in the room when and so forth.

PCK: What was the audience reaction to the early plays you directed: *Imperceptible Mutabilities in the Third Kingdom, The Death of the Last Black Man in the Whole Entire World, Betting on the Dust Commander*, and *The America Play*?

LD: With *Imperceptible Mutabilities* the reaction was amazing. BACA Downtown sold out. The word of mouth was incredible. We had waitlists and long lines out the door to get into the few performances we had. Mac and Greta invited us to do it again in 1989 and again the response was huge. Erika Munk wrote a beautiful review in the *Village Voice*; Yale's *Theater* published Alisa Solomon's exquisite essay; and then the OBIE Committee gave us OBIES for Best New Play, Best Direction, and for Best Performance (to Pamela Tyson). Then this tiny show was chosen as one of the *NY Times'* top ten shows of 1989.

PCK: It was almost like *Funnyhouse of a Negro*, Adrienne Kennedy's ground breaking play in 1964.

LD: That's an apt comparison. *Betting on the Dust Commander* enjoyed a similarly positive response. In both cases, audiences tended to be young, and ready for the new. *The Death of the Last Black Man in the Whole Entire*

World, which we did at Yale Rep, seems to me, looking back, to have been the production that brought Suzan-Lori to national attention, into what she slyly referred to as "the Big House." [The slave-owner's house.] There the response was complicated. We would receive standing ovations and have people walking out of the same performance. We had a brilliant cast, a superb design team, and the resources of a powerful regional theatre. And a very mainstream, mostly middle-aged, white audience. For many in the house, Suzan-Lori's play was a revelation. One guy wrote to me about how the experience of seeing her play felt as he imagined seeing *The Rite of Spring* must have felt in 1913. He, and many, felt thrilled to be discovering this voice, this vision. Others were alienated, upset, threatened. That show was written about in the *Times*, *Atlantic Monthly, The New Republic*. Critics loved writing about it and wrote eloquently about it; the play and production seemed to give them something they felt was genuinely important to write about. *The America Play*, which we also did at Yale Rep and then at the Public Theater, was again, a critical success, and again won Obie Awards for Best New Play and for two of our brilliant actors, Gail Grate and Michael Potts. Again we experienced angry walkouts and passionate applause at nearly every performance. The walkouts were not easy to take, believe me. We soul searched—were we failing these people in some way? We were not smug about this. But ultimately, we both believed that what we had created onstage was important—and that the kinds of disturbances the work was creating in the hearts of some of our audience needed to happen.

PCK: You mention altarpieces. I am intrigued by the ways in which Suzan-Lori uses religious rituals. Certainly the Cain and Abel story unfolds in *Topdog/Underdog* and in *Black Man* we have the bells associated with the Catholic Mass. And during *In the Blood*, it seems to me, Hester LaNegrita's accusers sound like Job's accusers. Why do you think Suzan-Lori has incorporated so many rituals and rites into the fabrics of her plays?

LD: Because these are part of the fabric of her life. They are part of the cultural capital she draws on. They come from her Catholic upbringing and from her cosmopolitan education. Her family's expatriate life and travels, and her education exposed her to the history and works of Western art and culture. It's part of who she is. And of course, growing up Catholic is going to feed the theatrical instinct! Every Sunday, witnessing all that holy water, gold, brocade, stylized gesture, ponderous speech, song put in service to the magic act of the transubstantiation—surely got into the ground water of Suzan-Lori's being. But Greek tragedy, and Shakespeare—they got in there, too. So did jazz, the blues, the Harlem Renaissance, Faulkner…

PCK: I like thinking of *Third Kingdom, The Death of the Last Black Man in the Whole Entire World,* and *The America Play* forming a trilogy on black identity and black history. Even though the plays are different, each one of them in its own way does get us into the great (w)hole of history. Would you agree?

LD: I think you could see these plays as a trio of meditations on what it meant/ means to be black in the America of our time. An artist's singularly honest attempt to understand and own that history, by *writing it down*.

I believe the power of this work will endure and grow. These plays are built on ancient dramatic structures. *Imperceptible Mutabilities in the Third Kingdom,* as I remarked earlier, echoes the narrative action of a medieval altarpiece, and of a passion play, illustrating, in episodes, not the life of one man—but of a people. *The Death of the Last Black Man in the Whole Entire World* operates like a Requiem Mass. It performs the ritual and communal act of remembering the Black Man's history, of resurrecting it and re-enacting it so that He can finally be laid to rest. *The America Play* might be seen as the ultimate family reunion play (like *Oedipus Rex*) or tragic recognition play—the great drama of the reunion of the holy (the pun is irresistible) Father with the Son and Mother. These deep structures are part of what make the plays so resonant. But it's important as well to remember that these great big plays by Parks are not solemn, even when they are heartbreaking. They are loaded with comedy, slapstick, farce.

PCK: How did each of Parks's plays challenge you as a director?

LD: With each of these plays the main directorial breakthrough, apart from understanding the purpose of the stylization of the language, was about discovering the container of the whole action.

In *Imperceptible Mutabilities in the Third Kingdom,* the location that contained the whole was the Third Kingdom or Middle Passage—that watery realm between Africa and America plied by the slave ships.

With *Black Man* it was discovering, again, what space would contain the whole. Where is this strange empty space where Black Woman comes to claim the body of her dead husband, and which becomes animate with the restless spirits of the ancestors? The ground zero of this play is not the front porch of Black Man and Black Woman. The "panels" in this play are, in effect, plays within the play. The main action needs to take place in a place that will contain the largest action of the play—which is the Chorus' struggle to get the Black Woman to own her husband's history. Before she can claim her husband's body, they must get her to hear, and accept, HIS story. This Chorus, made up of recent and long dead spirits, are themselves caught, trapped in this ice-cold limbo. Like the Ghost of Hamlet's Father, they cannot rest as long as their stories are forgotten or suppressed. They cannot "cross the river"; the Black Man cannot finally be buried, until their story is known. The scenographic breakthrough for me was to see the action in a space suggestive of a vast, empty morgue, which, in its austere grandeur, could evoke the ice-cold, historic "cold storage"—the limbo where Black Woman has come to claim her husband's body. The second breakthrough was to discover, with set designer Riccardo Hernandez, how to transform this cold, cruel space into a kind of cathedral in green nature—the restored roun' worl'—where the Black (unremembered, forgotten) Man, and his Ancestors, could finally be acknowledged, honored, and laid to rest.

The big discovery of *The America Play* was that the whole thing took place in a hole. Which we discovered one day after a reading of the play at New Dramatists, when Suzan-Lori worried aloud about where the hole should be onstage in relation to the Foundling Father, and I jokingly bent my head way back and looked up, as if into a great opening high up—and Suzan-Lori said, "But that's it!" And then I realized—my god that IS it! And of course we both fell out laughing, because the idea had been there all along, we just hadn't seen it yet.

PCK: You and Suzan-Lori have often said you share the same sense of humor. How is that reflected in the plays? Besides the puns such as Foundling Father, would you let us in on some of the jokes? In *Last Black Man* there are some hilarious lines and even in *In the Blood,* despite its links to Greek tragedy, there are moments that reverberate with humor.

LD: Well… there are the names, first of all, which are never accidental: Brazil in *The America Play* recalls Brazil nuts, which, in racist parlance, were once called "nigger toes." The broken family at the end of *Imperceptible Mutabilities* goes by the iconic WASP family name of Smith. These are jokes, excruciating jokes. In *Black Man* you have the stunning Ham's Begotten Speech which is as sustained a piece of subversive wordplay as any you'll find in Shakespeare. "Yo be wentin' much too long without hisself a comb in from thuh frizzly that resulted sprung forth…" and so on.

In our productions, Suzan-Lori's wordplay, or punning, and time warps, were echoed in the playing, in the props, in the clothes… In *Black Man* we put Queen-Then-Pharaoh-Hatshepsut in a gold lamé gown that Diana Ross or Cleopatra might have worn—she was the Mother of All Divas! Bigger and Bigger Thomas we conceived as the son or grandson of Richard Wright's Bigger Thomas—Black Panther beret, shades, with hip hop accents. And again, all in gold—a holy spirit after all. The marble slab on which Black man's corpse lay became an altar, a bier, a desk. In *Imperceptible Mutabilities in the Third Kingdom,* Mrs Smith and her daughters wore perfect brown and white polka-dotted Swiss dresses straight out of the 1950s, and little white gloves. They moved their gloved hands in ways that recalled the graceful gestures of the idealized 50s TV female—but the shadow of minstrelsy was also there, in the white gloves, and the patterned gestures. In *The America Play* we covered the stage floor in glittery black sand, and what Brazil unearthed in his "digging" for his father were little black boxes, perfect replicas of the big black coffin Brazil and Lucy had dragged along with

FIGURE 9 *The America Play* by Suzan-Lori Parks, directed by Liz Diamond, Yale Repertory Theatre, 1994. Michael Potts (Brazil) and Reg Montgomery (The Foundling Father). Photo by T. Charles Erikson. Courtesy of the photographer.

them. Eventually the stage was dotted with tiny black coffins, with red velvet interiors, containing the curious remains of the Foundling Father's lost Hall of Wonders. When the Foundling Father appeared in a vision to Lucy, performing a fragment from *Our American Cousin*, the play Lincoln watched the night he was shot, he introduced the act with a little riff from James Brown. Some of these ideas began as jokes that we thought up to crack one another up. They'd stay in if they kept doing so. Some of the ideas came to us as ways to make a painful moment hurt even more.

PCK: Are there any plans to stage revivals of these early plays?

LD: Not yet, not in the "Big Houses," but that will change.

PCK: Several years ago there was a revival of *Funnyhouse of a Negro* and people came from all over the world to see it simply because the play hadn't been done often. Certainly with the great success of a play like *Topdog,* I do foresee revivals on the horizon but it's these early plays that also need the exposure and need the benefits of revisiting them.

LD: It's a little like O'Neill's *The Hairy Ape* and his other gorgeous early plays. It took the Wooster Group to dig up—to dig—that great play. Let's not wait that long to dig these great plays.

PCK: Well let me say how grateful I am for all your work. Your responses today tie in so beautifully with the theme of this collection, *Suzan-Lori Parks in Person*.

23

BONNIE METZGAR ON SUZAN-LORI PARKS

Harvey Young

February 2013

Bonnie Metzgar is an award-winning producer, director and playwright. She served as Artistic Director of About Face Theatre in Chicago, Associate Artistic Director of Curious Theatre Company in Denver, founding producer of Joe's Pub (Public Theater) and Director of the graduate playwriting program at Brown University. Metzgar has collaborated with Parks since 1988, including her early plays at BACA Downtown and, later, 365 Days/365 Plays. This interview occurred on 1 February 2013 by telephone with a subsequent conversation in August.

Harvey Young: What circumstances led to your first collaboration with Suzan-Lori Parks?

Bonnie Metzgar: I am a student of Paula Vogel. Not just because I studied with her at Brown, but also in a more cosmic way. Paula Vogel and Mac Wellman were young theater artists in New York together. I had started my graduate work in 1987 at the University of Iowa in the Graduate Playwriting Program after having studied with Paula. It was a terrible fit—because the type of experimental work that I was writing was not the type of work that was going on at Iowa back then in the late 1980s. That year, Mac Wellman was one of the festival guests and I had a piece in the festival. He said to me, "This is not the right place for you. You should really come to New York. Jeff Jones and I have this workshop of young artists that had first started at New Dramatists as a class and now it's at BACA Downtown. You should come to New York and you can join this group." So, I left graduate school because Mac Wellman told me that I should come to New York and join this group [*laughter*]. Suzan-Lori was one of the people at the New Works Project at BACA Downtown when I arrived in fall 1988.

New Works Project. Basically, you signed up—I believe it was—every other week for slots to show new work. What made it interesting was the mix of artists working in hybrid forms—it was writers and directors and performers and designers. It was multidisciplinary—dance, alternative composition, visual art—but at the heart of it was experimental theater. Mac Wellman and Jeff Jones kind of presided over it—Mac used to command us to make as much strange and joyful noise as possible. The NWP was run by a committee structure. Each week a different artist would host. Usually, we would present two works in progress or something like that. That was really dynamic. It stayed at BACA until BACA closed, 1991. That was when JoAnne Akalaitis took the New Works Project to the Public Theater. She hosted it for a while during her tenure.

I became the Artistic Director of BACA Downtown. Greta Gundersen, the painter, had opened [BACA Downtown] and had a gallery downstairs and a theater upstairs. She decided to leave in fall 1989, after I was in NWP for a year. I was the only one around who had grant writing [experience]—I had raised $5,000 for the New Works Project. She was like, "Clearly, this person knows how to raise money." My day job was working at the Theatre on Film and Tape Archive at Lincoln Center for Betty Corwin. I wrote grants as part of my job. Even though I want to say that it was because I'm a brilliant artist, [the artistic directorship] was also because I had experience raising money [*laughs*].

I was the Artistic Director there for *Death of the Last Black Man in the Whole Entire World*. Greta had produced *Imperceptible Mutabilities* the year before I took over. *Death of the Last Black Man* was the first project of Suzan-Lori's that I ever produced.

HY: How would describe that first production relationship?

BM: At that point, Suzan-Lori and I lived upstairs/downstairs on a fire escape. We lived right above each other in Brooklyn. We were in each other's everyday lives. When we moved, we moved around the corner from each other. This continued for years. We had this—I think of it as a 19th century neighborly [relationship]… I don't know what it was. "Come on over for some tea…" or something. She would write certain things and she would just come up and read them. She liked to read them out loud and I liked to hear them. I think it started with her just reading her plays to me usually at home, out loud.

Death of the Last Black Man. There was lots of drama. Beth [Schachter] will remember this better than me. Did we lose an actor? There was something that happened just prior to going into rehearsal. Maybe it was a designer. I can't really remember. I think it had something to do with the electric chair?

Watching the collaborations that SLP had with both Beth Schachter and Liz Diamond from a producer's standpoint, it was very clear that

Suzan-Lori had a unique vision. This has been true throughout all the projects that I have done with SLP. That vision was on the page back then but she also already had a very strong idea of how her work was going to come out of the mouths of actors, how it was going to manifest itself in terms of space and time. And as smart directors, they listened to her. It was a very open room. Suzan-Lori could speak freely which is not always the case in a new play situation. The directors function[ed] as interpreters of her intention. As a piece would develop in real time and space—as there was an actual electric chair, they would hear from her how she felt it was living. I don't want to go so far as say it was a co-directing situation but in a certain way as far as staging and as far as language, Suzan-Lori acted like a co-director.

HY: How did audiences respond?

BM: Suzan-Lori was anointed by the alternative press from the second she started. She had this piece, *Dust Commander*, that was done at a gas station on Avenue B with Laurie Carlos. A lot of the right people who were tracking experimental theater saw that piece. So, when *Immutabilities* happened, it was the thing to see. It got *"[Village] Voice* Choice," which at the time really made things happen to you. Erika Munk wrote this big [article] about Suzan-Lori. Alisa Solomon supported her work. It started to build… For people interested in alternative art, it became known that the work that she was doing everyone needed to see. We were in downtown Brooklyn. People were not used to coming to Brooklyn at that time. This was right off of Fulton Mall and Fulton Mall was not glamorous. And now you had limousines pulling up with fancy people coming to see the show. Audiences, they were very excited. The thing about Suzan-Lori's work… it's funny. There may be some kind of cultural critique buried deep inside of it but the experience of it—it was really on its own terms. People really dug it. It was exciting.

HY: As a person who has produced and directed her works? What did you do differently when you were wearing those hats?

BM: When Suzan-Lori was in a venue like BACA Downtown which was created for experimental and hybrid works, audiences who were coming to it—they're adventurous, they are cultural adventurers. That's what they want to be doing—going to the borderlands. My job at BACA was to really push so we achieved the full extent of the vision. Flash forward to *Venus*. Here I am now, the Associate Producer at the Public Theater. Different reality. Also, it was a co-production with Yale directed by Richard Foreman. All three of those entities—Richard Foreman, Yale, and the Public Theater—they all have their huge legacies and visions. Very different situation for Suzan-Lori Parks. In particular, and most interestingly, Richard Foreman as a collaborator. I still think that was an extraordinary piece even though people hated the production. A lot of people hated it. I remember it was quite difficult for Suzan-Lori as a collaboration, given the active role she had up to that point in staging her works. Mostly because Richard wasn't used to working with a playwright who isn't himself. My job in that case was to identify the torturous aspects of the process that could be addressed, then to try to get folks at the Public Theater and Yale all onboard, then finally engage with Richard Foreman, all without undermining the project. It was hard. It was hard to have a world premiere be so shaped by someone outside of Suzan-Lori. I think it was her first experience with something like that—collaborating with another artist whose own aesthetic, to some degree, was overpowering her own. In a really simple way, at the front of the stage there's all that string, right? That shouldn't be a surprise to anyone. That's who we hired to direct the show, to collaborate with SLP. I was supportive of the idea of Richard as director. I believe that disturbing the process is one of the most powerful tools a producer has to use. Collaborating artists forced to work outside their comfortable rhythms—that is when something incredible gets born. But in this particular example, Suzan-Lori was not prepared to be on the outside and it was very difficult. Once we were on the road at Yale, my job was to take care of her needs as much as possible, and to help communicate those needs to Richard Foreman when I could.

Each of the projects, from a producing standpoint, was very different. When you're directing, it's a craft. The role of the director is so much simpler than producing. Producing—you're deciding who to put in the room to make this thing happen. You also have to manage all the relationships at these big institutions where thousands of people are involved and they're run by artistic directors with huge personalities like George [C. Wolfe]. For instance, Marcus Stern was supposed to direct *In the Blood*. He fell down in the middle of the street when we were casting and he broke his knee and he couldn't move. We ended up replacing him. Whatever people think about that decision, David Esbjornson came in. He inherited the cast. We moved the show into a totally different theater like three seconds before we started. It was a crazy mess. Now, the show ended up being great [*laughter*]. Each production, there's a certain amount of, "Yes, I planned for this to be brilliant in this way," and there's the other thing—called producing—which is when we respond to all the things that happen in real time when people fall down and we make the show anyway, in all its broken glory.

Here's the thing that makes Suzan-Lori's career really strange. From the second she starts writing, she's basically anointed into the canon of work that's important. But then her work does not get widely done. She is not Lynn Nottage. Her work is not done at *every* single regional theater. That's not what happens. She gets taught at every university. She speaks all over the world, at conferences. Then she goes to LA to write screenplays or whatever. But it's not really until *Topdog* that people pay any attention or really know her work. So, when you think about the Public Theater, it's not like she does the Public Theater then she goes away and does four other big productions then she comes back to the Public Theater. She didn't get a lot of production experience as a playwright. I don't know. It's strange to her that she never really had these many, many productions of her major works when they were first produced.

HY: In terms of the play script, is the play complete when rehearsals begin or is it developed as part of the production process?

BM: As you amass a body of work, like me, where you've worked with seventy different playwrights, what you end up having to accept is that that answer is very different depending on the writer. In these MFA programs, they don't teach writers to know their own process. Writers can't even narrate to you what they need. They don't know if you put actors in a room for a two-week workshop if it will help them rewrite the play, so that each night they can go [home] and come back with pages for the next day. They don't know if they can do that. Or if they work better to hear a one-day reading, then go off on their own for two weeks to do a rewrite, and come back for another reading of their new draft. These are two very different processes.

Suzan-Lori is very protective of the play. She will rewrite herself on her own. She will do that internally before she shows it to anybody. And then she will secretly, really on the DL, show some of it to one person and then maybe she will give it to the person who is supposed to produce it. Very secret. I don't even know if she tells herself she is doing it.

Suzan-Lori really believes in actors in the rewriting process. When she's hearing the play with the people who are actually going to do the play in early rehearsal and they have the words in their mouths and they are saying it for the first time—that's when she might make changes. We did this epic read-through of *365*. We did it because we were publishing the play before it was ever produced. She wanted to hear it come out of the mouths of actors before it was published. It's in that moment— either with an actor saying, "Wait a minute. This doesn't... or what's the rhythm here... or something's missing," that she'll be like, "Oh, I see what you're talking about," and she'll write the line that's missing right then and there. That's when it happens.

HY: I know of playwrights who will go away after rehearsals and will return having rewritten parts of a scene.

BM: I would say—to a large degree—that's the norm. With Suzan-Lori, that's very, very rare. She might cut a line. She might add a few words or add a line. The big radical thing that I remember happening is that in *Topdog/Underdog* she switched the order of two scenes but they were fully written. She didn't change anything [*laughter*]. That's not really her deal.

That's not really her thing except in that first read-through, first couple of days, when she's with actors.

HY: How did you become part of *365*?

BM: I was the producer on *Fucking A* at the Public. We were in rehearsal in early 2003. We were just hanging out—that's when she was writing *365*. She's like, "I'm doing this thing that at the end of the day; I write this little play. Ha, ha, ha." I was like, "Ha, ha, that's cool." It was not a big deal and she just mentioned it like that. *Fucking A* was the last show that I did at the Public Theater. After I left, I spent a lot of time in Colorado and I was working at Curious Theatre in Denver. Suzan-Lori contributed [a] song to this War Anthology project that I did out there, a long ballad which is very cool. She would come out every couple months and I said to her, whatever happened to that play-a-day thing? She said, "Oh yeah, I finished it. I did it for a year and then I stuck it in a drawer. It's done." "Let's do it. We gotta do it." She was like, "What are you talking about?" and I said, "Oh yeah, we're going to do that thing. Pull that thing out." It was like that.

We got theater and we got show business. It's heavy. We got the show business and we got the art that we are making. Here's something that was not written for show business. It was written as art. At the time, I was not attached to an institution or working on a Broadway show. So since I didn't have to care about show business, or the ego of any institution, there was a space for this big glorious sprawling weed to take root. If we just squint and ignore the system of delivery of theater to the masses—the resident theater movement and Broadway and all that—and just say, "What is theater? What is art? What role does it have in our lives?" Lots of new things can grow. SLP and I took this piece that was not written like other plays, not shaped like anything we usually put on as theater… It was a completely impractical thing that she did, writing this huge cycle. Is there room for this? What could it look like? I convinced SLP it was important that we produce it in a new way.

HY: What is the most memorable experience of *365* that you frequently revisit when looking back?

BM: *365* really lives with me. So many people's lives intersected with the project. The moment that I most visit… was in New York. I really remember being in this room at the Public. Let me just say that New York is not good at building community in general. Plus, joining a community art movement is the antithesis of cool in New York. I remember being in a circle of all these *365* participants who are introducing themselves. These are artists who spend everyday of every year making theater in the same town and many, many, many of them said, "Oh, I don't think I have ever seen you before." Really? Wow. And through *365* I got to be in the room where they started to invest in each other. Those kinds of moments where lots of artists came together and were able to share their experience while making something. This was just before everyone was on Facebook every day and connected in that way on social media. I feel like now we have a daily way that we're all connected which may be more sophisticated. But we were in the same room. Not visiting each other's pages. I'm happy that we didn't wait.

HY: How would you describe Suzan-Lori Parks's influence on your life?

BM: She's one of my closest friends. Suzan-Lori Parks the person has deeply impacted me as a human being. As an artist, she inspires me, my language, my loves. And our professional lives have been so intertwined in our careers. We share so many different and profound things. Both of our fathers had Parkinson's. Things that are not apparent to other people. We used to think that our lives were a reality TV show. We live in New York together. I'm white and gay. You're black and fabulous with dreads. Whatever. We're theater people. We're groovy. When you look back on it, her impact… she's an incredibly focused friend in the same way that she's an incredibly focused artist on her own work. She is very aware of her light. Sometimes, she has enough light for herself to hear the voices and have them come through her and what's leftover she wants to share with other people. Those other people might be students, those other people might be the people who come out to hear her speak, they might be her friends. Her first priority is her light, which I think she thinks is spiritual. A feeling. That's like understanding and creating a relationship with a higher power: you may not recognize it as God but you recognize it as a life force. Before Suzan-Lori, I don't think that I would have believed it. She lives it every day. That's been a really powerful inspiration to me.

INDEX

Taylor & Francis

eBooks

FOR LIBRARIES

Over 23,000 eBook titles in the Humanities, Social Sciences, STM and Law from some of the world's leading imprints.

Choose from a range of subject packages or create your own!

Benefits for **you**

▶ Free MARC records
▶ COUNTER-compliant usage statistics
▶ Flexible purchase and pricing options

Benefits for your **user**

▶ Off-site, anytime access via Athens or referring URL
▶ Print or copy pages or chapters
▶ Full content search
▶ Bookmark, highlight and annotate text
▶ Access to thousands of pages of quality research at the click of a button

For more information, pricing enquiries or to order a free trial, contact your local online sales team.

UK and Rest of World: **online.sales@tandf.co.uk**

US, Canada and Latin America:
e-reference@taylorandfrancis.com

www.ebooksubscriptions.com

ALPSP Award for BEST eBOOK PUBLISHER 2009 Finalist
sponsored by

Taylor & Francis eBooks
Taylor & Francis Group

A flexible and dynamic resource for teaching, learning and research.